KU-702-129

TRANSPORT AND ECONOMIC DEVELOPMENT IN THE NEW CENTRAL AND EASTERN EUROPE

To my parents, Lily and Bob

LIVERPOOL HOPE
UNIVERSITY COLLEGE

Order No./Invoice No. £17.47.

L097000815/050506066

Accession No.
308204

Class No.
914.7 HAL

Control No.
ISBN.

Catal.
MDK 12/98

Transport and economic development in the new Central and Eastern Europe

Edited by

Derek R. Hall

on behalf of the Transport Geography Study Group
of the Institute of British Geographers

Belhaven Press
London and New York
Co-published in the Americas by Halsted Press,
an imprint of John Wiley & Sons

Belhaven Press
(a division of Pinter Publishers Ltd.)
25 Floral Street, Covent Garden, London, WC2E 9DS, United Kingdom

First published in 1993

© Editor and contributors, 1993

Apart from any fair dealing for the purposes of research or private study, or criticism or review, as permitted under the Copyright, Designs and Patents Act, 1988, this publication may not be reproduced, stored or transmitted in any form or by any means or process without the prior permission in writing of the copyright holders or their agents. Except for reproduction in accordance with the terms of licences issued by the Copyright Licensing Agency, photocopying of whole or part of this publication without the prior written permission of the copyright holders or their agents in single or multiple copies whether for gain or not is illegal and expressly forbidden. Please direct all enquiries concerning copyright to the Publishers at the address above.

Co-published in the Americas by Halsted Press, an imprint of
John Wiley & Sons, Inc., 605 Third Avenue, New York, NY 10158–0012

British Library Cataloguing in Publication Data

A CIP catalogue record for this book is available from the British Library.

ISBN 1 85293 270 8

Library of Congress Cataloging-in-Publication Data

A CIP catalog record for this book is available from the Library of Congress.

ISBN 0 47022 003 1 (in the Americas only)

Typeset by Mayhew Typesetting, Rhayader, Powys
Printed and bound in Great Britain by Biddles Ltd., Guildford and King's Lynn

Contents

Notes on the contributors

Dr Richard A. Gibb is a Senior Lecturer in the Department of Geographical Sciences, University of Plymouth, England. Recently, he has been publishing prolifically with Wiesław Michalak on aspects of economic development and integration in post-communist Europe. Other research interests include the Channel Tunnel and southern African development.

Dr Derek R. Hall is Chair of the IBG Transport Geography Study Group and Principal Lecturer in Geography in the School of the Environment, University of Sunderland, England. He is a member of the International Editorial Board of the *Journal of Transport Geography*. A regular visitor to the region since 1968, he has edited a companion Belhaven volume, *Tourism and economic development in Eastern Europe and the Soviet Union*, published in 1991.

Dr Jan S. Kowalski is Professor of Economics, Department of Comparative Economic Systems, University of Münster, Germany. His research interests have focused on comparative economic systems, regional development and policy.

Ms Anu Kull, Institute of Economics, Academy of Sciences of Estonia, Tallinn, Estonia. In addition to her interests in transport, she has published on the development of human geography in Estonia.

Dr Wiesław Z. Michalak is a Senior Lecturer in the Department of Geographical Sciences, University of Plymouth, England. Recently, he has been publishing prolifically with Richard Gibb on aspects of economic development and integration in post-communist Europe. His own research interests have particularly focused on foreign investment in Central and Eastern Europe.

Dr David Pinder is Professor of Economic Geography in the Department of Geographical Sciences, University of Plymouth, England. He has written extensively on European development issues and, since the mid-1980s, has conducted extensive research into the restructuring of Western Europe's oil refining industry. In 1991–92 he was awarded a Leverhulme Fellowship to research oil-based energy in Central and Eastern Europe.

Dr István Prileszky is Professor of the School of Transport and Logistics, Széchenyi István College of Technology, Györ, Hungary. He has degrees in transport economics and management sciences from the University of Economic Sciences, Budapest, and was formerly employed in the road transport industry. In 1991 he spent three months at University College, London.

Dr Zofia Sawiczewska is Professor of Maritime Economics in the Institute of Economics, University of Gdańsk, Poland. She has published widely on maritime matters, most recently in *Maritime Policy and Management*, and has undertaken research in London, Boston and California. She was the first woman to be elected Dean of the Faculty of Transport Economics and Deputy Rector of Gdańsk University.

Ms Bridget Simmonds is a graduate of the University of Cape Town. She is currently a Leverhulme-funded Research Assistant in the Department of Geographical Sciences, University of Plymouth, England, and has worked extensively on energy structures and trends in Central and Eastern Europe.

Emeritus Professor Leslie J. Symons recently retired from the Geography Department and Centre of Russian and East European Studies of University College, Swansea, Wales. He has long held a particular interest in aviation in the erstwhile socialist world. Amongst his many works are the jointly-edited *Soviet and East European transport problems* (Croom Helm, 1985) and *Transport and economic development: Eastern Europe and the Soviet Union* (Duncker & Humblot, Berlin, 1987), in addition to several authored volumes on the Soviet Union.

Dr Zbigniew Taylor is a Research Associate in the Institute of Geography and Spatial Organisation, Polish Academy of Sciences, Warsaw, Poland. His research interests include transport and social geography, and he is currently researching into accessibility of facilities and the daily mobility of rural dwellers. He has published widely in Western as well as in Eastern Europe – for example, co-authoring *Transport Geography*, published in Warsaw and Barcelona. He is a member of the International Editorial Board of the *Journal of Transport Geography*.

Dr Colin Thomas is Reader in Geography in the Department of Environmental Studies, University of Ulster, Coleraine, Northern Ireland. His previous appointments have included a post in the University of Birmingham's Centre for Russian and East European Studies. He has also held research scholarships at the University of Ljubljana, and has been a visiting scholar at a number of European centres, including the Institute of Geography, Bucharest, Moscow State University and the

USSR Academy of Sciences' Institute of Geography. He has published widely on questions of regional development within the former Yugoslavia, and one of his current projects is a study of internal migration up to 1990.

Dr David Turnock is Reader in Geography at Leicester University, England. His interest in Eastern Europe in general, and Romania in particular, is renowned. In 1988/9 Routledge published his four-volume set on the geography of Eastern Europe. Most recently he has jointly edited a volume on *Eastern Europe's environmental problems* (Routledge, 1992). His contribution in the current volume arises out of ESRC-funded research on economic and demographic change in the Romanian Carpathians and on earlier work dealing with the exploitation of Carpathian forests.

List of figures

List of plates

LIVERPOOL HOPE UNIVERSITY COLLEGE

List of tables

Preface

This volume arises from initiatives begun in 1990 by the Transport Geography Study Group (TGSG) of the Institute of British Geographers (IBG). The need to examine and understand crucial interrelationships between transport development and the restructuring economies of Central and Eastern Europe suggested to the Group an appropriate theme for its contribution to the Institute's January 1992 Annual Conference, to be held at University College Swansea. As a sounding board for ideas and themes for papers, and to broaden the disciplinary perspective on the analysis of transport questions, a joint workshop was convened at the then Polytechnic of Central London (PCL) in April 1991 by Mike Browne (University of Westminster) and Roger Mackett (University College London (UCL)) jointly with the Universities Transport Study Group (UTSG), and partly funded by the IBG and UTSG. The participants were mostly drawn from the UK. An exception was István Prileszky, of Széchenyi István College of Technology, Györ, Hungary, who was temporarily attached to UCL. The breadth of discussion at the workshop was sufficient to provide a number of themes which could act as the basis for papers required for the Annual Conference. It also underlined the necessity of direct participation from researchers and practitioners from the region in question.

The TGSG sessions of the Swansea conference, convened by the editor of this volume, were held over the two half-days of the afternoon of 8 January 1992 and the morning of the 9th. With some financial assistance from the IBG, the sessions were able to host three papers presented by contributors from Central and Eastern Europe (in addition to one from Belgium and five from the UK), while further delegates from the region were able to participate in the debate from the floor. In all, Estonia, Hungary, Poland, Romania and Russia were represented during the session. Unfortunately, Dr Prileszky, who had taken part in the original April 1991 workshop, was prevented through illness from attending.

The programme progressed from analyses of general trends to assessments of specific aspects of the relationship between transport and economic development in the region. Within this framework, each of the four modules had a specific sub-theme. The emphasis which ran through every paper, however, was that of the impact of political change and the problems and opportunities of economic transition. At the outset, it was emphasised that given the dynamism of the region and the relatively short time to have elapsed since political and economic restructuring were

LIVERPOOL HOPE UNIVERSITY COLLEGE

initiated, the papers presented were to be seen as somewhat speculative, being designed to stimulate debate and suggest frameworks for future research agendas.

From the diversity of papers presented, a number of common methodological problems emerged, including that of continuing data source shortcomings. Questions relating to new spatial orientations, changing modal splits, differing impacts on passenger and freight transport, the widening gulf between Central Europe and the Balkans and the long-term impact of conflict were all seen to provide fertile ground for subsequent enquiry.

This present volume has therefore built upon these earlier stages of development by inviting the participants of the Swansea TGSG modules to revise and update their papers for publication in the light of the often energetic debate which ensued during the conference, and in response to subsequent events within the region. Further researchers and practitioners in the field who were unable to take part at Swansea were invited to provide additional chapters to assist balance and breadth. In this way, Chapters 2, 3, 4, 8, 9, 10 and 12 of this book build upon the papers presented at the conference, while Chapters 5, 6, 7 and 11 have been commissioned specifically for this volume. Only one of the Swansea participants, Jacques Charlier, of the Catholic University of Louvain, Belgium, was unable to provide material for the final work, due to ill health.

The editor would like to take this opportunity to thank a wide range of people for their assistance and encouragement during the evolution of this volume. The participants of the original workshop at PCL, those taking part in the Swansea sessions, the final contributors to this volume and the TGSG Committee have all lent a great deal of support. Pat Cowell and Neil Purvis transformed a number of the original maps and diagrams into publishable artwork under far from easy circumstances, and Neil also made a valuable editorial contribution. The production team at Belhaven, as ever, went about their task with efficiency and good humour: particular mention should be made of Jane Evans and Patrick Armstrong, and of course Iain Stevenson, rail enthusiast and bon viveur.

Derek R. Hall
Newcastle upon Tyne
October 1992

Glossary of abbreviations and acronyms

An-	Antonov
BAe	British Aerospace
CEL	Central European [Pipe] Line
CIS	Commonwealth of Independent States
CMEA	(former) Council for Mutual Economic Assistance
CoCom	Coordinating Committee for Multilateral Export Controls
ČSA	Československe Aerolinie
CSCE	Conference on Security and Cooperation in Europe
DB	Deutsche Bundesbahn
DR	Deutsche Reichsbahn
dwt	deadweight tonnes
EBRD	European Bank for Reconstruction and Development
EC	European Community/Commission
ECAC	European Civil Aviation Conference
ECE	East-Central Europe
EIB	European Investment Bank
EFTA	European Free Trade Area
GAL	Polish Transatlantic Shipping Company: Gdynia-America Line
GATT	General Agreement on Tariffs and Trade
GDP	gross domestic product
GDR	(former) German Democratic Republic
GNP	gross national product
GRT	gross registered tonnes
IATA	International Air Transport Association
IBG	Institute of British Geographers
ICAO	International Civil Aviation Authority
Il-	Ilyushin
ILG	International Leisure Group
ILO	International Labour Office
ILS	instrument landing system
IMF	International Monetary Fund
IUCN	International Union for the Conservation of Nature and Natural Resources (World Conservation Union)
IUOTO	International Union of Official Travel Organisations
JAT	Jugoslovenski Aerotransport
JTG	Journal of Transport Geography

kph	kilometres per hour
LOT	Polskie Linie Lotnicze
MALÉV	Hungarian Airlines
OECD	Organisation for Economic Cooperation and Development
PCL	(the former) Polytechnic of Central London
PHARE	Poland/Hungary Assistance for Restructuring Economies
SEM	Single European Market
SEPL	Southern European Pipeline
STEG	Staatseisenbahngesellschaft
TAL	Trans-Austria [Pipe] Line
TAROM	Romanian state airline
TEM	Trans-European Motorway
TER	Trans-European Railway
TGSG	Transport Geography Study Group
TNC	Trans-national corporation
Tu-	Tupolev
UCL	University College London
UDR	Uzine de Fier şi Domeniilor din Reşiţa
UNESCO	United Nations Education and Science Organisation
UTSG	Universities Transport Study Group
WTO	World Tourism Organisation
WWF	Worldwide Fund for Nature

1 Introduction

Derek Hall and Jan Kowalski*

1.1 Transport and economic restructuring

Although the literature on the relationship between transport and economic development in the erstwhile Soviet bloc had begun to expand in the 1980s (e.g. Ambler *et al.*, Tismer *et al.*, 1987; Taylor 1984a, 1987, 1989; Turnock, 1986), this volume, focusing on Central and Eastern Europe (Figure 1.1; Table 1.1), presents one of the first major attempts to appraise that relationship during the period of transition from communist to market-based economies. Such an undertaking can be fraught with analytical and methodological problems yet is pregnant with longer-term research applications and cooperation possibilities.

With a Central and Eastern Europe in economic, political and social transition acting as the ever-changing context for this volume, the shelf-life of too hasty assumptions and intemperate generalisations can be perilously short. The countries of the region under review are moving towards market economies and are developing pluralist political systems at differing speeds, from varied points of departure, and with varying degrees of upheaval. Additionally, several dynamic regional factors will continue to interact for some time to influence national developments. These include the consequences arising from the demise of the Council for Mutual Economic Assistance (CMEA or COMECON), collapse of the old Soviet economy, adoption of hard currency accounting, influx of selective Western investment and technology, and continued political instability, particularly in the Balkans. All continue to generate shifting patterns of trade relations and transport flows within the region.

Those states of Central and Eastern Europe politically and socially dominated by communist parties had been hidebound by inflexible economic policies based on rigid five-year plans and large-scale public ownership of the means of production, trade and transport. Full employment was guaranteed: indeed, every able-bodied adult was theoretically obliged to work as part of a social contract between the individual and the state. 'Full employment' meant that there were no unemployment

---

* Professor Kowalski contributed the draft text of section 1.3.

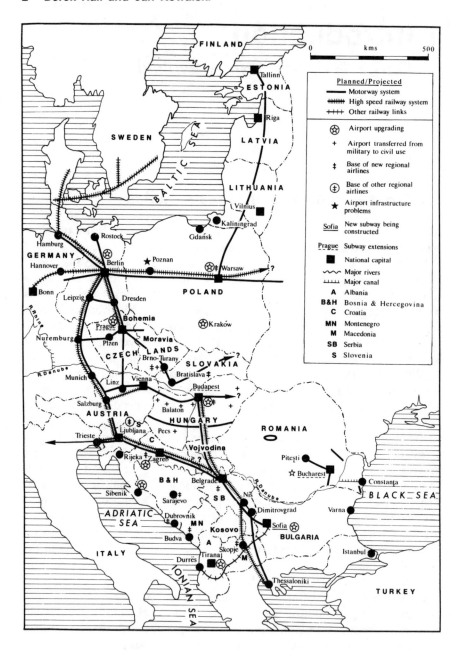

Figure 1.1 Central and Eastern Europe: transport upgrading

Table 1.1 Central and Eastern Europe: basic national data

Country	Area ('000 sq km)	Population		$ per cap GNP (1988)	Currency*
		In millions (1990)	Density per sq km		
Albania	27	3.3	114	930 [*]	Lek
Bulgaria	111	9.0	81	5,633	Lev
Czechoslovakia[‡]	128	15.7	123	7,603	Koruna
Former GDR	108	16.6[¶]	154	9,361	Deutschmark
Hungary	93	10.4	112	6,491	Forint
Poland	313	37.9	121	5,453	Złoty
Romania	238	23.3	98	4,117	Leu
Former Soviet Union European components:				5,552	
Armenia	30	3.3	111		Rouble/Dram
Belarus	208	10.2	49		Rouble/voucher/Taler
Estonia	45	1.6	36		Kroon
Georgia	70	5.4	77		Rouble
Latvia	65	2.7	42		Rouble
Lithuania	65	3.8	58		Rouble/Litas
Moldova	34	4.4	129		Rouble/Leu
Russia	17,000	148.0	9		Rouble
Ukraine	506	51.5	102		Coupon/Grivna
Former Yugoslavia				4,898	
Bosnia-Hercegovina	51	4.1[†]	80		Dinar
Croatia	57	4.8	84		Dinar/Crown
Macedonia	26	1.9	73		Dinar
Slovenia	20	1.9	95		Tolar
Yugoslavia (Serbia and Montenegro)	135	12.0[†]	89		New Dinar

*   as at July 1992
[†]   estimate
[‡]   at the time of writing Czechoslovakia was preparing to become divided into two separate states, with Bratislava becoming the capital of Slovakia, and Prague retaining capital status for the Czech lands only (Hall, 1992a).
[¶]   1988 figures
[*]   1986 estimate

Sources: *Business Europa*, 1992 1(2): pp. 60, 62; *Europa World Yearbook*, 1992, p. 306; Hall, 1991c, p. 9.

benefits, and dismissal from employment was a convenient way of under-mining dissidents. Overmanning, poor service quality, dated technology and low productivity were the norm. Personal social and physical mobility (Fuchs and Demko, 1978) was severely constrained through a variety of mechanisms (Adam, 1984; Compton, 1972; Sjoberg, 1991a, pp. 51–62, 1991b, 1991c, pp. 26–9) and structural barriers (Hall, 1988a; Kapitany *et al.*, 1984). Private initiative within the informal economy flourished (Aslund, 1984a, 1984b; Kenedi, 1981).

As from mid-1989, most Central and East European communist parties lost power or 'reformed' themselves. German unification consolidated a society of almost eighty million people situated in a pivotal position within Europe. Generating the world's highest value export performance, the 'new' state appeared to be in a prime position to act as the major economic influence on Central and Eastern Europe's transport future. As the Soviet Union withered away, centrifugal forces increased the potential for instability on the region's eastern flank. New states, new dominant political ideologies, uncertain economic circumstances and continuing instability and conflict have thus provided the far from optimistic 1990s circumstances within which 1980s free market dogmas could be imposed on the region.

The two-way interaction between transport and economic development represents in many ways a struggle between, on the one hand, the forces of post-communist restructuring and the emergence of a 'new Europe', and the inertia and shortcomings inherited from communism on the other. In the first instance, the influence of political and economic restructuring on transport can be summarised under four headings (Hall, 1993):

1. New organisational and management structures. These have arisen from the various processes of decentralisation, de-monopolisation and privatisation, and the establishment of new independent states and growth of foreign economic involvement (see Chapters 4, 6, 8 and 9). The imposition of new financial stringencies has been reflected in such secondary impacts as the closing down of unprofitable routes and modal shifts in the carriage of freight (Chapters 4, 6 and 7).
2. New linkages and routes. These have been developed through (a) the generation of new trade relationships and orientations westwards, rather than following the previous eastward bias of the region (Chapters 2, 3 and 7); (b) the breaking down of East–West (or at least West–East) constraints on personal movement with often substantial increases in tourism (Chapter 12); and (c) German unification (Chapter 5). Negatively, the repulsion effect of conflict, most notably in the former Yugoslavia (Chapter 11), has provided an additional short- to medium-term dynamic influence on route and network development (Plate 1.1).
3. New equipment and technology transferred to the region. This is largely derived from cooperation with Western (including Japanese) partners, involving either direct sale or lease, as in the case of Boeing and Airbus aircraft (Chapter 4), or the purchase of manufacturing

Plate 1.1 With the opening of Albania, the potential of this road around Lake Ohrid between that country and Macedonia, part of the historical route between the Adriatic and Bosphorus/Black Sea, has been constrained by events in neighbouring regions of the former Yugoslavia. (Derek Hall)

licences for production of new transport technology within the region itself, as in the motor vehicle industry (Chapters 6 and 13).

4. A quantitative and qualitative upgrading of infrastructure and services, ranging from international freight and passenger termini to catering, retailing, ticketing, fuel provision and equipment servicing, as a consequence of the market orientation of the region's economies, joint ventures with Western companies and the growing trade and political relationships with Western Europe and North America (Chapters 2, 3, 4, 6 and 7). Out of these new opportunities has arisen increasing competition between states for regional hub status, most notably in the air and inland waterway transport sectors (Chapters 4 and 13), and competition between Western contractors to provide the necessary infrastructure and services.

Problems inherited from the communist period do underpin many contemporary transport developments and dilemmas within the region. These may be summarised under eight headings:

Plate 1.2   A barely signposted difficult mountain road not untypical of the transport infrastructure in a number of the region's rural areas. (Derek Hall)

1. Poor infrastructural maintenance. This has been experienced in all transport sectors, but it is most notably evident, given current modal shifts, in the region's road network. Inadequate lane capacity, poor road surfaces, alignment, maintenance and signposting (Plate 1.2), and insufficient roadside services such as petrol filling stations, catering, and other retailing outlets all present major shortcomings.
2. Inferior technology, ranging from Soviet-built aircraft, with their high levels of fuel consumption and excessive maintenance and ground staff requirements, to obsolete and underpowered motor vehicles, widespread use of animal power (Plate 1.3) and hopelessly outmoded and overloaded telecommunications systems. Emblematic of the Soviet-style economic system, this factor has been endemic in the transport systems of all countries in the region. Substantial upgrading and replacement is now a major task.
3. Organisational and structural obstacles and bottlenecks express themselves in poorly developed transport logistics (Chapter 2), in tensions between government departments involved in transport and economic development, between the public and emerging private sectors, and between old and new public sector organisations.

Plate 1.3 An almost timeless Balkan scene. Horse-powered goods transport and ancient Skoda buses lined up in an alfresco mosque-side bus station in Berat, Albania. (Derek Hall)

Shortcomings in legislative and regulatory provision for privatisation and joint venture development, including insurance and guarantees, may inhibit Western investment. Further obstacles are presented by the manner in which elements of the old communist *nomenklatura*, through their resilient networks of influential contacts, have managed to hold on to positions of economic power while nominally relinquishing the political reins.

4. Neglect of human resources. The quality of the region's passenger transport services, in particular, has been generally low and very variable by accepted Western standards, reflecting poor working conditions, low staff morale and lack of incentives. Some Western financial institutions and management consultants have begun to respond to the huge requirement for staff training in all sectors of the transport and travel industry. Needs are now most pressing in, particularly, such areas as computing, telecommunications and foreign languages (Hamilton, 1991).

5. Mobility constraints. Since the events of 1989, most exit formalities for Central and East Europeans have been abolished. But while

mutual reductions of impediments between a number of Western and Eastern European countries have come about, others remain. Bottlenecks at inefficient border crossing points are an obvious constraint which requires attention, particularly for those countries of Central Europe aspiring to EC membership. Hungary completed a computerisation of all its 723 crossing points in 1992 in readiness for handling the coded EC passport, and by 1995 the country should have installed 5,000 professional border guards to replace the present 22,000 soldiers.

6. Fiscal problems. Most of the region's currencies continue to be inconvertible. The introduction of completely new currencies (in Slovenia and Croatia, the Baltic states and members of the Commonwealth of Independent States (CIS)) has added complications to the region's already unstable fiscal position. Although devaluations since 1989 have rendered official exchange rates more realistic, currency constraints remain for investment planning, joint venture development and export pricing. While adoption of hard currency accounting for all international transactions has drawn the region into the world market, it has further emphasised the general unmarketability of much of the region's manufactures. It has also considerably increased international travel costs (the requirement to pay for Russian fuel in dollars coinciding with the shedding of transport subsidies), and of contributing to hard currency shortages.

7. Neglect of environmental considerations. The region's environmental debate has largely avoided addressing transport questions (Carter and Turnock, 1992). Widespread use of electric public transport was a positive element of communist transport policy, especially in high-density urban areas (Plate 1.4). But traffic congestion, particularly in the more advanced cities such as Budapest and Prague, has long been recognised as a major source of atmospheric pollution and health problems, resulting from poor engine technology, use of low-grade fuel and an over-burdening of public transport. The environmental impacts of transport and travel activities and opportunities in the region will need to be very carefully monitored. In the short term, rapidly increased tourism, for example, is placing severe pressures on specific, often fragile, environments, both rural and urban (Chapter 12).

A more specific problem is the environmental inheritance of former Soviet military airfields, which, when vacated, were found to be very poorly maintained and often heavily polluted with fuel seepage. At two sites in Poland alone (Stara Kopernia and Szprotawa), environmental damage is estimated at $175 million; and jet fuel so heavily saturates the ground that residents have been charged for the right to dig holes and pump it out. In Hungary, reclamation of the former Soviet military airfields at Halasztelek and

Plate 1.4 An aged two-car tram unit on reserved track at the multi-mode transport interchange (bus, tram, metro, rail) in the high-density Budapest suburb of Ors. Vezer Tere. (Derek Hall)

Tokol is being undertaken with Danish assistance. The danger of well pollution is particularly critical, as Tokol is Budapest's main water supply area.

8. Imbalanced investments. Dominated by centralised five-year plans' emphasis on quantitative output, investment tended to be concentrated in a few grandiose projects rather than on improving quality and infrastructural support. In Polish ports, for example, early post-war physical and economic reconstruction was followed by stagnation. Quay modernisation was undertaken, but with a continuation of traditional stevedoring; increasing numbers of vessels were purchased at the expense of improving port infrastructures, such that by the 1990s, Poland, as one of the region's most important maritime nations, found itself with outdated infrastructure, poor technology and insufficient deepwater capacity to cope with rapidly changing conditions (Chapter 8). For example, only about 15 per cent of general cargoes were containerised (Lijewski, 1982; Sawiczewska, 1992; Taylor, 1984a, 1987, 1989, 1993).

Since the fall of the ruling communist parties in Central and Eastern Europe, the region's already far from satisfactory transport infrastructure has actually experienced some short-term deterioration. This is a reflection of several factors:

1. The movement of often heavy public subsidies away from public transport (as a forerunner to privatisation);
2. A modal shift of freight transport away from heavily subsidised rail onto roads;
3. A deterioration of road conditions, resulting from both past under-investment and a current rapid increase in motor vehicle use, reflecting modal shifts and a substantial increase in tourism and cross-border leisure traffic; together with:
4. The conflict in former Yugoslavia, necessitating avoiding routes both on land and in the air away from a major trunk corridor between Central Europe and the Balkans. Most notably, this has contributed to substantially increased transit road traffic through Hungary;
5. The long lead-times for aircraft and shipping fleet replacement (partially mitigated by leasing arrangements and second-hand purchases) and port and airport rebuilding/expansion programmes;
6. The uncertainty of private sector and international funding provision.

1.2 Regional transport data

While national yearbooks of each country are an obvious prime source to turn to for data compilation, most of the statistics in the tables which follow are culled from the publications of Euromonitor (1991, 1992) and the *Europa World Yearbook* (1992). There are a number of reasons for this: (a) such international compilations provide comparative data in readily digestible form; (b) they attempt to iron out or highlight inconsistencies in the data; and (c) with national fragmentation it is becoming increasingly difficult to gain adequate access to all appropriate national yearbooks. These factors tend to outweigh the major drawback of using international compilations: that of the inevitable time lag (now improving) between data collection and its initial publication in the appropriate national yearbook, and its subsequent publication in the international compilation, usually rendering the latter a year behind the former.

Table 1.2 Central and Eastern Europe: road network, 1989 (kilometres)

	Total	Motorway		Highway (national)		Secondary (regional)		Others (local)		Density km/
		a	b	a	b	a	b	a	b	sq km
Albania*	7,201	–		–		–		7,201	100.0	0.23
Bulgaria	36,934	266	0.7	2,935	8.0	3,796	10.3	29,937	81.1	0.33
Czechoslovakia	73,113	527	0.7	9,659	13.2	17,935	24.5	45,519	62.3	0.57
Hungary†	105,370	311	0.3	6,379	6.1	23,024	21.9	75,656	71.8	1.13
Poland	360,864	243	0.1	45,231	12.5	128,746	35.7	186,644	51.7	1.15
Romania	72,816	113	0.2	14,570	20.0	26,967	37.0	31,166	42.8	0.31
USSR*	1,609,900	nd		nd		nd		nd		nd
Yugoslavia†	122,062	871	0.7	16,772	13.7	31,964	26.2	72,455	59.4	0.47

Notes: a : length
b : percentage of country's total
nd : no data
* : 1987 figures
† : 1988 figures

Sources: Euromonitor, 1992, p. 412; *Europa World Yearbook*, 1992, p. 317; author's additional calculations.

1.2.1 The infrastructure

Table 1.2 outlines the nature of the region's road network as it was on the eve of political and economic change. Notable is the minute proportion of motorway length and the contrasting predominance of local roads.

Aside from the significant growth of the small Albanian network (Plate 1.5), Table 1.3 indicates that during the 1980s, at least, little change took place in the region's public rail network. Within Central Europe, only Poland shows any significant absolute change, adding over 2,000 km to its system during the decade. Incomplete USSR data suggest somewhat more extensive Soviet development, however.

No overall pattern emerges from looking at the changing sizes of shipping fleets during the 1980s (Table 1.4). Overall, increasing fleet size is the trend, with Romania (115.7 per cent) and land-locked Czechoslovakia (109.8 per cent) more than doubling the sizes of their fleets during the decade. Yugoslavia and Hungary also increased their fleets significantly, the latter again emphasising an apparently growing role for inland waterway transport. Poland showed some retrenchment.

While types of vessel vary (Table 1.5), it is notable that ore and bulk carriers make up a sizeable proportion of the tonnage of Bulgaria, Czechoslovakia, Poland, Romania and Yugoslavia's fleets, while over

Plate 1.5 A Czech-built T669 diesel locomotive hauls a passenger train past the village of Lin, with its hillside propaganda slogan, on part of the Albanian rail system constructed in the mid-1970s. (Derek Hall)

Table 1.3 Central and Eastern Europe: length of public rail network, 1977–88 (kilometres)

	1977	1980	1982	1984	1986	1988	1980–88 % change
Albania	330	330	330	330	330	509	54.2
Bulgaria	4,295	4,267	4,273	4,279	4,297	4,300	0.5
Czechoslovakia	13,190	13,131	13,142	13,114	13,116	13,104	0.2
Hungary	8,063	7,826	7,823	7,830	7,836	7,614	2.7
Poland	23,953	24,356	24,348	24,353	24,333	26,545	9.4
Romania	11,127	11,110	11,125	11,169	11,221	nd	0.1*
USSR	228,800	239,400	242,600	246,400	nd	nd	2.9[†]
Yugoslavia	9,967	9,465	9,389	9,279	9,246	9,349	− 1.2

Notes: nd: no data
   *   1980–86 % change
   [†]   1980–84 % change

Sources: Euromonitor, 1992, p. 416; author's calculations.

Table 1.4 Central and Eastern Europe: merchant shipping: size of fleet, 1977–90 (thousand GRT)

	1977	1980	1984	1986	1988	1990	1980–90 % change
Albania	55.9	56.1	56.1	56.1	56.1	55.8	– 0.5
Bulgaria	964.2	1,233.3	1,283.0	1,385.0	1,392.4	1,360.5	10.3
Czechoslovakia	148.7	155.3	184.3	197.9	157.9	325.8	109.8
Hungary	63.0	75.0	80.0	86.4	76.1	98.3	31.1
Poland	3,447.5	3,639.1	3,267.3	3,457.2	3,849.4	3,369.2	– 7.4
Romania	1,218.2	1,856.3	2,666.8	3,233.9	3,560.7	4,004.6	115.7
USSR	21,438.3	23,443.5	24,492.5	24,960.9	25,784.0	26,737.4	14.1
Yugoslavia	2,284.5	2,466.6	2,681.9	2,872.6	3,476.4	3,816.0	54.7
Total	29,620.3	32,925.2	34,711.9	36,250.0	38,353.0	39,767.6	20.8

Sources: Euromonitor, 1992, p. 424; author's calculations.

three-quarters of Hungary's and virtually all of Albania's tonnage consist of general cargo vessels. Oil tankers have some significance for Bulgaria and Romania – the two Soviet bloc states which were not connected to the Soviet oil pipeline system – and for the USSR itself. The proportion of container ships throughout the region in 1990 was pitifully small, indicating significant shortcomings in freight-handling technology and logistics.

Turning to civil aviation in 1990, what is particularly striking about Table 1.6 is the similarity between several of the region's fleets regarding numbers of passengers carried (five with between one and two million), kilometres flown (six between 21 and 44 million), aircraft departures (four in the band 18–29,000), hours flown (six within the 62–68 per cent range), and freight carried (five between five and ten thousand tonnes). Civil aviation activity increased during the 1980s (Table 1.7), with Bulgaria outstanding in raising scheduled distances flown between 1980 and 1989 by nearly 160 per cent, reflecting Balkan's development of intercontinental routes. Other increases were more modest, ranging from 7.7 to 36.2 per cent, with Czechoslovakia actually recording a slight decrease. The most significant development, which was hidden by such trends, was the dramatic decline in activity in Poland in the early 1980s during the Solidarity and subsequent martial law periods. Poland's 1982 figure shows a more than 66 per cent reduction in activity compared to 1980. The dips in the figures for Czechoslovakia and Romania at this time might also reflect secondary effects of the Polish situation.

Table 1.5 Central and Eastern Europe: merchant shipping: principal types of vessels, 1990

a. In thousand GRT

	Tankers			Carriers		General cargo		
	Oil	Oil/ chemical	Chemical	Liquid gas	Ore & bulk	Single deck	Double deck	Container ships
Albania	0	0	0	0	0	15.7	38.8	0
Bulgaria	287.7	0	6.1	0	611.0	78.6	197.4	19.1
Czechoslovakia	0	0	0	0	241.2	10.0	74.5	0
Hungary	0	0	0	0	17.3	13.9	67.2	0
Poland	126.3	27.8	0	0	1,602.6	184.6	716.7	61.0
Romania	645.2	0	0	0	1,890.7	207.2	864.5	15.2
USSR	4,041.0	125.9	7.5	125.3	3,147.4	2,287.4	3,297.9	626.0
Yugoslavia	306.0	0	8.1	0	1,803.0	260.6	905.9	130.6
Total	5,406.2	153.7	21.7	125.3	9,313.2	3,058.0	6,162.9	851.9

b. As percentages of national totals

	Tankers			Carriers		General cargo			Other
	Oil	Oil/ chemical	Chemical	Liquid gas	Ore & bulk	Single deck	Double deck	Container ships	
Albania	0	0	0	0	0	28.1	69.5	0	2.4
Bulgaria	21.1	0	0.4	0	44.9	5.8	14.5	1.4	11.9
Czechoslovakia	0	0	0	0	74.0	3.1	22.9	0	0
Hungary	0	0	0	0	17.6	14.1	68.4	0	0
Poland	3.7	0.8	0	0	47.6	5.5	21.3	1.8	19.3
Romania	16.1	0	0	0	46.5	5.2	21.6	0.4	10.2
USSR	15.1	0.5	0.1	0.5	11.8	8.6	12.3	2.3	47.8
Yugoslavia	8.0	0	0.2	0	47.2	6.8	23.7	3.4	10.7
Total	13.6	0.3	0.1	0.3	23.4	7.7	15.5	2.1	37.0

Sources: Euromonitor, 1992, p. 427; author's calculations.

Table 1.6 Central and Eastern Europe: national airlines data, 1990

	Aircraft departures			Passengers		Freight carried
	'000s km travelled	number	hours flown	carried ('000s)	load factors (%)	(thousand tonnes)
Bulgaria	31,442	37,150	49,466	1,907	68	5
Czechoslovakia	23,900	22,349	32,599	1,095	66	5
Hungary	18,998	18,974	34,703	1,363	66	5
Poland	39,240	28,618	60,759	1,510	62	10
Romania*	21,300	23,652	36,927	1,281	62	9
USSR	161,014	62,053	199,785	137,198	87	2,901
Yugoslavia	43,156	49,455	81,828	3,258	68	34
Total	339,050	242,251	496,067	147,612	–	2,969

Notes: * 1987 data

Source: Euromonitor, 1992, p. 423.

Table 1.7 Central and Eastern Europe: civil aviation: scheduled distances flown, 1977–90 (million kilometres)

	1977	1980	1982	1984	1986	1988	1989	1990*	1980–89 % change
Albania	nd	nd	nd	nd	nd	nd	nd	nd	nd
Bulgaria	10.6	12.7	19.5	25.8	28.5	32.4	33.0	31.4	159.8
Czechoslovakia	26.8	24.7	19.5	21.6	23.5	25.7	24.6	23.9	–0.4
Hungary	12.4	16.2	17.6	17.6	18.2	17.8	20.3	19.0	25.3
Poland	29.4	35.1	11.8	22.8	27.7	30.1	37.8	39.2	7.7
Romania	19.4	19.7	17.1	19.5	21.0	21.9	22.5	21.3	14.2
USSR	nd	nd	125.1	125.0	113.0	155.2	146.8	161.0	17.3[†]
Yugoslavia	31.9	34.8	28.5	29.8	39.3	46.4	47.4	43.2	36.2

Notes: nd: no data
  *: 'national airline' only, as in Table 1.6
  [†]: 1982–89 % change

Sources: Euromonitor, 1992, p. 420, 423; author's calculations.

1.2.2 Goods transport

The trend of goods transport by road, as measured in tonne-kilometres, during the 1980s (Table 1.8) reveals no apparent pattern: while Romania (– 57 per cent) and Czechoslovakia (– 38 per cent) recorded considerable overall decreases, Bulgaria's figure increased by half and Hungary and Poland showed substantial gains. However, Yugoslavia aside, all

Table 1.8 Central and Eastern Europe: goods transported by road, 1977–89 (million tonne-kilometres)

	1977	1980	1982	1984	1986	1988	1989	1980–89 % change
Albania	nd	1,302	nd	nd	1,268≠	1,269	1,269	−2.5
Bulgaria	9,449	10,078	10,577	7,262	7,495	14,725	15,148	50.3
Czechoslovakia	17,305	21,335	20,962	20,919	12,201	13,079	13,247	−37.9
Hungary	9,550	10,258	11,883	9,716*	12,175	13,120	nd	27.9"
Poland	40,277	44,546	34,024	36,577	37,029	38,796	38,448	13.7
Romania	nd	11,756	11,150	7,300	5,520	4,929†	5,070	−56.9
USSR‡	nd	131,000	143,000	138,000	489,811	491,955≠	nd	–
Yugoslavia	12,510	18,997	19,267	21,540	22,342	20,882	nd	9.9"

Notes: nd: no data
* 1985 figure
† 1987 figure was 4,851
‡ new data series introduced 1985
≠ 1987 figure
" 1980–88 % change

Sources: Euromonitor, 1992, p. 415; Europa World Yearbook, 1992, p. 311; KPS, 1989, p. 105; author's calculations.

Table 1.9 Central and Eastern Europe: freight carried by rail, 1977–90 (million tonne-kilometres)

	1977	1980	1984	1986	1988	1989	1990	% change 1980–89	% change 1989–90
Albania	nd	477	nd	629*	626	626	nd	31.2	–
Bulgaria	17,076	17,676	18,132	18,324	17,580	17,040	14,124	– 3.6	– 17.1
Czechoslovakia	71,544	72,636	73,992	75,156	75,288	71,976	64,260	– 0.9	– 10.7
Hungary	23,556	23,868	22,308	22,092	20,568	19,368	16,776	– 18.9	– 13.4
Poland	135,408	134,736	123,504	121,776	122,208	110,208	83,532	– 18.2	– 24.2
Romania									
USSR†	3,331	3,440	3,600	nd	nd	nd	nd	–	–
Yugoslavia	22,224	24,996	25,812	27,564	25,416	25,800	nd	3.2	–

Notes: nd: no data
     *   1987 figure
     †   figures in thousand million tonne-kilometres

Sources: Euromonitor, 1992, p. 418; Europa World Yearbook, 1992, p. 311; LPS, 1989, p. 105; author's calculations.

countries recorded substantial downturns in the early to mid-1980s, from which some recovered while others did not, as reflected in the above trends. Perhaps two factors are at work here. First, the slowing down of these increasingly inefficient economies witnessed a general reduction of goods movement. That some countries' road goods sectors were able to recover, secondly, may reflect a combination of a modal shift from rail to road, as would appear from Table 1.9, and the degree of flexibility of individual economies and their contact with the West. For example, the marked disparity in overall performance between the neighbouring land-locked states of Czechoslovakia and Hungary would appear to be in large measure due to the stark contrasts in political and economic flexibility prevailing between the two at that time.

In reflecting a downward trend, substantially accelerated between 1989 and 1990, Table 1.9 would appear to highlight the less flexible nature of railway transport and the resultant decline in the amount of the bulk goods and raw materials transported by rail. This has meant an overall reduction in freight most suited to rail transport, and a modal shift to road of goods more sensitive to door-to-door delivery and market requirements. The events of 1989 clearly hastened this process in most instances.

What incomplete data were available for analysis in Table 1.10, concerning sea-borne goods transported, suggest no clear overall trends. Poland recorded a general decline in the level of unloaded goods with a less clear pattern for those loaded, while Bulgaria was recording an upward trend in the latter, revealing some export success, and a downward pattern for the former. Romania and Yugoslavia were showing growth in both elements up to 1988.

Although Table 1.11 records a general upward trend in airborne freight, with the exception of Hungary, this overall pattern masks significant national variations. Poland, for example, recorded a decline of 28 per cent between 1980 and 1988, never having fully recovered from the post-Solidarity martial law period, but then for 1988–89 showed a 113 per cent growth. Czechoslovakia's figures rose to a 1986 peak and then declined, while both Romania and the Soviet Union, while recording overall upward trends, also experienced successive increases and decreases during the decade, Soviet airborne freight being the only example actually to show a decline for 1988–89.

1.2.3 Passenger transport

As might be expected given the administrative and financial constraints, numbers of passenger cars in use showed only modest gains in the second half of the 1980s, although significant national variations were recorded (Table 1.12). For example, of the two least developed countries (aside

Table 1.10 Central and Eastern Europe: international sea-borne goods, 1977–90 (million tonnes)

	1977 a	1977 b	1980 a	1980 b	1984 a	1984 b	1988 a	1988 b	1989 a	1989 b	1990 a	1990 b
Albania	nd	nd	1.0	0.5	1.2	0.6	1.1	1.0	nd	nd	nd	nd
Bulgaria	3.1	24.8	3.6	28.1	3.8	25.3	5.5	22.0	nd	nd	nd	nd
Czechoslovakia	nd	nd	nd	nd	nd	nd	nd	nd	nd	nd	nd	nd
Hungary	nd	nd	nd	nd	nd	nd	nd	nd	nd	nd	nd	nd
Poland	37.8	24.0	28.1	22.8	39.4	15.9	32.0	18.2	27.3	17.0	30.7	12.5
Romania*	nd	nd	7.2	27.0	8.6	28.5	13.8	33.3	nd	nd	nd	nd
USSR*	nd	nd	151.2	69.8	166.5	75.9	160.6	85.6	nd	nd	nd	nd
Yugoslavia	4.7	16.5	5.2	23.1	6.5	22.3	8.5	25.5	8.1	25.3	nd	nd

Notes: a: loaded
b: unloaded
nd: no data
*   1980 figures are for 1982

Sources: Euromonitor, 1992, pp. 425–6; *Europa World Yearbook*, 1992, p. 311.

Table 1.11 Central and Eastern Europe: freight transported by air, 1979–89 (million tonne–kilometres)

	1979	1980	1982	1984	1986	1988	1989	1980–89 % change
Albania	nd	nd	nd	nd	nd	nd	nd	–
Bulgaria	nd	nd	nd	nd	nd	9.0	9.0	–
Czechoslovakia	18.0	14.6	17.1	16.9	21.0	17.2	17.3	18.5
Hungary	7.8	9.2	9.2	8.6	9.4	5.8	5.8	–37.0
Poland	18.4	18.8	6.4	9.3	12.0	13.5	28.8	53.2*
Romania	11.9	10.0	9.0	11.2	10.1	12.8	14.5	45.0
USSR	2,099.0	2,151.8	2,185.7	2,744.9	2,650.4	2,720.8	2,644.5	22.9
Yugoslavia	nd	nd	53.6	81.4	100.2	124.4	135.4	152.6†

Notes: nd   no data

   * 1980–88 change was −28.2%; 1988–89 change was 113.3%

   † 1982–89 % change

Sources: Euromonitor, 1992, p. 422; author's calculations.

Table 1.12 Central and Eastern Europe: passenger car use and distribution, 1985–9

	1985		1987		1989			
	a	c	a	c	a	b	c	d
Albania	nd	nd	nd	nd	nd	nd	nd	nd
Bulgaria	600.0	67	775.0	86	781.4	30.2	87	263
Czechoslovakia	2,575.0	166	2,700.0	173	2,853.0	10.8	183	519
GDR	3,306.2	198	3,462.2	208	3,660.1	10.7	220	555
Hungary	1,435.9	135	1,660.3	156	1,660.3	15.6	157	429
Poland	3,450.0	93	3,650.0	97	3,917.6	13.6	103	319
Romania	250.0	11	260.0	11	270.0	8.0	12	36
USSR	11,000.0	40	11,750.0	42	12,827.4	16.6	45	191
Yugoslavia	2,849.4	123	2,972.8	127	3,255.0	14.2	137	440
Total	25,466.5	62	27,230.3	65	29,224.8	14.8	72	267

Notes: a: cars in use (thousands)
b: cars in use % change 1985–89
c: cars per thousand population
d: cars per thousand households

Sources: Euromonitor, 1991, p. 586; author's calculations.

Table 1.13 Central and Eastern Europe: railway passengers, 1977–90 (million passenger-kilometres)

	1977	1980	1984	1988	1989	1990	% change 1980–89	% change 1989–90
Albania	nd	369	nd	703	nd	nd	90.5‡	–
Bulgaria	7,344	7,056	7,536	8,148	7,596	7,788	7.7	2.5
Czechoslovakia	19,176	18,048	19,320	20,029*	19,572	nd	8.4	–
Hungary	13,020	12,372	10,512	10,764	9,612	11,400	–22.3	18.6
Poland	44,316	46,320	53,184	52,128	55,884	50,376	20.6	–9.9
Romania								
USSR	322,200	332,064	347,856†	nd	nd	nd	–	–
Yugoslavia	10,464	10,272	11,736	11,568	11,748	nd	14.4	–

Notes: nd: no data
* 1987 figure
† 1982 figure
‡ 1980–88 % change

Sources: Euromonitor, 1992, p. 417; Europa World Yearbook, 1992, p. 311; KPS, 1989, p. 107; author's calculations.

Table 1.14 Central and Eastern Europe: civil aviation passengers, 1979–89 (million passenger–kilometres)

	1979	1980	1982	1984	1986	1988	1989	1980–89 % change
Albania	nd	nd	nd	nd	nd	nd	nd	–
Bulgaria	nd	nd	nd	nd	2,100*	2,279	2,400	–
Czechoslovakia	1,740	1,536	1,596	1,692	1,872	2,242	2,195	42.9
Hungary	960	1,020	1,212	1,200	1,092	1,178	1,379	35.2
Poland	2,316	2,352	804	1,776	2,196	2,701	3,734	58.8†
Romania	1,179	1,209	1,145	1,372	1,427	1,669	1,646	36.1
USSR	150,708	160,296	172,212	183,276	194,352	213,169	226,734	41.4
Yugoslavia	nd	nd	nd	3,845‡	4,284≠	3,245	5,123	–

Notes: nd: no data
*   1987 figure
†   1980–88 change was 14.8%; 1988–89 change was 38.2%
‡   1985 figure
≠   1987 figure was 5,229

Sources: Euromonitor, 1992, p. 421; author's calculations.

from Albania and the USSR), Bulgaria showed the greatest proportional gain in the region, just over 30 per cent, as might be predicted for a country with a narrow base. Yet Romania, from a much lower base figure, recorded the smallest increase, just 8 per cent, reflecting the deteriorating economic and political conditions being experienced in that country.

The period saw a trend of generally modest overall growth in railway passenger loads, with the notable exception of the small expanding Albanian system (Table 1.13). However, a longer-term decline in Hungary was evident, as were occasional short-lived downturns, such as those for Bulgaria and Czechoslovakia in 1989 and Poland in 1986 and 1990, as well as an uncertain pattern for Yugoslavia in the second half of the 1980s.

Air passenger transport appears to show a healthy growth for most countries of the region during the 1980s (Table 1.14), although a considerable downturn in Poland in the early 1980s reflected the country's domestic economic and political turmoil, and a blip in Yugoslavia for 1988 may have reflected tourism difficulties.

1.3 Economic restructuring in perspective

1.3.1 Components of economic restructuring

In Soviet-type planned economies, money, prices, costs, interest rates and microeconomic considerations played a very minor role: acknowledged in theory but not employed as the basis for actual economic behaviour (Kornai, 1980, 1982; Kowalski, 1983, 1987; Funck and Kowalski, 1987). The behaviour of enterprises was influenced primarily by the existence of 'soft' budgets, permitting them to disregard the financial aspects of their activities and therefore also the markets for their output. All reform programmes currently being executed in Central and Eastern Europe are directed towards the 'hardening' of these budget constraints, and towards changing the ways in which economic actors perceive the role of financial levers in the functioning of the economy.

The major components of economic restructuring packages in Central and Eastern Europe can be summarised as follows:

1. Privatisation: an efficient market economy with budget constraints requires the elimination of predominant state ownership of fixed assets, the formation of bankruptcy laws and the establishment of stock exchange activities. This issue is arguably the most important

one in the reform programmes of post-communist Europe, but it faces numerous obstacles (Lipton and Sachs, 1991; Milanovic, 1991: Kowalski, 1990).

2. Elimination of the planning apparatus and institutions administering the traditional economic system. Experience from the earlier reforming countries of Central Europe (Poland, Hungary and Czechoslovakia) has shown that, despite massive resistance from the employees of these institutions, implementation of this step has not been too difficult.
3. Introduction of currency convertibility related to a reform of the price system, based on market mechanisms.
4. Establishment of a private banking system. Recent experience in Poland and elsewhere has shown that the lack of an efficient system for the execution of payments can be a major bottleneck on the way to a market economy.
5. Introduction of a tax system commensurate with a market economy.
6. Reform of the laws governing activities of foreign capital, and of the regulations with respect to foreign trade.

Such preconditions represent an interrelated system, the components of which need to be addressed simultaneously. Experience gained during the initial years of implementation of reform programmes in Central Europe has highlighted substantial impediments, arising largely from the behaviour patterns implanted in economic actors during the long decades of central planning, and from the absence of the institutional and legal frameworks that form the organic fabric of market economies in the West (Kowalski, 1991). While such constraints are substantial even in such relatively well-informed societies as those of Central Europe, for the less developed, more fissiparous and ideologically indoctrinated Balkans, they pose greater and more complicated problems.

1.3.2 Privatisation

This is probably the most important, and also the most complicated, of the tasks of economic restructuring. It encompasses three elements: small privatisation, large privatisation and reprivatisation. The first entails the transfer of ownership of small enterprises from the state or local authorities to the private sector. These enterprises tend to be small shops, garages and workshops. Although small privatisation often leads to tensions and conflicts, such as between the pre-communist owners and present employees and managers, general experience of such processes is relatively favourable. Most of the retail trade, catering, tourist-related services and small handicrafts enterprises have been successfully privatised in Hungary, Poland and Czechoslovakia. This has been

LIVERPOOL HOPE UNIVERSITY COLLEGE

accompanied by reprivatisation – giving back small businesses to their former owners who had been expropriated by the communists – and by the establishment of numerous small new businesses, especially in services: in Poland, for example, 1.3 million new small enterprises were established between the start of 1991 and mid-1992.

In Central Europe, the privatisation of printing, newspapers and other printed media was almost totally implemented during the first two years following the demise of communism, reflecting the negative experiences of the communist era. The privatisation of newspapers and creation of a multi-mode media environment was given top priority, although at the time of writing (1992) privatisation processes relating to the most effective communication medium, television, had not moved beyond the discussion stage.

Major and sometimes insurmountable problems have arisen in the process of large privatisation – transferring the ownership of large, mainly industrial, enterprises. These units tended to dominate the national economy in terms of productive capacities, and the local economies in terms of monopoly employment. They were usually grossly inefficient, in terms of both technology and manpower, and were thus burdened with extremely high overhead costs. These circumstances were exacerbated by often excessive levels of atmospheric emissions and water-borne waste discharges, lamentable working conditions and other major environmental problems.

Also falling into the large privatisation category have been the transformations of large state transport enterprises such as railways, airlines and centralised road passenger and freight carriers.

In the course of justifying privatisation, Western economists argue that as state ownership of the means of production was considered a precondition for the existence of the planned socialist economy, so private ownership constitutes the fundamental precondition for the market economy. In this context, privatisation, and particularly large privatisation, is seen as an element of a comprehensive systemic change; and secondly, only in the case of private enterprises can budget constraints be 'hard'. Additionally, as in the case of the UK government's 'selling the family silver', the privatisation of large state enterprises is seen as an essentially short- to medium-term means of boosting state income and easing budgetary problems.

The privatisation of large industrial enterprises may also be a means of escaping from a political dilemma with which post-communist governments are faced: they are on the one hand the owners of the enterprises, but on the other hand they rely politically on the workers and, in particular, the support of the unions. Given that in the transition phase standards of living either stagnate or actually fall, and that the establishment of an efficient market economy results in often substantial redundancies, governments are placed in a precarious position. This conflict between the role of government as owner and representative of capital on the one hand, and as representative of the working people on the other, has been especially acute in Poland, but has been felt all over Central and Eastern Europe. Thus governments wish to remove their responsibility as 'capitalists' and transfer the problems of wage and work-conditions bargaining to the newly established private employers' organisations and the unions.

The task of the reformers in Central and Eastern Europe is without precedence in its scope and dimensions. Privatisation – in a possibly short period of time – of almost the whole economy has never before been implemented. Experience gained in the UK, France and elsewhere appears of limited value and relevance. Privatising a small number of enterprises in the established functioning market economy, as in the case of recent West European privatisations, is much easier and poses fewer problems than the transformation being undertaken in Central and Eastern Europe, where the whole institutional, legal, and even psychological basis for privatisation has been absent.

Various approaches to the implementation of the privatisation process are being discussed and experimented within the region. Generally four variants can be distinguished:

1. The 'quasi-Yugoslav' approach (the nomenclature may now need to be revised): workers' participation. The employees of the privatised enterprises receive shares in 'their' enterprise, either free of charge or for a small payment.
2. Participation of all citizens, whereby all adult citizens of a country should obtain the right either to receive or to buy some shares in the privatised enterprises. A sub-variant of this scheme consists in the distribution of vouchers for which shares can be bought, instead of distributing the shares themselves.
3. Participation of the 'nomenklatura': whereby former higher-level party and government officials are given access (and possibly priority) to privatisation as a means of overcoming resistance against political and economic change from influential power groups.
4. Participation of all economic actors, regardless of their nationality or institutional form, in the purchase of shares in the privatised enterprises. Economically the most rational approach, this has the least likely chance of success in the region.

The programmes which have been implemented in Poland, Hungary and Czechoslovakia are a mixture of the above schemes, with the Hungarians attempting to stay closest to the fourth approach. The former East Germany represents a special case, with a central agency, the Treuhandanstalt, supervising and financing the restructuring and privatisation of the former state enterprises.

Privatisation programmes have proved to be much more difficult to implement and have proceeded much more slowly than was expected. All aspects of ownership, wealth and, consequently, power awake strong emotions and passionate actions. Additionally, a number of technical problems have slowed down privatisation efforts. Often entrepreneurial mechanisms and 'effective ownership' – control of management and efficiency – are very weak, especially in the case of privatisation schemes resulting in an atomised ownership of many small shareholders. Current privatisation schemes aim therefore at the establishment of 'controlling' shareholders, who would own a considerable part of the enterprise.

In Central and Eastern Europe generally it has been assumed that privatisation *per se* leads to increased efficiency in the functioning of enterprises and to frictionless coordination, control and allocation; but real-life situations are not optimal. Complications may be connected particularly with confused property rights and the largely unresolved question of how to privatise enterprises which are monopolist, or near monopolist, without simply creating private monopolies. The regulation of such monopolies is an unknown field in Central and Eastern Europe, and not a notably successful one in the West. Most of the issues connected with the controlling of agents by principals, be it by state or private share-owners, are also virtually unknown. One line of action is to open economic sectors to foreign interests, although potential international monopolies, held by the multinational companies, may thus be further encouraged. However, learning from the experience of foreign competition and investment is generally seen to be beneficial for the fledgling market economies.

The evidence linking ownership change to increases in efficiency is mixed (Boardman and Vining, 1989; Vickers and Yarrow, 1988, 1991): some studies suggest that privatisation has resulted in increased efficiency (as in the case of Canadian railways), others relate improved efficiency to increased competition and rivalry, and maintain that publicly-owned enterprises can match the private sector in efficiency when placed within a competitive environment.

West European experience points to a rather limited potential for the privatisation of transport infrastructure. There are some examples of privately built and operated highways, railways, bridges, tunnels, airports and seaports, but on the whole the share of privately constructed and operated infrastructure is very small. The time-horizons of private transport infrastructure projects are usually very long, with profitability often doubtful. A lack of private and public investment capital for all types of projects is an acute problem, and the purchasing power of potential customers will remain relatively low for a long time. Therefore, the only realistic route to private rail and road networks is through international financing by the IMF, World Bank and similar organisations.

With respect to transport enterprises using the infrastructure, privatisation potential is certainly higher, but varies by sector. In Central Europe, most of the shipping, haulage and dispatching companies had been privatised at the time of writing, either through employee and management buy-outs, liquidation of the 'old' firms, or through joint ventures with foreign capital. Also, many new firms had been established. In Poland, in the field of shipping even large former state companies had been privatised, in that they had received the charter of a private company, although it was usually owned by various public institutions (see Chapter 8).

In the case of railways, the potential for privatisation is high in service sectors such as catering, but the privatisation potential of whole railway companies seems doubtful in the short to medium term. The same applies to national airlines, where it is easy to privatise some elements, while leaving the bulk of the enterprises in public hands. It should be noted, however, that a number of privately-owned small airlines started operating in Central Europe in 1991 (see Chapter 4).

It is generally considered that the most promising way to privatise national carrier companies is to change their status to a private company while retaining public ownership in the majority state of shares. Even such a relatively minor change can result in economic behaviour which is better oriented towards profit, efficiency and subsidy minimisation.

1.3.3 Economic consequences of reform

Economically, the most important consequence of reform is a reduction of corporate demand for production inputs. The introduction of the market economy brings about a more efficient use of materials, energy and transport services. The hoarding of inputs has become financially impossible and organisationally unnecessary. Paradoxically, this reduction in demand for inputs, coupled with the introduction of hard budget constraints, relieves existing pressures on the transport and energy sectors in the short to medium term (Funck and Kowalski, 1987), despite an obvious need for infrastructure investments and modernisation in these fields.

The transition to a market economy also results in major structural adjustments. The share of services in employment and generation of GDP will certainly increase: service activities were traditionally underdeveloped in the communist economies. The share of manufacturing will, at the same time, diminish substantially, that of agriculture and forestry more slowly. Table 1.15 shows the shares of these sectors in the mid-1980s and the expected changes by the year 2010 (Kessel *et al.*, 1990).

Table 1.15 Central and Eastern Europe: GDP (per cent sectoral share),
1985 and 2010

Country	Agriculture/Forestry		Manufacturing		Services	
	1985	*2010*	*1985*	*2010*	*1985*	*2010*
Bulgaria	16.0	3.9	42.0	41.4	42.0	54.7
Czechoslovakia	9.8	1.8	49.1	50.7	41.1	47.5
'GDR'	7.0	1.5	55.0	44.5	38.0	54.0
Hungary	16.1	4.7	39.3	40.1	44.6	55.2
Poland	16.0	5.6	42.0	36.5	42.0	57.9
Romania	16.0	5.5	42.0	36.7	42.0	57.8
'Soviet Union'	16.0	4.0	42.0	42.6	42.0	53.4

Source: Kessel *et al.*, 1990, p. 59.

1.4 Outline structure of the volume

This volume attempts to address a number of questions in relation to the
dynamic interaction between transport and economic development in
Central and Eastern Europe. The geographical emphasis inevitably falls
upon the more advanced countries of the region: Hungary, Czechoslovakia (about to be divided as this volume went to press) and Poland
(and, historically, eastern Germany). This reflects the observation, made
by a number of contributors to this volume, that a cleavage is developing
between Central Europe and the Balkans which is likely to grow rather
than diminish. This is a consequence of (a) differing degrees of vigour
in pursuing systemic transformation, (b) initial advantage, (c) an
imbalance of Western financing and investment, (d) proximity to
Western Europe, and (e) continued instability and conflict within the
Balkans. By contrast, the Baltic states, given the removal of Russian
occupying military forces, will be in a position to close the social and
economic gap between themselves and Central Europe.

In Chapter 2, Wiesław Michalak and Richard Gibb provide a useful
introductory overview of the position of Central Europe and its developing relations with the West. They recognise the increasing polarisation
between Central and South Eastern Europe noted above, which they see
as being reinforced by the Central European countries' association
agreements with the EC. The authors of this chapter also point to the
poor quality of available data, a problem long recognised by researchers
of, and in, the region. Michalak and Gibb graphically characterise
government statistical offices within command economies as the interface
between the theory of the plan and the reality of economic performance.
From the perspective of transport network development they suggest that

the most important current trend is the dramatic increase in trade with the West, with an expected growth rate of 4.25 per cent per annum between 1991 and 2010. Most notably, Germany has assumed a paramount importance in the external trade of Hungary, Czechoslovakia and Poland, supplanting the former Soviet Union, and thereby explicitly symbolising political and economic reorientations and transformations. This leads the authors to argue that the future development of both the road and the rail networks in these countries will proceed along pre-war spatial patterns, although the enormous investment required will delay an East–West reintegration of transport systems. They conclude that, while logistics will play an important part in the region's developing transport systems, the short- to medium-term contraction of economic activity will constrain Western involvement in this area. Further, post-1989 reorientations in transport have exposed the inadequacy of the existing transport infrastructure to cope with the demands of the modern market-led economy. Michalak and Gibb consider it unlikely that short-term solutions can be expected.

In Chapter 3, focusing on oil pipeline development, David Pinder and Bridget Simmonds again emphasise the importance of developing links with the West and argue that, almost paradoxically, north–south oriented infrastructure in particular requires substantial investment. They examine three interrelated questions: the likely scale of future international oil movements and variations in import dependence within the region; the nature and potential of the existing infrastructure for reorientation; and, thirdly, the links and investments required for reorientation. The authors conclude that the Friendship pipeline and its branches provide the basis for further elaboration within the region, and that investment in such ports as Rostock could improve the capability of the region's oil import facilities to feed existing pipelines. Above all, substantial opportunities exist to construct short linking pipelines of both east–west and north–south orientation in order to provide a more comprehensive supply network and to connect the region to major Western oil ports. The authors point out, however, that no overall plan exists to build on the existing foundations, and that the pace and nature of reorientation will depend upon Western private investment, and, implicitly, upon the Western transnational companies controlling the skills and capital required.

Leslie Symons, in Chapter 4, appraises one of the most dynamic sectors of transport in the region. As the prestige end of transport development and the focus of much business and tourism travel, air transport is a very explicit symbol of the region's fortunes. Flag carriers such as MALÉV, even before the events of 1989, were aware of the image projected through this medium and acted as the region's vanguard in hiring Western consultants and leasing Western equipment in an effort to compete with Western airlines on a more equal basis. Four areas of activity have been influenced by the events of 1989: moves towards the privatisation of state-owned flag carriers and the growth of new private airlines; the take-up of Western technology, most notably Boeing and Airbus aircraft, bought outright or on lease; de-monopolisation and the contracting of Western servicing companies to run air-related activities ranging from in-flight catering and computerised ticketing arrangements to aircraft servicing and fuel provision; and the development of new routes.

Jan Kowalski, well known for his work on economic restructuring, assesses in Chapter 5 the implications of change on German transport developments. The twin impacts of German unification and restructuring in the East have posed major problems, but have also opened up substantial possibilities for the German economic machine. Drawing on work undertaken with colleagues, the author discusses projections of trends to the year 2010, particularly in connection with the promulgation of the 1991 Federal Government programme 'Transport for German Unity' and the 1992 German transport plan.

In Chapter 6, István Prileszky undertakes a detailed assessment of changes taking place in the Hungarian transport industry, emphasising some of the benefits and shortcomings of decentralisation and privatisation. He points to the leading role taken by Hungary in restructuring processes in the region, and emphasises the lack of precedent for such transformations. This is exemplified by the different forms of market aimed at in the freight and public transport sectors. In the face of substantial infrastructural shortcomings and short-term economic retrenchment, the attraction of foreign investment to aid Hungary's transport development is seen as the only solution to a rapidly mounting crisis.

Zbigniew Taylor reiterates many of these sentiments in Chapter 7, in his wide-ranging discussion of Polish transport. As a consequence, he notes that processes of restructuring and privatisation have been slower in the transport industry than in other economic sectors, notably the retail and wholesale trades. It is pointed out, however, that rapid changes occurring in neighbouring countries are exerting a direct impact on the country's transport infrastructure, most notably in the development of the Via Baltica road project.

In Chapter 8, Zofia Sawiczewska complements the previous contribution by concentrating on Polish maritime questions. She notes that the international nature of this transport sector has meant that there has been a strong awareness, and continued experience, of Western practices and standards. However, bureaucratic obstacles remain to constrain the industry's efficiency.

In a pioneering study, Anu Kull's contribution (Chapter 9) on Estonia provides a very welcome insight into restructuring processes taking place within the Baltic states, so soon after being freed from Soviet domination.

As her chapter emphasises, however, new problems have replaced previous ones, and the Baltics present a particular situation which, while having much in common with the rest of Central and Eastern Europe, also has very specific characteristics. While the chapter concentrates upon the decentralisation of public transport, it well articulates the problems of extricating the transport sector from the former Soviet organisational and operational systems. The concurrent questions of consolidating Estonian statehood and coping with economic and energy crises act as the backdrop to detachment and restructuring. It is hardly surprising that, under these circumstances, any forward-looking view of Estonian transport development is constrained by economic, political and technological uncertainty.

Moving south to the Balkans, David Turnock's contribution on Romania, Chapter 10, complementing much of his earlier work on that country, concentrates upon the role of transport in rural development, and sets this within an historical perspective. He suggests that there exists an effective infrastructure to support a large number of rural projects where modest capital reserves can exploit resources of cheap labour. On the other hand, a selective improvement in the transport infrastructure is likely to emphasise inter-urban links and thereby to reinforce a high level of locational concentration of large businesses attracting foreign capital. This 'core–periphery dichotomy' will increase the need for traditional peasant resourcefulness.

Chapter 11 provides Colin Thomas, in an appraisal of developments in the former Yugoslavia, with a difficult task, which he has undertaken with great effectiveness. Not surprisingly emphasising the impact of geopolitics, together with the role of historical forces and the natural environment, he provides an analysis of recent developments in transport, and hazards some conclusions for the future relationship between transport and economic development in the south Slav lands. The author argues that the disruption to the transport and communications systems brought about by the dismemberment of the Federation came at a time when the socio-economic gulf between the more and less developed republics was continuing to widen. He concludes that central to the region's material and social progress is the extent to which all the communities are physically linked to each other and functionally integrated with broader European transport systems.

Heavily dependent upon transport availability, tourism, as one of the world's leading economic activities, is put into regional perspective in Chapter 12. The differential impacts of increasing tourist numbers between Central Europe and the Balkans is noted, reinforcing statements made in earlier chapters concerning the increasing disparities between the two sub-regions.

The final chapter outlines a number of key themes and agendas, and concludes on a somewhat pessimistic note concerning the region's transport and economic restructuring prospects in the short- to medium-term.

2 Development of the transport system: prospects for East–West integration

Wiesław Michalak and Richard Gibb

2.1 An introduction to the region

The political events which have taken place in Eastern Europe since 1989 have transformed the entire economic and spatial environment of this region to a degree unparalleled since the end of the Second World War. It is clear that the entire process of economic and social transformation, in which transport has a crucial role to play, depends on the success of the political reforms. The principal objective of these reforms, now well advanced in East-Central Europe (ECE: defined here as Czechoslovakia, Hungary, Poland and the lands of the former East Germany; Figure 2.1) is a simultaneous creation of both stable parliamentary democracy and a market economy. The difficulties involved in this transformation are formidable, not least because a transition from a centrally planned to a market orientated economy has never been attempted before. Although this chapter will focus on the reforms in the economic sphere, the success of the entire process of restructuring depends on the concurrent reform of the political environment. For example, political legitimacy and cohesion are clearly necessary for a sustainable economic transformation, as well as for the complex process of political change from a totalitarian one-party system to a multi-party democracy. Nonetheless, in the last four years, the countries of ECE have initiated major reforms aiming at creating a Western-style market economy.

This chapter focuses principally upon the transport developments in the ECE countries following political and economic change. The objective is to examine the implications of these changes for the region's transport systems. Specifically, the focus is on the rail and road networks, and the infrastructure of the transport sector. It is argued that the success of the economic reforms in ECE depends, to a large degree,

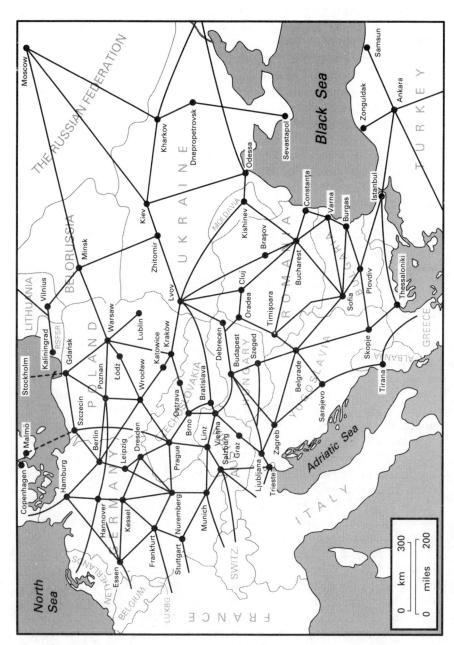

Figure 2.1 East-Central Europe: main transport links, 1991

on the integration of the transport systems of ECE countries with those of Western Europe. Clearly, the most significant institutional and economic framework for such integration, capable of overcoming the present state of crisis in the transport sector, is the European Community (EC) (Abbati, 1986).

The problems involved in integrating the transport networks of Eastern and Western Europe are compounded by the recent developments in the European Community. The political and economic opening of ECE coincided with moves towards the creation of the Single European Market (SEM) and the integration of EFTA (European Free Trade Association) countries into the EC (Kostrzewa and Schmeiding, 1989). The existing transport network linking ECE and Western Europe is not capable of handling the unforseen increase in East–West trade, passenger and transit traffic (ECMT, 1991). Such an increase in traffic, both commercial and passenger, is the most tangible consequence of the political and economic opening of ECE. At present, however, the transport networks and infrastructure, designed in the era of political and economic isolation from Western Europe, are not capable of coping with the new demands. The creation of SEM, the integration of EFTA countries and the opening of ECE put a new set of pressures on the transport system in Western Europe and the EC in particular. Thus, it is likely that the transport integration of Eastern and Western networks will be much more difficult than expected. The difficulties involved have been principally of three kinds. First, after forty years of the command economy, the institutions and system of incentives in ECE are far removed from those required for market orientated economies. Therefore, significant changes in institutions and the system of incentives are required. The significant changes needed in the structure of the transport sector are bound to result in important short-term adjustment costs. Second, important political problems will emerge as a result of the fundamental remodelling of political and social institutions. Finally, the transition is likely to be significantly longer than previously assumed due to the depth of the economic crisis in the region as well as economic recession in the West.

Poland, Czechoslovakia, Hungary and eastern Germany have been selected from the countries of the former 'Eastern Europe' because they have all embraced a radical reform approach to transforming their command economies. These reforms led to the speedy unification of East Germany with its Western counterpart. The massive transfer of resources and capital to the eastern part of Germany sets this region ahead of the other three countries in terms of political and economic reforms (Hamilton, 1991). On the other hand, whereas Poland and Hungary have a history of economic and political reforms dating well back before 1989, Czechoslovakia had a hard-line Stalinist government (with the exception of a few months in 1968) which continued to insist on the orthodox principles of the Soviet-style socialist economy (Myant, 1989) (Plate 2.1).

Plate 2.1 Symbolic of the differing Hungarian and Czechoslovak approaches under communism is the fact that the bridge linking the two countries across the River Danube was never restored after wartime destruction. Instead, a ferry has continued to ply commuters between Štúrovo in Slovakia on the far, northern bank, and Esztergom. (Derek Hall)

However, in January 1991, the newly elected Prague government committed itself to a radical economic transformation programme. The clear commitment of the four countries to a radical programme of economic and political reforms distinguishes ECE from South-Eastern Europe, where the pace of the reforms has been much slower (Romania, Bulgaria, Albania), or crippled by a civil war (Yugoslavia), and the former Soviet Union, where such a programme was adopted much later.

The division between the countries of ECE committed to a radical systemic transformation of their command economies and the rest of what used to be known as 'Eastern Europe' is reflected in the policies emanating from the West. The EC, the European Investment Bank (EIB), the European Bank for Reconstruction and Development (EBRD), together with the International Monetary Fund (IMF) and the World Bank, have all favoured these four countries (Corbo *et al.*, 1991). The clearest indication of the increasing polarisation between ECE and South-Eastern Europe is the series of association agreements between Poland,

LIVERPOOL HOPE UNIVERSITY COLLEGE

Czechoslovakia and Hungary and the European Community (Rzecz-pospolita, 1991, 1992). In particular, these agreements recognised formally the close economic and political relationships between ECE and its Western neighbours which pre-dated the Soviet imposition. Clearly, the association agreements will have a significant impact on the future of the transport network in this part of Europe.

Before proceeding to an analysis of the legacy of the socialist management of the economy and transport sector, it is worth emphasising the poor quality of the economic data produced throughout this region (Blades, 1991). Before 1989, in most of ECE the official statistical agencies performed an overtly political function. The principal task was to monitor and report the 'success' of central plans. Since these plans prescribed in minute detail the production targets for each enterprise, the statistical offices would perform an audit-type function, exercising regular and detailed supervision of the state industries. In effect, statistical offices acted as an interface between the theory of the plan and the reality of economic performance. Statisticians were therefore under pressure to report success and to ensure that the economic targets set by the communist government were being achieved. On occasions this led to outright falsification of data; more usually it meant the suppression of unwelcome statistics or the presentation of data in misleading or uninformative ways (Blades, 1991 p. 16). Statistics relating to transport issues were no exception to this general rule.

2.2 The socialist legacy and central planning

The seemingly irreversible socialist experiment in ECE came to a sudden and largely unexpected end in 1989. The collapse of the Soviet-style socialism has both economic and political roots. These are well illustrated by the developments in the transport sector of the centrally-planned economy (Kowalski, 1986).

Central planning led to endemic shortages, slow technical change, low quality of goods and an over-expanded public sector of which transport played an important part. In practice, full employment and the system of social safeguards were bought at the price of economic backwardness and the absence of political freedom (Kornai, 1980, 1982). The poor performance of the transport sector within ECE has both contributed to and reflected the disappointing economic record of the centrally-planned economies. The one factor that is common for all aspects of the transport network performance of ECE is the influence and systemic constraints of the centrally-planned economy (Winiecki, 1988).

In theory, central planning was a top-down process whereby the detailed physical plans for state enterprises were formulated at the centre

– usually by a state planning commission – to allocate inputs and outputs to their various uses. However, in practice the centre invariably had less information than the individual enterprises about the production possibilities and constraints (Kowalski, 1983). To facilitate control, state enterprises were aggregated into large conglomerates with highly monopolistic structures.

The operational complexities of the transport system relied little on highly distorted markets. Transport enterprises emphasised plan fulfilment rather than profitability. The transport sector was distorted by pervasive production, price and trade controls. This, in turn, severely distorted input and output prices and divorced resource use from resource costs. As a result, investment in the transport sector always lagged behind demand and emphasis was nearly always upon the quantity rather than the quality of the services (Mieczkowski, 1980; Tismer *et al.*, 1987).

Another feature of the centrally planned transportation systems in ECE was their relative isolation from each other (Korboński, 1990). The deliberate policy of economic autarky was introduced to avoid dependence of ECE countries on the resources of their neighbours. Distorted price structures were unsustainable because of the relative isolation of the centrally-planned economies within the protected CMEA market. The arbitrary wage structures, job security, and extensive in-kind benefits led to low productivity and overmanning. This resulted in a large-scale hoarding of labour in all ECE countries. The workers and management of the transport sector had few incentives for process and product innovation (Tarski, 1981). These factors ultimately led to extremely slow and uneven technological progress.

Finally, the abolition of the private sector severely inhibited individual entrepreneurship. Small private firms were extremely rare within the transport industry. In other words, the planned economies lacked the 'creative destruction' characteristic of the market economies (Winiecki, 1988). The transport system also lacked the ability to coordinate, specialise, and innovate, which seriously effected the economic vitality of the ECE countries. Furthermore, transport is by nature peculiarly subject to distortions not caused by the market (White and Senior, 1983). A very important part of the planning legacy common to all the countries of East-Central Europe was the absence or weakness of core market-orientated institutions, both inside and outside of government. Legal and accounting institutions were weak, standards did not conform to those generally accepted in the West, and there was no tradition of independent audit (OECD, 1991). As a result, the transport sector lacked marketing and strategic planning capabilities and effective inventory controls, and had little information on the relative profitability of the various products it provided.

2.3 Demise of the CMEA and its impact on the transport sector

Perhaps the most important institution which shaped the East European transport networks at the intra-regional level was the Council for Mutual Economic Assistance (CMEA). The CMEA, or Comecon as it is known in the West, was a brainchild of Stalin, who ordered the creation of the organisation in 1949 in response to the perceived threat to the region presented by the 1947 Marshall Plan (Korboński, 1990). The CMEA was never intended as an evolving organisation like the EC, with its own political institutions and supranational powers transcending the local jurisdiction of member states. It was a committee, or rather a series of committees, whose main functions, at least superficially, were to promote industrialisation and a high rate of economic growth, coordination of economic plans, specialisation in production and maximisation of regional trade (Grzybowski, 1990).

However, from the hindsight of forty years it is clear that the reasons for establishing the CMEA were of a political, rather than an economic, nature. The Soviet Union rejected the Marshall Plan and forced Czechoslovakia and Poland, which had originally accepted aid from the United States, to reverse their decisions. The CMEA provided the Soviet Union with an instrument of political and economic control over the East European Soviet Republics (Estonia, Latvia, and Lithuania) and East-Central Europe (Hamilton, 1990). In effect, the CMEA assured coordination of intra- and extra-regional trade initially to the advantage of the Soviet Union and later to the 'socialist bloc'. It was a political instrument leading to a complete reorientation of the traditional economic linkages with Western Europe and involved the reorganisation of the transport network towards the East and away from the West (Turnock, 1989a).

The ultimate demise of the CMEA after the collapse of the communist regimes in Europe can be partly attributed to those early days of this institution, which solidified a perception in East-Central Europe that the CMEA was merely an instrument of the Russian imperialism. Even though in the 1960s and 1970s there were clearly advantages in CMEA trade, particularly of raw materials, for ECE countries the introduction of the so-called transferable rouble (which was neither transferable nor convertible) substantially contributed to the systematic distortion of the economic mechanism. Because intra-CMEA prices did not relate in any way to world market prices for raw materials, in particular energy resources, the effective subsidy induced by Soviet oil prices led to the development of an extremely energy-intensive type of industrial production (Plate 2.2). The transport network reflects this structure of intra-CMEA trade. An overwhelming proportion of the trade was by rail. The bulk of the trade was in raw materials imported from the USSR. Some of the largest and most capital-intensive transport investments during forty years of the

Plate 2.2 Heavily-polluting lignite power station with adjacent heavy industry and unsegregated apartment blocks, with arable fields beyond. Part of the landscape of energy-intensive industrial development. (Derek Hall)

CMEA were designed to increase the volume of such trade (ECMT, 1991). Thus, the strongest transport linkages in terms of freight volumes were in an east–west direction. The cross-border north–south linkages between ECE countries are exceptionally weak by Western European standards.

The CMEA did not make the progress in transport and the economic sphere experienced by the EC. Even though some significant projects were completed during the 1960s and 1970s, throughout its existence (and particularly during the 1980s) there was no consensus over, and little enthusiasm for, enhancing transport integration between CMEA members.

In theory, the programmes introduced by the CMEA Standing Commission for Transport should have emphasised physical planning and the rational shaping of the transport potential from the perspective of a central plan. In practice, however, the solutions proposed by the CMEA were characterised by: (a) an extremely inefficient structure of expenditure on transport development; (b) disharmony, contradiction and imbalance in the development of domestic transport systems in member

countries; (c) a lack of sufficiently effective incentives to ensure allocation of the factors of production in the transport system; (d) automatic
reproduction of outmoded equipment and organisational patterns; and
(e) abandonment of all efforts to improve quality, reduce costs or adopt
innovation (Drozik, 1991).

As a consequence, ambitious plans such as the well-known Trans-
European North–South Motorway project (TEM) and the Trans-
European North–South Railway project (TER) were never finalised. Only
a small proportion of the TEM project was completed by 1991 (in
Hungary 38 per cent of target, Czechoslovakia 37 per cent and Poland
twenty per cent). Construction was slowed down or abandoned altogether
after 1989 owing to financing problems and shortages of material
resources (Timar, 1991).

The collapse of the Soviet economy at the end of the 1980s wholly
discredited the Soviet model of the planned economy. The introduction
of hard currency as the mode of payments for intra-CMEA transactions
dealt a terminal blow to the process of economic and transport integration in ECE. The end of the CMEA was a 'fait accompli' when the two
Germanies united, eliminating one of the most significant trading partners in ECE. By the end of 1990 the CMEA had become largely irrele-
vant both in terms of trade and as an institutional framework for
transport integration (Corbo *et al.*, 1991).

The most important present trend from the perspective of transport
network development is the dramatic increase of trade with the West
(Table 2.1). Until 1989, overall trade volumes between Eastern and
Western Europe were relatively low (Zloch-Christy, 1991; Rothengatter
and Kowalski, 1991). The opening-up of ECE markets and the increase
of exports to the EC countries has had a massive and, most likely,
permanent impact on the structure of the transport system in Europe.
The predominance of trade between former member states of the CMEA
has given way to a much more intensive trade with the EC countries and
Western Europe in general. It is expected that the East–West trade will
grow by 4.25 per cent per year between 1991 and 2010 (Seidenfus, 1991).
In the case of the former East Germany the increase is expected to be
even more significant. By comparison with the intra-German trade in
1985, the increase is expected to be twenty-fold by the year 2010 in real
value terms (Kassel and Rothengatter, 1990).

Even though there are still significant economic and political barriers
between ECE and the EC, it is clear that future adjustments of the
transport network in Poland, Hungary and Czechoslovakia will be geared
towards a very substantial increase of transport flows especially with
Germany and Austria. The 'second generation' association agreements
signed on 16 December 1991 formally institutionalised this trend
(Rzeczpospolita, 1992). The most immediate result of these agreements,
which are explicitly limited to the economic sphere, will be a further

Table 2.1 Foreign trade of the ECE countries, 1985–2010 (in million US dollars)

	Exports				Imports			
	'CMEA'		'The West'		'CMEA'		'The West'	
	1985	*2010*	*1985*	*2010*	*1985*	*2010*	*1985*	*2010*
Czechoslovakia	2,712	4,448	782	5,443	2,797	4,587	732	5,345
ex-GDR	3,259	5,346	1,794	11,381	3,116	5,112	1,570	10,401
Hungary	1,027	1,685	681	3,152	921	1,511	724	3,146
Poland	1,238	2,031	1,059	4,311	1,317	2,161	849	3,827

Source: Seidenfus, 1991, pp. 269–71.

strengthening of economic, and thus transport, links with Germany and Austria. In the space of eighteen months from the summer of 1990, Germany had taken over from the former Soviet Union as Hungary's largest trading partner. Some 27 per cent of the entire Hungarian export trade in 1991 was with Germany. Conversely, German exports to Hungary increased by 36 per cent: far more than with any other country. Similar developments have occurred in Czechoslovakia and Poland, where trade with Germany has assumed a paramount importance since 1990 (Kassel and Rothengatter, 1990).

Of course, historically there is nothing particularly new in these trends. Germany and Austria were very significant economic players in ECE before the Second World War. Germany's drive towards the war directly affected the economies of these countries. The aim of the 'war economy' introduced in 1933 was to accelerate economic growth of Germany and secure agricultural products and raw materials to support re-armament. As a result, the countries of ECE increased their trade with Germany toward the second half of the 1930s (Solimano, 1991). Today many in the East and West regard ECE as a natural sphere of economic and cultural influence for Germany and Austria, simply because of geographical proximity (Ash, 1990). The physical layout of the transport network and the location of the major industrial agglomerations in ECE reflect this traditional impact of German economic weight. There is no doubt, in the author's opinion, that the future development of both the rail and road networks in Poland, Hungary and Czechoslovakia will proceed along the traditional pre-war spatial pattern. However, the sheer magnitude of the necessary investment will significantly delay the coming re-integration of transport systems.

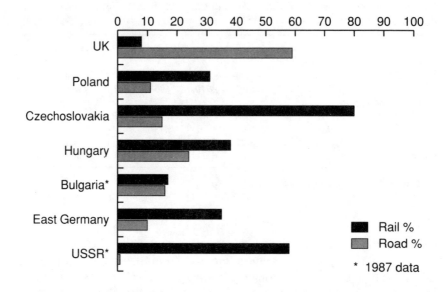

Figure 2.2 Share of inland and cross-border freight by mode in ECE and the UK, 1988

Source: Coopers and Lybrand, 1991, p. 5.

2.4 Transport characteristics of the region

The current structure and state of maintenance of the transport system differs appreciably among the four countries of ECE. By and large, however, there are a number of common characteristics shared by all transport systems in ECE. The most striking feature is a high proportion of goods and passengers carried by rail. Over half of the entire traffic of people and goods is by this mode (De Waele, 1991). In all ECE countries rail freight transport accounts for at least one-third of the entire freight (Figure 2.2). Conversely, the motorway networks and road traffic in general are, by Western standards, in an embryonic state. The only country with a significant network of motorways is the former East Germany. However, most of this network was constructed before the partition of Germany. Very little investment was directed toward the maintenance of this network during the forty years of communist rule. As a result, most motorways are in a very poor state of repair.

The high priority given to rail transport was a result of both economic and ideological factors. First, the bulk of freight transport before 1989 consisted of raw materials and half-products destined for the primary and heavy industries. This resulted in large investments in the rail system, which continued in ECE for over forty years until the fall of the communist regimes. Moreover, priority was given also to heavy freight traffic in terms of infrastructure and frequency of railway network use. Such policies led to very serious restrictions in the frequency and speed of passenger traffic. Second, individual car ownership was considered a symbol of excessive Western consumerism and a manifestation of Western cultural decadence (Winiecki, 1988). Of course, behind the official ideological phraseology there were more prosaic reasons such as the lack of necessary resources, technology and know-how for a successful development of the domestic car industry.

The short-term improvements in the rail transport system are expected to be fairly modest in all ECE countries except the former East Germany (Drozik, 1991). Even though the rail network and infrastructure requires major improvements, it has been impossible to obtain any substantial investment resources due to the massive economic crisis in ECE. The short-term changes in the rail system and traffic will focus on the following areas: (a) adoption of new transport technologies, such as container traffic; (b) increased use of automatically controlled traffic; (c) a modest increase in train speeds; (d) logistic improvements; and (e) coordination and modernisation of cross-border traffic.

In contrast, road transport is expected to change very significantly in all ECE countries. Specifically, the traffic volume and quality of service are expected to rise dramatically. This is because the level of initial investment required in order to upgrade substantially the road transport is much lower than that required by the rail system. Moreover, according to recent estimates (Drozik, 1991), there is a considerable excess capacity relative to demand in the road haulage sector. The road transport potential can be easily increased by deregulating the market as well as by shifting costs in the transport system towards the consumers. Both measures were introduced in 1990–91 in ECE.

At present, however, the physical distribution system within ECE is characterised by a very limited choice between some very basic and often low-performance services. The existing state of infrastructure, in terms of roads, railways, airports and communications, will limit the potential to achieve performance levels assumed in Western Europe. However, within that constraint, the moves to allow greater competition are likely to lead to a sharp improvement in the range of service and standards in the next two or three years.

The performance levels of ECE transport systems are low for four major reasons: (a) lack of competition; (b) inadequately developed management; (c) low motivation levels; and (d) severe over-manning. These are a product of three main influences. First, private sector operators have generally been very small scale and local in their scope. Value added services are virtually non-existent. Second, under the command economy, investment in transport infrastructure was concentrated largely on the railways (Figure 2.2). Third, the failure of the command economy to optimise efficiency has given rise to major capacity constraints and maintenance backlogs which need to be addressed if ECE is to achieve operating effectiveness levels associated with the EC countries.

For example, East German Railways (DR) estimated that in addition to the existing $2 billion investment programme, they needed to spend an additional $2 billion per annum over the next ten years to bring the infrastructure and rolling stock up to the standard of West German Railways (DB). The problems in the road sector are even worse, typified by poor road maintenance and shortages of vehicle spare parts. According to the Federal Ministry of Transport, a total investment of DM 500 billion (*sic*) is necessary to maintain and modernise the transport system of former East Germany (Kassel and Rothengatter, 1990). Over 5,000 road and 4,000 rail bridges need repair and upgrading to West German standards. The estimated costs of upgrading the transport structure are too high even for the German economy. However, just to maintain the present transport infrastructure would cost approximately DM 119 billion; a staggering figure considering that these costs would not include any investment for modernisation. In 1992, the Federal Ministry of Transport has set the official costs for seventeen selected transport projects (Deutsche Einheit) in eastern Germany at DM 56 billion until the year 2000.

In less than two years after the collapse of the communist government in 1989, much of East German industry has disintegrated and unemployment has reached three million in a region with a total population of 16.3 million. Up to 1989, East German Railways carried 75 per cent of all freight. Since then its volume has fallen by 40 per cent (ECMT, 1991). The dilemmas are several: such a volume decrease is devastating for the business economics of any firm.

Additionally, its traffic flows are moving from a north–south axis to an east–west direction from the Rhine. Over the next twenty years north–south volumes are expected to decline by twelve per cent with east–west volumes rising seven-fold. By contrast, the road network has seen virtually no improvement since its construction before 1939, giving rise to congestion and low driving speeds.

Hungary's experience with a market economy is of a longer standing than that in eastern Germany, Poland and Czechoslovakia. Government policy has been working at both ends of the market system. On the one hand, it has been splitting up its large state monopolies into smaller, medium-sized units to make them more cost effective. On the other hand, increased competition is being licensed; for example, the freight forwarding monopoly has been terminated (Timar, 1991).

To date the pace of change has been restrained. For example, only 10

Table 2.2 Hungary: share of freight by mode and number of operators, 1990

	Per cent share of tonne/km	No. of organisations
Rail	38	2
Road	24	130
Waterways	26	7
Air	–	2
Pipeline	11	1

See also Table 6.1.

Source: Coopers and Lybrand, 1991, p. 4.

per cent of Hungary's 150,000 truck fleet licences are held by private hauliers. Table 2.2 demonstrates the degree of concentration in all sectors. The entire railway network is operated by only two firms, only one of which is privately managed. By contrast, road haulage is serviced by 130 firms. However, the majority of these enterprises are recent start-up ventures operating on a very small scale. By comparison, in the UK, with a population only five times larger, there are a total of 90,000 operators' licences, with 32,000 held by third-party carriers (Coopers and Lybrand, 1991). However, the impact of creating smaller business units encouraging competition, and the loosening of price controls, has been severe for existing road transporters, some of whom have shed up to 50 per cent of their staff and vehicles.

2.5 Conclusions and the future

It is unrealistic to expect a significant improvement of rail and road transport systems in ECE in the short term. Considering the massive costs of modernising the physical infrastructure, it is likely that efforts will be directed towards improvements in management and organisation. One of the most important challenges facing ECE is the establishment of a successful logistic operation for the transport system. Logistics is vitally important to the success or failure of any business. Simply defined, it is getting the right product to the right place at the right time, in the right condition. Optimum logistics means providing the correct level of service at the minimum cost. Logistic costs as a percentage of sales have declined dramatically in the West over the last decade, In ECE they remain extremely high, reaching up to 35 per cent of the total sales. However, new suppliers are emerging to create a more competitive logistics service environment. The entry of major forwarders like Kuhne and Nagel, Danzas, LEP and Schenkers, no longer excluded by state monopolies, is facilitating international movements. Unfortunately, these organisations are unlikely to have a major impact on the availability of domestic storage and transport costs in the medium term.

In this respect, the well-publicised penetration of the integrated carriers such as TNT, DHL and Federal Express may have more impact. These companies will have to compete with the newly established private carriers in ECE. However important these additions to the transport network are, they must be seen against a bleak economic outlook for ECE. The economic results of 1990/91 reveal a large-scale contraction in economic activity, particularly in Poland and Hungary which are much further ahead of Czechoslovakia in terms of reforms implementation. These trends are worrying, as they may undermine public support for the reform process. The present situation does not bear much room for optimism, given the monumental task of transforming a very obsolete transport system within the framework of ECE economies into a market-orientated one.

In conclusion, the future of the transport infrastructure and network in ECE depends, to a large extent, on broader political developments in both East-Central Europe and the European Community. The prospects for a smooth transition of the command economies to market equivalents are not very good. The social and political costs may prove too great to bear by the already overstretched societies. Yet, there seems to be no alternative to a radical and quick reintegration and alignment with the West. Transport issues are very closely linked to economic reform, foreign debt, and institutional relationships within the EC framework. The most immediate impact, thus far, of the post-1989 developments in ECE is a radical reorientation of transport linkages towards Western Europe, which has exposed the total inadequacy of the existing transport infrastructure to cope with the demands of the modern market-led economy. The demise of the CMEA further stresses the need for a rapid improvement in the facilities for trade with Western Europe. The recently completed 'association agreements' are early signs of the emerging trend towards a much greater degree of transport coordination between the two parts of Europe.

There is no doubt that the transport system must be improved if a successful transition to a market economy is to be accomplished. The legacy of systematic under-investment in transport facilities, mobile equipment, infrastructure and maintenance of the existing system makes any significant improvement unlikely in the short term. A significant investment, including foreign capital, is needed to upgrade the existing transport facilities to modern standards. However, considering the magnitude of economic reforms such as privatisation and currency stabilisation, and the extent of the foreign debt exposure of Poland and Hungary, it is unlikely that short-term solutions can be expected.

3 Oil transport: pipelines, ports and the new political climate

David Pinder[1] and *Bridget Simmonds*

3.1 INTRODUCTION

Although energy is fundamental to economic development, energy transport is an under-researched field. Passenger transport and freight movement have attracted widespread attention, yet there is often an implicit assumption that energy is available as and where required. To a great extent this reflects the nature of Western economies, where most transport research is undertaken. Here, heavy investment by public- and private-sector interests has created stable distribution systems which, while they require continuous maintenance and minor adjustment, deal effectively with energy movement. Western Europe's port system provides ready access to crude oil; pipelines move crude oil, natural gas and a range of refined products efficiently over considerable distances; fleets of road tankers transport oil products to countless destinations; railways link collieries and ports with power stations; and highly developed grid systems distribute electricity – whatever its source – to virtually all areas. Only rarely are these systems faced with challenges, such as the need to restructure oil product distribution following the oil crises of the 1970s, that are capable of stimulating interest in energy transport issues.

However, this stable situation is not typical of all world regions. Energy transport still poses major problems in developing countries, and there is now a widening realisation that former communist states possess energy transport infrastructures and systems that are so woefully inadequate that they pose a major threat to attempts to cultivate market-oriented economies (Gorst, 1991). In these types of economy the need for energy transport research is substantial. Although recent transport research, as exemplified by Hoyle and Knowles (1992) focuses on a broad range of issues, it provides little information on energy movement, particularly in the debilitated states of Central and Eastern Europe.

Table 3.1 Central and Eastern Europe: consumption of oil products, 1989 (per cent)

	Albania	Bulgaria	Czecho-slovakia	East Germany	Hungary	Poland	Romania	Yugoslavia
Industry	17.60	1.94	43.27	8.98	24.54	9.31	15.80	21.72
Transport	40.46	87.03	30.78	52.34	40.21	59.03	17.15	24.87
Commercial/public	N/A	N/A	N/A	N/A	N/A	N/A	N/A	N/A
Residential	5.76	4.79	0.61	18.19	12.08	1.30	7.96	N/A
Non-energy	7.06	2.82	N/A	13.15	3.61	20.80	6.57	12.78
Other	29.07	3.41	25.34	6.62	13.90	9.55	52.52	3.45
Total	100	100	100	100	100	100	100	100

Notes: Data exclude intermediate consumption for purposes such as electricity generation and combined heat and power production. N/A: Not available; in most instances where this appears, energy has been consumed but is recorded in the 'Other' category.

Source: International Energy Agency (1991), pp. 239, 321–334.

This chapter contributes to an understanding of the major energy transport issues facing these areas. Since these questions are both numerous and broad, however, it does so on a selective basis. While it is recognised that research is needed into many aspects of energy provision, oil has been selected as the focus of the investigation and attention has centred particularly on the international movement of this energy source.

At first sight this choice may appear unusual: in sharp contrast to Western Europe, oil is not a dominant fuel, and on average accounted for only 28 per cent of all energy consumption in Central and Eastern Europe in 1989 (International Energy Agency, 1991). Moreover, as will be shown below, oil demand in the 1980s was variable and, in sharp contrast to natural gas consumption, did not show a strong upward trend.[2] Yet oil is a vital source of energy in terms of the sectors which consume it (Table 3.1), even though solid fuels still account for some 60 per cent of all energy consumed. Moreover, there is every prospect that increased consumption of oil and oil products will be necessary if economic modernisation is to succeed. One recent estimate is that total energy consumption will rise by between a quarter and a half by 2005, and that oil will satisfy a third of the additional demand (Anon., 1990a). The sector likely to be particularly important in the growth of oil product consumption is transport and, perhaps above all, road transport. On the one hand the economically vital road haulage industry will be dependent upon the availability of transport fuels while, on the other, petrol consumption is likely to rise as car ownership increases.[3]

Given the fact that indigenous oil resources are limited, it is evident that the satisfaction of demand will require the cross-border movement of crude oil, or oil products, on a significant scale. In this connection an important point is that the oil-refining industry's infrastructure, like that of many other industrial sectors, requires heavy investment to raise it to Western standards. One indicator of its backwardness in many areas is the scant provision of cracking technologies, which are commonplace in Western Europe. These break down heavy refined products, converting them into lighter, more valuable fractions, such as transport fuels. Poland, Czechoslovakia and Hungary, for example, have nineteen refineries, but only two of these have any cracking capacity (Thrash, 1991). In view of this handicap, it is arguable that imports should mainly comprise oil products produced elsewhere as efficiently as possible. However, this solution discounts the fact that oil products would be significantly more expensive to import than crude oil, and would therefore impose an increased balance of payments burden on these economically weak countries. This factor suggests that it is strongly in Central and Eastern Europe's interests to maintain its refining industry as best it can, and to achieve efficient access to crude oil supplies. Hence we arrive at our focus on the consumption and international transport of this commodity.

Against this background, the chapter addresses three interrelated questions. First, on what scale are international oil movements likely to be necessary, and to what extent does the need for imports vary from one part of Central and Eastern Europe to another? Secondly, what infrastructures currently ensure crude oil supplies, and in what ways do economic, political and strategic factors suggest that they should be reoriented towards Western Europe? Third, if reorientation is desirable, what infrastructural links and investments are necessary to ensure that it is achieved?

Before turning to these questions, a number of additional introductory points are necessary. The newly independent states of Latvia, Lithuania and Estonia have been excluded from the analysis, chiefly because data for these areas are not yet available, but also because the former Soviet Union is not the focus of the discussion. Conversely, the former East Germany has been included in the investigation, even though political integration of the two Germanies has been achieved. Despite political progress, the oil supply system of the eastern and western parts of the country are not yet effectively coordinated and, as will be shown, eastern Germany's oil infrastructures remain relevant to the problem of ensuring efficient supplies to neighbouring fledgling democracies, particularly Poland. Finally, the foreign exchange implications of oil imports, and the reduction of imports through the development of indigenous alternative energy sources, have been excluded from the discussion. These major questions justify separate examination, and it is sufficient for this chapter to proceed on the widely accepted assumption, outlined below, that significant oil imports will in any event be necessary.

3.2 Crude oil demand and indigenous supplies

Although total oil consumption in the early 1980s naturally varied between states, in most countries demand was in the range 14–18 million tonnes per year, and total Eastern bloc requirements stood at 112 million tonnes (Table 3.2). In comparison, the calorific value of coal and lignite consumed in 1980 was equivalent to 257 million tonnes of oil. Trends during the 1980s were variable, but most countries consumed less oil at the end of the decade than at the start and, overall, in 1989 total demand in the former communist countries was approximately 100 million tonnes. In the later 1980s a slight upward trend in oil usage was evident in a number of countries, but economic upheaval following the fall of communism has precipitated further consumption cutbacks on a scale that is as yet unknown. As has already been indicated, however, growth is expected to re-emerge as market economies become established, and total demand may well rise beyond 100 million tonnes by the turn of the century.

Table 3.2 Central and Eastern Europe: oil consumption changes during the 1980s

	1980	1989
	(million tonnes)	
Albania	2.2	1.6
Bulgaria	14.7	13.9
Czechoslovakia	18.3	14.7
East Germany	17.7	13.4
Hungary	11.2	8.3
Poland	16.8	17.3
Romania	18.1	14.6
Yugoslavia	13.6	15.8
Total	112.6	99.6

Source: International Energy Agency (1991), pp. 68–73.

Table 3.3 Central and Eastern Europe: oil production and consumption relationships, 1989

	Production	Consumption	C/P ratio 1:
	(million tonnes)		
Self-sufficient			
Albania	1.7	1.6	0.94
Import-reliant			
Hungary	2.7	8.3	3.07
Romania	9.7	14.6	1.51
Yugoslavia	3.4	15.8	4.64
Import-dominated			
Bulgaria	0.1	13.9	139.00
Czechoslovakia	0.2	14.7	73.50
Poland	0.2	17.3	86.50
East Germany	0.0	13.4	–
Total	18.0	99.6	Average 5.53

Source: International Energy Agency (1991), pp. 23, 68–73.

Compared with Western Europe, these current and predicted levels of demand are small. For example, in 1990 Italy alone consumed 92.3 million tonnes of oil. However, in the context of the economic problems experienced by the former communist states, oil consumption on this scale is substantial, particularly in view of the fact that indigenous oil supplies are sparse. Only Hungary, Albania, Romania and the former

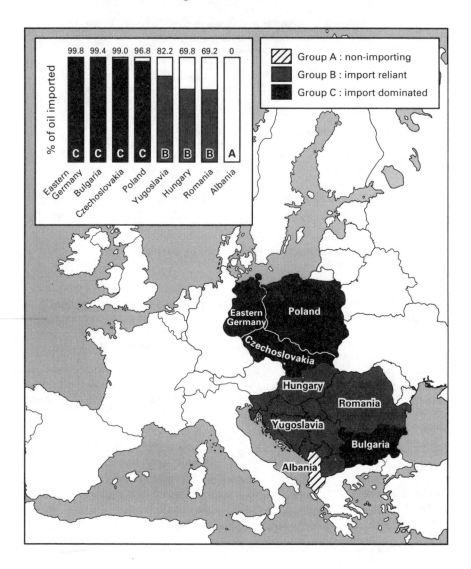

Figure 3.1   Central and Eastern Europe: oil import dependence

Yugoslavia produced more than one million tonnes of oil a year during the 1980s and, except in Hungary, output in all these countries fell significantly during the decade (Table 3.3). Total production in 1989 was less than 20 million tonnes, causing a high consumption–production ratio throughout most of Central and Eastern Europe (British Petroleum Company, 1991).

Using consumption–production ratios to classify the former communist states, three categories of import reliance in the late 1980s can be identified (Figure 3.1). First, Albania was the only *non-importing country* in which production was entirely capable of meeting domestic consumption. Second, Hungary, Romania and Yugoslavia were *import-reliant* states where production covered only part of requirements. Third, Poland, Czechoslovakia, Bulgaria and the former East Germany had virtually no domestic reserves and were, therefore, entirely *import dominated*.

Given access to Western technology and support, it is theoretically possible for these groupings to change. Exploration in countries currently lacking known reserves could identify new resources, while exploration might well enhance the existing known reserves in Hungary, Albania, Romania and the former Yugoslavia. Similarly, Western exploitation technologies might also raise yields from existing oilfields and thereby narrow significantly the production–consumption gap in countries with indigenous resources. But, for technical, economic and political reasons, such changes would naturally have a significant lead time. One important obstacle to exploration and enhanced exploitation is that it is likely to be some time before Western companies, which possess many of the necessary technologies, consider that economic trends make Central and Eastern Europe an attractive investment area. This is despite the fact that the former Soviet Union, with its more promising investment environment, is proving attractive to Western energy-related capital (Gorst, 1991). It can therefore be concluded that, for the foreseeable future, the large majority of Central and Eastern Europe will remain strongly, or totally, dependent on imported oil. Indeed, the example of Romania, which moved from self-sufficiency to 40 per cent import dependence between the mid-1970s and 1989, demonstrates that substantial oil imports may become necessary if resource depletion and the problems of economic disintegration permanently damage oil production (International Energy Agency, 1988, 1991).

In global terms the volumes of oil to be moved will not be great. Western Europe, for example, imports approximately 500 million tonnes of oil a year, while the annual capacity of the pipelines connecting Rotterdam with the western part of Germany and Belgium exceeds 40 million tonnes. But, although Central and Eastern Europe's import requirements may be modest by outside standards, the efficient movement of perhaps 80 million tonnes of crude oil a year is a challenging goal.

3.3 Current infrastructure and supply issues

Pipelines provide the dominant form of oil transport throughout Central and Eastern Europe. In some instances, particularly in Eastern Europe, these pipelines are essentially national facilities. Bulgaria uses this form of transport to carry oil from its offshore Tjulenovo oilfield inland to the Pleven refinery; in Romania the port of Navodari is linked by pipeline to inland oilfields and refineries; and, prior to the civil war, the former Yugoslavian refining industry was heavily dependent on the Adria pipeline. In contrast, Central European countries have been obliged to look eastwards for their supplies throughout the post-war period and, consequently, to rely on an international pipeline network. Today, therefore, their oil supply infrastructures are dominated by a pipeline system connecting Central Europe with the former Soviet Union (Figure 3.2). Two oilfields (the Volga Urals field, and the Ob field) are the chief sources of supply, and pipelines currently extend through Hungary, Czechoslovakia and the former East Germany (Andrews, 1991). The international supply system therefore extends for more than 3,000 km, its chief arterial element being the Friendship pipeline. To illustrate the significance of this link for just one country, in the 1980s it handled more than 80 per cent of East Germany's imported crude oil, typically amounting to almost 20 million tonnes a year (Baum, 1990).

Port facilities provide less dominant elements in the supply system (Figure 3.3). Thus Gdańsk has its Port Polnocny crude oil terminal, capable of handling vessels up to 150,000 dwt. Also on the Baltic, the eastern German port of Rostock is linked to the Schwedt refinery by pipeline but is only accessible to tankers of 45,000 dwt. On the Bulgarian Black Sea coast, meanwhile, Burgas is able to accept tankers up to 70,000 dwt while, in the Adriatic, the former Yugoslavian ports of Ploče (Kardeljevo), Koper, Rijeka and Omišalj all have crude oil import facilities. The largest of these are terminals accessible to ships of 200,000 dwt at Rijeka and, 25 km away on the island of Krk, to ones of 350,000 dwt at Omišalj (Cuny, 1991).

While this is the broad geometry of the oil supply infrastructure, several other features should be noted. First, because distances are extensive, transport costs are high. Moreover, since harsh environments in the former Soviet Union mean that new sources of oil are unlikely to be readily accessible, these costs are likely to increase. The days of 'easy oil' from the East are therefore past (Gorst, 1991).

Second, it may be that the condition of the Friendship pipeline system is far from satisfactory, especially along those sections which pass through the difficult environments near the source regions. This possibility is raised by the low standards known to exist along the pipelines built to export natural gas from the Soviet Union. Many sections of this gas network were originally constructed in haste, to

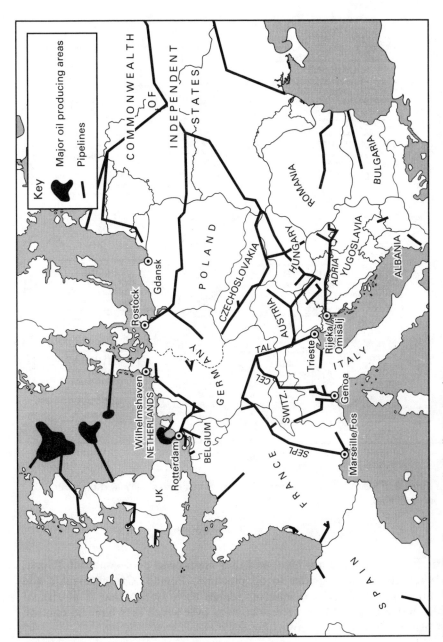

Figure 3.2 The European oil pipeline network

LIVERPOOL HOPE UNIVERSITY COLLEGE

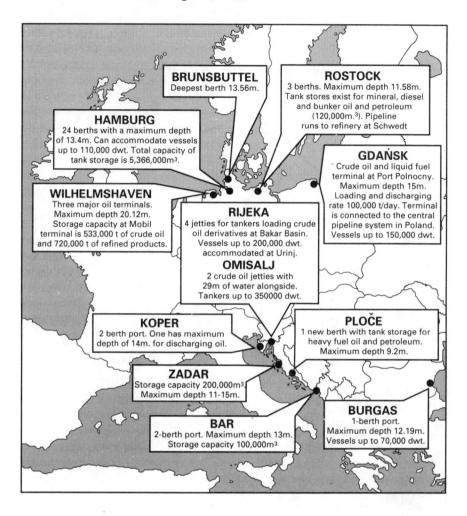

BRUNSBUTTEL
Deepest berth 13.56m.

ROSTOCK
3 berths. Maximum depth 11.58m.
Tank stores exist for mineral, diesel
and bunker oil and petroleum
(120,000m.^{3}). Pipeline
runs to refinery at Schwedt

HAMBURG
24 berths with a maximum depth
of 13.4m. Can accommodate vessels
up to 110,000 dwt. Total capacity of
tank storage is 5,366,000m^3.

GDAŃSK
Crude oil and liquid fuel
terminal at Port Polnocny.
Maximum depth 15m.
Loading and discharging
rate 100,000 t/day. Terminal
is connected to the central
pipeline system in Poland.
Vessels up to 150,000 dwt.

WILHELMSHAVEN
Three major oil terminals.
Maximum depth 20.12m.
Storage capacity at Mobil
terminal is 533,000 t of crude oil
and 720,000 t of refined products.

RIJEKA
4 jetties for tankers loading crude
oil derivatives at Bakar Basin.
Vessels up to 200,000 dwt.
accommodated at Urinj.

OMISALJ
2 crude oil jetties with
29m of water alongside.
Tankers up to 350000 dwt.

KOPER
2 berth port. One has maximum
depth of 14m. for discharging oil.

PLOČE
1 new berth with tank storage for
heavy fuel oil and petroleum.
Maximum depth 9.2m.

ZADAR
Storage capacity 200,000m^3.
Maximum depth 11-15m.

BAR
2-berth port. Maximum depth 13m.
Storage capacity 100,000m^3.

BURGAS
1-berth port.
Maximum depth 12.19m.
Vessels up to 70,000 dwt.

Figure 3.3 Central and Eastern Europe: port accessibility and oil-related port facilities

standards that were not high, and they are now in poor condition (Gorst, 1991). If this also applies to oil pipelines, Poland, Czechoslovakia and Hungary will all find themselves served by a system that is at risk of disruption as a result of defects in areas over which they have no control. Clearly this would be unsatisfactory.

Third, from the viewpoint of countries such as Poland or Czechoslovakia, the existing pipeline network has become less attractive because it no longer originates in a politically stable area. This has yet to pose real problems, and it may be that in the long run the new political and economic realities create no serious supply threat. Nonetheless, poorly managed oilfields are now struggling to maintain output,[4] the disintegration of the Soviet Union has undermined old supply certainties, and in the natural gas market there is evidence that former eastern bloc countries plan to broaden their sources of supply (Anon., 1990b). Moreover, the power of political conflict to disrupt energy structures has been graphically demonstrated by the break-up of the former Yugoslavian federation. Because oil import terminals and the Adria pipeline have come under Croatian control, refining centres outside this new state are now denied free access to imports.

Lastly, because of the new political climate, Russian oil is no longer sold to Central and Eastern European countries at preferential prices. Formerly the pricing system not only ensured that CMEA members received oil at a fraction of the rate charged to Western customers, but also gave them a substantial financial advantage over developing countries buying Soviet oil. In addition, the terms of trade were eased still further by the negotiation of soft payment terms and bilateral barter agreements (Gorst, 1990). However, since early in 1990, oil has been traded at world market rates and payment in hard currency has been required. This, too, has inevitably reduced the attractions of the supply structures that have prevailed throughout the post-war years. In addition, one recent prediction is that, because of difficult production conditions, during the 1990s Russian oil prices may rise significantly above those of OPEC countries (Osayimwese, 1991).

From this survey it is evident that, in much of Central and Eastern Europe, any policy which attempts to maintain past eastwards-oriented oil supply patterns may well encounter substantial disadvantages. Moreover, in addition to the problems cited above, past practices must be called into question because they are monopolistic and deny consumer countries the advantages of supply competition between a range of producers. Taking the region as a whole, the difficulties are least severe in Bulgaria and Romania, chiefly because their oil imports are effected by sea and do not entail dependence on pipeline deliveries from the CIS. While these countries face the problem that incoming oil involves foreign exchange payments, therefore, they have flexibility in terms of their potential areas of supply. Conversely, Poland, Czechoslovakia and Hungary – with their heavy reliance on the CIS pipelines – lack this flexibility. And, as has been indicated, political turmoil in what was formerly Yugoslavia has isolated part of the refining industry from world markets by severing its Adria pipeline link with what are now Croatian port facilities at Rijeka. Consequently these countries all pose an important strategic question: how may the oil supply system be reoriented in order to ensure that current disadvantages are minimised and access is gained to secure sources at competitive prices? It is on this question that the remainder of this chapter is focused.

3.4 Infrastructural investment and supply reorientation

In an ideal world a heavy investment programme, especially one aiming to provide a new westward-looking pipeline system, might be envisaged, but in the current economic climate it is unrealistic to propose such a strategy. The discussion therefore assumes that current infrastructures will be retained whenever possible, and that reorientation of the supply system should be achieved by modest infrastructural additions. In practical terms, this assumption relies heavily on the fact that, with appropriate changes at pumping stations, the direction of flow through pipelines can be reversed. The additions proposed mainly comprise the construction of missing pipeline links, but they also entail limited investment in ports; they are presented as a menu from which choices may be made, rather than as a comprehensive investment programme to be implemented as a whole; and their analysis can best be undertaken by considering the current oil supply system in terms of its northern and southern components.

3.4.1 The northern supply system

This system supports much of the Polish refining industry and extends into the former East Germany, where it is linked to the refining centres of Schwedt and Leipzig. Physically it comprises the northern branch of the Friendship pipeline, plus the Polish port of Gdańsk and the eastern German port of Rostock. Both ports give access to world oil markets, and in this sense a potential orientation towards the West already exists. However, both ports also have limitations which must be overcome if this potential is to be fully exploited.

Gdańsk is relatively well equipped as an oil import port (Figure 3.3). Crude oil can be handled at a rate of 100,000 tones per day, and the 15 m channel allows access to vessels up to 150,000 dwt (Cuny, 1991). Drawing a comparison with Western Europe, in these respects it resembles the UK port of Southampton, which supports the country's largest refinery, Esso Fawley. However, viewed from the national and international perspectives, Gdańsk is not well equipped to exploit its oil trans-shipment facilities to the full because it is not connected with the Friendship system. Consequently crude oil must either be processed locally, at the three million-tonne refinery, or be transported to inland refining centres by rail. Much more efficient transport to the hinterland would be ensured by the construction of a short (about 210 km) crude oil pipeline extending southwards from Gdańsk to link the port with the northern branch of the Friendship pipeline (Figure 3.4). The most appropriate point for the connection with the latter would be Płock, where it would allow Poland's largest (9.8 million tonnes) refinery to be supplied directly from Gdańsk (Thrash, 1991; Burles, 1991).

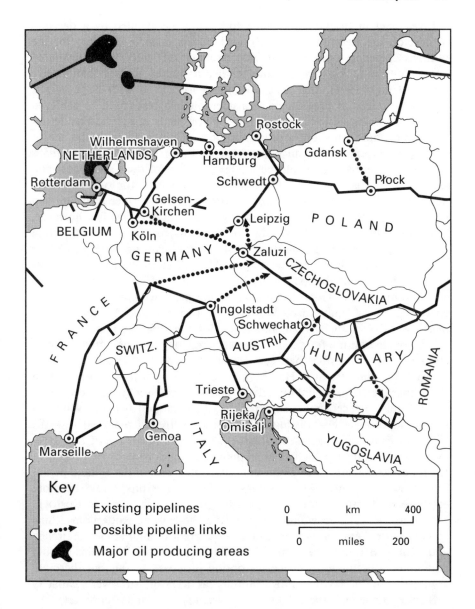

Figure 3.4 Central and Eastern Europe: opportunities to integrate oil supply systems with Western Europe

Investment in the Gdańsk–Płock link could be avoided by a decision to develop the German port of Rostock as the main feeder port for the northern pipeline system. Rostock's primary difficulty is its restricted access for oil tankers. With channel depth limited to less than twelve metres (Cuny, 1991), the scale economies associated with large vessels cannot be gained at present, but considerable progress could be achieved through dredging and relatively limited investments in supertanker jetties and appropriate on-shore storage facilities. Compared with the major developments undertaken in many western European ports in the 1950s and 1960s, these works would be modest in terms of their scale, cost and technological challenge. For Germany the motivation for such improvements would be an upgraded supply system for the former East German refining centres of Schwedt and Leipzig. Internationally, however, Poland's Płock refinery would also stand to gain by importing competitively priced oil eastwards along the existing Rostock–Płock section of the pipeline network. Expressed in these terms, German investment in the port of Rostock could have the same effect in Poland as the construction of the Gdańsk–Płock pipeline proposed above. Unless the latter were to be financed by Western aid, therefore, the Rostock option might well be financially advantageous for the Polish economy.

Two other options for the northern system may also be noted. First, a 200-km link is possible between Hamburg and the existing Rostock–Schwedt pipeline. Because Hamburg is already served by a pipeline from Wilhelmshaven, this would effectively give the northern system access to a seaport able to accept most supertankers. (The deepest berth at Wilhelmshaven handles vessels drawing up to twenty metres). Compared with the strategy of improving access in Rostock, the chief advantage of this development would be a reduction in shipping costs and hazards as a result of fewer tankers passing through the complex waters east of the Jutland peninsula. Conversely, however, the construction of this link would be more costly than the straightforward upgrading of maritime access to Rostock.

A more radical step would be to extend the existing Rotterdam–Rhine pipeline system eastwards from one of its current termini at Gelsenkirchen and Köln. Because the gap to be bridged is 400 km, this would undoubtedly be the most expensive option proposed so far, but there are arguments in its favour. For example, as a result of severe capacity cutbacks made in the 1980s in Germany's inland refineries, the Rotterdam–Rhine pipeline system has excess capacity. The excellent port facilities available in Rotterdam would allow full advantage to be gained of economies of scale. And, as with the Wilhelmshaven solution, the costs and hazards of tankers navigating the waters east of Jutland would be reduced. In addition, new pipeline construction from the Rotterdam network eastwards across Germany offers the opportunity to link the northern and southern pipeline systems in Central Europe. This is a strategic consideration to which the discussion will return.

3.4.2 The southern supply system

The southern pipeline system has two elements. The first is the southern branch of the Friendship pipeline, which bifurcates as it leaves CIS territory to give branches serving Czechoslovakia and Hungary. In southern Hungary the extremities of this network collect oil from small fields for delivery to convenient refineries, while one branch pipeline extends into what is now Croatian territory in order to gather oil. The second element is the Adria pipeline, which extends from Rijeka eastwards to the vicinity of the Romanian border. As was previously indicated, with the break-up of Yugoslavia this link has come under Croatian control, ensuring that only Croatian refineries have secure access to the deepwater port facilities at Rijeka and nearby Omišalj.

In view of the disruption caused by the civil war, it is unlikely that the port facilities of Rijeka and Omišalj will play a significant role in the reorientation of this system towards Western oil supplies. At best, these high-grade deepwater facilities – which could have become a key element for the entire southern supply system – are likely to be used to sustain refining in Croatia alone. Trieste, in contrast, has much to offer consumers in Czechoslovakia, Hungary and, perhaps, parts of former Yugoslavia outside Croatia. This Italian port is accessible to supertankers of 160,000 dwt; can be made accessible to ones of 200,000 dwt (Cuny, 1991); and is the origin of the TAL pipeline to Austria and Germany, the capacity of which is 50 million tonnes per year. In Austria a branch of the TAL line terminates at Schwechat near Vienna, only 80 km from the main Czechoslovak pipeline, which could therefore be connected with the West through relatively minor construction work. This development would not simply link Czechoslovakia with the Adriatic but, through reversals of flow in the existing system, could also serve Hungary. Moreover, it might also make feasible a new crude oil pipeline running from Hungary to serve parts of the former Yugoslavia now cut off from sea-borne oil supplies by Croatia.

The potential of Genoa and Marseille to serve Central Europe through their existing pipelines should also be recognised. At present the CEL line from Genoa terminates at the Ingolstadt–Vohburg–Neustadt refining cluster north of Munich, from where it is little more than 200 km to the existing Czech network. Construction of this link with Czechoslovakia would provide access to port facilities even more attractive than those currently available in Trieste. Although onshore berths in Genoa are limited to vessels of 130,000 dwt, two offshore single point moorings accept supertankers of 270,000 dwt and 500,000 dwt (Cuny, 1991). For all practical purposes, therefore, Genoa is able to offer the full advantages of scale economies. Moreover, the port is also well located for supertankers using the Straits of Gibraltar, whereas there are significant time and cost penalties associated with the diversion around the Italian peninsula and through the Adriatic to Trieste. Similar arguments also apply to the French port of Marseille-Fos. Locationally, it is even more favourably placed than Genoa; tankers of any size can be accepted; the SEPL pipeline already links the port with Germany; and a new 400 km extension would complete the connection with Czechoslovakia.

3.4.3 North–south system linkage

The preceding discussion of opportunities to achieve reorientation to the West has considered the northern and southern supply systems in isolation from each other. If these systems were to be connected, however, Central European countries in particular could achieve still greater advantages in terms of supply diversity. These advantages would be partly economic because countries would have greater freedom to seek competitively priced oil. But they would also be strategic in the sense that a broad, integrated network would provide protection against unilateral interruptions to supplies as a result of unforseen political difficulties in future decades. Given that the political futures of the new democracies, as well as their economic fortunes, are highly uncertain, this is an important consideration.

One opportunity for north–south integration, the eastwards extension of the Rotterdam–Rhine pipeline network, has already been noted. If this were to penetrate the former East Germany and then bifurcate, links with the Leipzig–Schwedt–Płock pipeline and the Czechoslovakian network could readily be established. In this scenario the branching pipeline would provide north–south integration, while the dominant axis of movement might well remain east–west as Rotterdam became a major supplier to both the northern and southern systems. This would have substantial attractions for interests in Rotterdam, where additional oil traffic could be handled without difficulty.

North–south integration in this part of Europe is not, however, entirely dependent on the extension of the Rotterdam–Rhine system. Integration could also be achieved by the construction of a 120-km pipeline between Leipzig and the Zaluzi refinery, just inside Czechoslovakian territory. The development of this link would require the installation of pumping equipment to allow oil to flow in either direction as necessary, and the existing pipelines to which it was connected would similarly require modification. But, once complete, this project would facilitate the north–south exchange of oil on a substantial scale.

3.5 Conclusions

Although the future of the Central and Eastern European economies is highly uncertain, a need for substantial international trade in oil can be predicted with some confidence. As countries make the change towards true market economies this need will grow, and in most instances it will be driven by the expanding demands of the transport sector. In some countries, especially Bulgaria and Romania, circumstances suggest that – provided the finance is available to import oil – the problem of obtaining it will not be great. This reflects the fact that these countries have not been crossed by the former USSR's Friendship pipeline and have instead relied on ports which can now give access to many sources of crude oil.

Where the Friendship pipeline has been a significant influence – primarily in Poland, Czechoslovakia, Hungary and the former East Germany – economic and political considerations indicate that a reorientation to a broader mix of markets, in which the West is strongly represented, is highly desirable. Except in Germany, this reorientation will not be entirely straightforward. The southern supply system, apart from the now-defunct Adria line in Yugoslavia, has had no access to ports providing links with world markets; ports in the north either have inadequate facilities or are not well connected to the international distribution network; and the east–west influence previously exerted by supplies from the Soviet Union has ensured that opportunities for north–south interchange are poor.

As the discussion has demonstrated, however, opportunities to overcome the problem faced by these countries do exist. The possibilities outlined above have three main facets. First, although the main arteries of the Friendship pipeline system may be far from perfect, at least for the time being they can be retained to form the main elements of a reoriented network. Second, particularly in the port of Rostock, limited investment could improve oil import facilities that are already connected to the northern supply system. Third, and more significantly, many opportunities exist to construct short, yet potentially highly effective, pipelines to create a far more comprehensive supply network. Some of these pipelines, such as a Gdańsk–Płock connection, would be internal to the former communist states. But, through connections with Western Europe's highly developed and well-maintained pipeline system, the majority would link former communist areas with a selection of the leading – and competing – European oil ports. Trieste, Genoa, Marseille, Rotterdam and Wilhelmshaven are outstanding candidates in this context. Thus a major implication of this chapter is that investment in Western Europe has already done much to lay the foundations for a major reorientation of oil supply patterns in the former heart of communist Europe.

What must be emphasised finally, however, is that no overall plan

exists to build on these foundations. While the opportunities can be identified, therefore, action is likely to depend on private-sector investment
in and from the West. This in turn suggests that the pace of reorientation
will be highly dependent on the extent to which economic recovery and
restructuring provide the necessary impetus for Western companies who
currently control the skills and capital that are required.

Notes

1. Research for this paper was made possible by the award of Leverhulme
    Research Fellowship to Professor Pinder in 1991/92. The provision of this
    support is gratefully acknowledged.
2. Natural gas consumption in Central and Eastern Europe rose from 373
    million tonnes of oil equivalent (mtoe) in 1980 to 637 million tonnes in 1990,
    and one estimate has suggested that the total will rise to between 840 and
    1050 mtoe by 2005 (Anon., 1990a)
3. Road transport already dominates the consumption of oil products by the
    transport sector. In Bulgaria, Romania, the former Yugoslavia and the
    former East Germany, road transport accounts for more than 80 per cent of
    this sector's oil consumption (International Energy Agency, 1991).
4. In the late 1980s an output decline of ten per cent underlined the importance
    of this problem.

4 Airlines in transition to the market economy

Leslie Symons

4.1 Introduction

In the social and economic upheaval which has followed the collapse of the Soviet Union and freeing of the Central and East European states from its domination, few sectors of the economy of any of these states have faced greater changes than the civil aviation organisations. Under the Soviet system, civil airlines enjoyed monopoly conditions and were protected by state subsidies from the economic pressures that they would otherwise have faced. The infrastructure – airports, air traffic control – was provided by the state, and the aircraft manufacturers enjoyed the patronage of the state with only limited competition between enterprises and virtually no exposure to foreign competition. Central planning also decided the routes to be operated and the level of service to be provided.

There were, of course, built-in drawbacks to this system. The lack of competition resulted in mediocre service levels in all areas: from aircraft design and airport construction to in-flight catering and ticketing arrangements. Nevertheless, the services provided were fairly comprehensive and cheap, and to that extent accessible to the public. In general, the operating standards were sound and schedules were adhered to. This was certainly true of the 1950s and 1960s, when civil aviation throughout the world had yet to experience the modernisation and expansion of the 1970s and 1980s. The occasional traffic jams that occurred when aircraft were taken out of service for technical reasons were hardly worse than might have been expected elsewhere, and when airport closure was forced upon the operators by weather conditions it could plausibly be argued that this would have happened anywhere under any system.

4.2 Aviation under the Soviet system

All the states of Central and Eastern Europe embraced by the CMEA had to accept the aircraft and operating systems supplied by the Soviet Union. The routes that they were permitted to operate were subject to the overall requirements of Soviet policy and the economic pre-eminence of the Soviet Union's monopoly airline, Aeroflot. In one sense, Aeroflot was not one airline but a grouping of semi-autonomous directorates, but the whole was totally subject to overall unified control. The central planners ruled absolutely over every aspect, from procurement to timetabling, and Aeroflot was claimed to be the biggest airline in the world.

Cracks began to appear in this monolithic structure in the 1970s. The Soviet Union was still claiming that it was 'catching up' with the United States and, at least in its successes in the exploration of space, it could point to some evidence for this. The terrible legacy of the Second World War could still be used to explain the lower standard of living of the peoples of the Soviet Union as compared with North America or Western Europe. The 'period of stagnation' under Brezhnev had not yet been confidently identified. But cracks there were, and in the world of civil aviation they were observable in the failure of aircraft design and procurement to advance in line with Western development. For the Soviet Union and for the countries of Central and Eastern Europe the signs were different. In the Soviet Union the problems were more evident, being epitomised by the failure of the intended flagship of Aeroflot, the Tupolev Tu-144 – the Soviet venture into civil supersonic flight. The Tu-144 was the first supersonic airliner to take to the air (31 December, 1968) and the first to exceed the speed of sound (5 June, 1969) (Taylor, 1976, p. 442). However, while the Anglo-French Concorde progressed, expensively but steadily, until it entered commercial service in 1976 (and continues in service in 1992), the Tu-144 was beset by successive problems, not least in its engines. Modifications were reported to be still in progress in 1981 (Taylor, 1982, p. 234), but shortly afterwards it became clear that the project had been quietly abandoned. At more mundane levels, but inevitably affecting Central and East European airlines as well as Aeroflot, were the more general problems with aero-engines which were also hindering development of other airliners, not only in design but in production and repair facilities. The number of aircraft grounded through lack of serviceable engines increased significantly, although this was not admitted publicly at the time. There was also failure to advance in air traffic control, instrument landing systems and radar, airport development and computerised ticket sales.

Importation of equipment was not in accord with the principles of the Soviet government, but in any case the export of any item with possible strategic value was strictly limited by the embargo imposed by the USA on its firms and all other companies inasmuch as their products utilised

American elements or components. Such embargoes applied equally, of course, to the Central and East European countries, such that they were almost entirely dependent on Soviet supplies.

In 1979, however, British Aerospace concluded an agreement with CNIAR of Romania for licensed construction of the BAC 1-11 twin-jet airliner in Romania, to be preceded by delivery of three complete aircraft (Taylor, 1982, p. 173). Romania had built the Britten-Norman (later Pilatus) Islander since 1969, but the decision by a CMEA country to build a major foreign airliner was a significant departure from previous policy. It was, however, not to be repeated, and the Central and East European countries (except Yugoslavia) remained dependent on equipment designed and, with few exceptions, built in the Soviet Union.

4.3 Aircraft construction in conjunction with the Soviet Union

Small aircraft industries existed in the Central and East European countries during the CMEA years, but they did not extend much beyond building light aircraft. These did, however, include small passenger aircraft for local and short-range regional services. In Czechoslovakia, the Let National Corporation plant was established in 1950. It produced training and agricultural aircraft, air taxis and gliders and, in 1966, began design of the Let L-410 twin-turboprop light transport.

Production of this model began in 1979, and it became the standard Aeroflot feederline aircraft. Aeroflot requirements included the ability to operate in temperatures ranging from -50 to $+45$ degrees centigrade with systems to be survivable in temperatures as low as -60 degrees (Taylor, 1982, p. 44). The Aero Vodochody and Zlin Moravan National Corporations, dating from 1953 and 1935 respectively, produced training and aerobatic aircraft which gained a world-wide reputation in their classes.

A wide range of light aircraft types have been built in Poland, where the industry began in 1910. Agricultural aircraft have been a recent specialisation, with a major commitment to supplying a large part of Soviet needs, to both Soviet and Polish designs. Responsibility for production of the Soviet Antonov An-28 twin-turboprop light transport was added to the PZL-Mielec activities in 1978. The An-28 was intended for the shortest routes in the Soviet Union, replacing the long-serving An-2 single-engined biplane, which had been produced in large numbers in Poland for many years (Plate 4.1).

These examples show that CMEA countries were enabled to develop their aircraft construction industries to some extent under Soviet influence. Indeed, it could be argued that these industries were on a scale

Plate 4.1　An Antonov An-2 biplane, of which several thousand were built by PZL, Poland for service in the Soviet Union for local airline services, medical, forest fire-fighting and agricultural work. (Leslie Symons)

appropriate to the size of the countries. Certainly they could hardly have expected to design and build airliners of modern complexity, though they might have been able to undertake more remunerative links through sub-contracting and cooperative projects with the West if given more freedom, as may be seen in the future.

The economic collapse of the Soviet Union brought severe problems for the Central and East European aircraft industries as for the airlines. The PZL-Mielec firm, having build twenty An-28s for Aeroflot, undertook to construct another thirty without having received payment for the first batch. A delegation went to Moscow to try to sort out the problem and, asked who ordered them, said 'Yasov'. This produced the retort 'He is in prison, go and get it from him' (Crawford, 1991a, pp. 32–3).

One reason cited for the failure of the Soviet Union to meet its debts was the Polish demand for payment in hard currency, which the Soviet Union could not meet. Early in 1992 it was said that the Polish state-owned aircraft construction firm, PZL, had supplied $30 million worth of equipment to the former USSR which had not been paid for. The possibility of barter deals was being considered. Meanwhile PZL still employed forty thousand people at twelve sites but stated that this level of employment could not be sustained in the existing conditions.

Construction of helicopters and of parts of Soviet aircraft had been brought to a halt. PZL reported that 85 per cent of its business had been with the USSR and this had totally collapsed. It was also owed money by its own Ministry of Defence, and had lost its market for Kruk agricultural aircraft in East Germany consequent upon German reunification. Offset agreements with Aerospatiale and Alenia following purchase of ATR-72 aircraft had provided some hope. Negotiations were being conducted with other foreign firms, and the Parliamentary National Defence Committee met in late January 1992 to try to work out a rescue programme to save the firm. Similar problems were reported by Czechoslovakia, which had lost its Soviet market for the Let L-410 and L-610 regional airliners and for training aircraft.

It was announced early in 1992 that the Russian Yakovlev firm had won the concept-definition stage of a competition for a trainer for CIS countries, which had been necessitated by the requirement of the Czech Aero firm for payment for its trainers in hard currency. The magnitude of the lost market was shown by the fact that out of a total of 1,020 L-410s built in Czechoslovakia, 872 had been for Aeroflot and 2,129 Aero L-39 advanced jet trainers had been supplied to the Soviet Union. It was considered that only Western support and business could save the Aero firm.

4.4 Airline reconstruction in Central and Eastern Europe

As soon as control by the Soviet Union was weakened and their own communist parties deprived of power, measures were taken in the states of Central and Eastern Europe to reconstruct their economic and social organisation. Attention to aviation varied in the different states, but was in all cases aimed at breaking the Soviet mould, extending routes to new destinations and developing links with Western countries. Early privatisation was generally a further aim. The developments in the former German Democratic Republic were a special case because of the early reunification of Germany, and these will be discussed after treatment of the other states, as will developments in the former Soviet Baltic republics.

4.4.1 Hungary

Hungary was the first of the former CMEA countries to announce its intention to privatise its state airline, MALÉV. It sought Western capital in the form of a minority stake to allow it to purchase modern aircraft to make it more competitive than with its old Soviet types. Credit Suisse First Boston, advising the Hungarian government, advocated beginning privatisation in 1991 but this was resisted by the new director of MALÉV, Tamas Dari, the first civilian to be appointed to this post. He denied that the airline was on the verge of bankruptcy but stated that privatisation should not be attempted until the airline was in a healthier condition (Gál, 1990). A compromise between the airline and the Property Trusteeship Agency resulted in the decision that the state would retain 51 per cent of the capital rather than the 25 per cent originally intended (Gál, 1991a). It was also agreed that privatisation should be delayed until 1992–3. The Tu-134s and Tu-154s were to be reallocated to charter operations under an independent company and an Il-62 was allocated to a new service to Japan (Gál, 1991b). Fleet renewal was planned to begin with Boeing 737-300s to be delivered in 1993 but Western aircraft were being leased meanwhile, supplementing the Soviet aircraft on which hitherto the airline was dependent. It was noted that the Boeing 737 uses only 40 per cent of the fuel required by the Tupolev Tu-154. Nevertheless, MALÉV's Deputy Chief Executive Officer said that the Tu-154 was a sound aircraft and that the Russians had been good partners.

Early in 1992 it was announced that negotiations for a joint venture with the American Lockheed Corporation were being completed. This would include arrangements for the maintenance of the mixed fleet of Soviet and Western aircraft. Hungary also plans to develop its airport system, again aiming to attract Western capital on a lease/buy-back arrangement so that eventually the ownership would be in Hungarian hands. Budapest Ferihegy airport needs $90 million for Phase 1 – the construction of a new terminal. This would service an increase from four to six million passengers a year, with the aim of being ready for the 1996 World Expo.

Also planned was the development of Kiskunlaachaza, a former Soviet airfield 30 km south of Budapest, into a new cargo hub. It already had a runway of 2,500 m, but this would be extended. As it is relatively remote, this airfield presents few environmental problems. The USA was to fund a study of seven ex-Soviet airfields with a view to development.

4.4.2 Poland

The Polish airline, LOT, quickly began making strenuous efforts to replace its ageing Soviet aircraft with Western types. It placed orders for nine McDonnell Douglas MD-80s, costing $350 million, for delivery in 1992–3. It decided to buy nine Boeing 737s (five Series 500 and four 400s) and entered into negotiations for two Boeing 707-300s and the lease of two Boeing 737s. It aimed to sell its Ilyushin Il-18s and Il-62s,

Tu-154s, Tu-134s and An-24s. Sales were bound to be difficult because of the spares problem, plus the fact that the ex-USSR constructors and, possibly, airlines, were wanting to sell the same types. On the other hand Aeroflot could usefully employ some of LOT's aircraft, which are fitted with Western avionics to enable the opening up of routes not possible previously. By January 1992, LOT had, in fact, sold seven Il-62s and ten An-24s to the Ukraine for $15 million, a low price considered to reflect the problems associated with the aircraft. The price of spares for all the Soviet aircraft had risen markedly and negotiations for their acquisition would have to be with individual factories instead of, as previously, Aviaexport, which further complicated matters.

The Poles hoped also to withdraw their Tu-134s by the end of 1992 and their Tu-154s by late 1993, to result in an all-Western fleet by the beginning of 1994, with an average age of no more than two and a half years.

LOT began in 1991 to operate the ATR-72 to Berlin and Prague, and Boeing 767s to North America in place of the Il-62s, which were withdrawn by December. A joint venture with Sweden was attempted: a new airline, LinjeLOT, was planned to start up in April 1992 operating ex-Linjeflyg Fokker 28s within Poland as well as to European and ex-USSR destinations. Redevelopment of Warsaw's Okęcie airport is also being undertaken.

Partial privatisation of LOT is planned when the airline returns to profitability. The government would retain 51 per cent of the capital, with foreign investors and airline staff being given opportunities to take shares (Crawford, 1991b, p. 49). It was announced early in 1992 that in the approach to privatisation a thousand jobs had been already eliminated and that many more would be lost during the year, reducing the airline's total employment to five thousand by the end of 1992.

4.4.3 Czechoslovakia

Českovslovenske Aerolinie (ČSA) was formed by the merger of two airlines in 1945. It became a major international airline, with a wide range of European and intercontinental services. In 1992 its aircraft were still predominantly Soviet-built types (including Tu-154s, Plate 4.2). It was intended that ČSA should be privatised by the mid-1990s with foreign investment of up to 40 per cent, with other airlines being favoured as foreign partners. The London merchant bank, J.P. Morgan, was providing advice. The Il-62s, which were used on trans-Atlantic and Far East routes, were replaced by two Airbus A310s. It was hoped to replace twenty Tupolevs during 1992, and delivery of five Boeing 737s was being undertaken in that year (Plate 4.3). Services to Havana, Ho Chi Minh City and Mexico were withdrawn and flights to other Central and East European countries were reduced.

Plate 4.2   A Tupolev Tu-154 medium-range Soviet airliner in the old livery of ČSA Czech airlines. (Leslie Symons)

Plate 4.3   All change: a Boeing-737 in the new ČSA colours (compare with Plate 4.2) with a USA registration. (ČSA)

In January 1992 it was announced that an agreement had been made for Air France to take a 40 per cent share in ČSA, valuing the Czech (*sic*) airline at $150 million. The 60 per cent majority share would remain with the Czechs, divided between the government and certain institutions. Four ATR-72s were to be bought to replace the Tu-134s. Services to Singapore, Bangkok and Jakarta were introduced and the Montreal service was extended to Chicago.

A new charter carrier, Air Moravia, was formed for cargo services, expanding into long-haul passenger charters in December 1991 with a 160-seat ex-ČSA Il-62M, a 350-seat Il-86 being added in January 1992. Singapore and Hanoi were the main destinations.

4.4.4 Bulgaria

Balkan Bulgarian Airlines dates from 1947, when, as TABSO, it was formed as a joint Bulgarian–Soviet undertaking, becoming wholly owned by Bulgaria in 1954. It adopted its present name in 1968, was reconstructed in 1985, and joined IATA four years later. In 1991 further reorganisation made it and three other carriers independent companies under the State Administration of Civil Aviation. These were Hemus Air, for medium-range operations, and Heli-Air and Bul-Air, for, respectively, specialised helicopter and agricultural operations. The international airports of Sofia, Varna and Burgas and seven domestic airports were also reorganised (Vankov, 1991).

Balkan operated with mainly Soviet-built aircraft in 1992, but was in the process of re-equipping with Western airliners. It leased two Airbus A320s, becoming the first East European carrier to operate this type, and wanted, if finance became available, to buy four more from Airbus Industrie. It thus also became the first airline in Eastern Europe to operate a fly-by-wire aircraft in commercial service.

With its fleet of some sixty aircraft, Balkan operated in 1992 a wide network of international services including African, Asian and North American destinations.

4.4.5 Romania

After several years of trying to modernise its fleet, TAROM, the Romanian state airline, was, in 1992, still having to rely largely on its Soviet-built Ilyushins, Tupolevs and Antonovs, together with Boeing 707s and BAC1-11s (as referred to above). It had developed a wide range of overseas services, some domestic routes rated of great importance to the economy, and a strong charter side. But the airline was seriously hindered by lack of ground facilities and support, made worse by

Bucharest's Otopeni airport having been damaged by an earthquake in 1990. A new airport was badly needed but this was impracticable unless financial constraints could be eased.

At the September 1992 Farnborough Air Show it was announced that TAROM had ordered seven Boeing 737s with options on a further six (Betts, 1992).

4.4.6 Germany

In the case of the former German Democratic Republic (GDR), after negotiations involving foreign airlines, the government of the Federal Republic decided that Lufthansa should take over the airline operations of Interflug, with its ancillary activities, notably agricultural aviation, being split up and sold off. Lufthansa took over early in 1991. The Soviet airliners used by Interflug were re-registered into the ownership of the federal government and were grounded until sold early in 1992. The Airbus which had been bought by Interflug was taken into government service, fitted with new doors and employed in cargo and ambulance duties. It was reported that three A310s had been bought by the Luftwaffe for freighter/tanker use.

The German case is particularly interesting because absorption of the former GDR territory into the Federal Republic makes possible direct comparisons and evaluation of the situation against the background of Europe's most successful economy. Owing to the many problems besetting Interflug, including finance, fuel supply, spare parts for the elderly Soviet aircraft and bureaucratic control which prevented the adoption of reforms and a competitive approach, Interflug's airline operations had become restricted to a number of international routes. In early summer 1990 Interflug was scheduled to operate from East Berlin to about forty destinations. These included Algiers, Bangkok, Beijing, Cairo, Dubai, Hanoi, Havana, Pyongyang, Singapore, Tripoli and Tunis, as well as a wide range of East and West European cities.

The network resembled a miniaturised version of Aeroflot's international services, omitting most of its long-haul destinations, which were outside the scope of Interflug's fleet. In addition to major cities, they included, on a seasonal basis, approved holiday destinations. Links with Paris, London, North America and other long-haul destinations were mainly through interchange at Amsterdam, Brussels, Copenhagen, Rome or Warsaw, or by flights provided by Aeroflot or other, mainly East European or Scandinavian, airlines.

It should be remembered that from the end of the Second World War until reunification all services into West Berlin were the prerogative of the airlines of the occupying powers. No German-operated services were available except by, for example, taking a British Airways, Air France or

Pan Am flight to Frankfurt and changing there to a Lufthansa service. Interflug's 1990 schedules also included services from Dresden to some ten destinations. Application had been made for a service to Paris. Erfurt had Interflug services to Budapest and to Varna, and a service from Leipzig to Düsseldorf had been inaugurated in August 1989.

To maintain these services Interflug had a fleet mainly made up of Soviet aircraft: seventeen Ilyushin Il-62/62M four-engine long-range airliners, twenty-nine Tupolev Tu-134A twin-jet medium-range airliners, twelve very elderly Il-18 4-turboprop transports and eight Let L-410 regional airliners, which did not feature in international schedules. These were only latterly supplemented by three A310-300 Airbuses, rendering Interflug the first airline to operate the type.

All the Soviet aircraft designs were fuel-thirsty and hence expensive to operate, and spare parts, even replacement engines, were subject to serious delays in delivery. Air traffic control was based on the Russian system so had to be replaced, and the landing aids were obsolete. Development of Berlin Schönefeld airport to ICAO Category 3A (full autoland) was taken in hand. A new control tower was necessary, the old one being too low and too small. The southern runway was found to be in bad condition, while the northern runway had environmental problems. It was hoped to expand the airport southward.

Schönefeld, belonging to the Länd of Brandenburg, was favoured by air transport interests as the new airport for Berlin, 'Berlin International', partly because it was close to the city. Environmental considerations, however, required other sites to be considered. These included former Soviet military airfields to the south of the city.

Finance for redevelopment would come from the federal government but the airports were owned by private companies. The structure was, to say the least, unusual. Schönefeld was controlled by one company, another controlled the Tegel and Tempelhof airports in West Berlin. A holding company was being sought. Schönefeld was used by Aeroflot in 1991 for their flights to Moscow and by ČSA to Prague, but all other major routes were served from Tegel or Tempelhof. Virtually all the old Interflug routes had been discontinued: the European capitals and some other large cities were now accessible direct from Berlin either by Lufthansa or another airline, and from most other important destinations via an interchange at Frankfurt or Munich.

A new airline, The Berline, was formed by ex-Interflug staff, based at Schönefeld, to operate passenger and cargo services, using ex-Interflug Il-18s. It obtained contracts to fly German workers to the Commonwealth of Independent States and to Mediterranean destinations.

4.4.7 Latvia

All three Baltic republics hastened to organise their own airlines as soon as, or even before, their independence was recognised. Latvia announced in September 1991 that it would privatise its Aeroflot directorate as Baltic International Airlines in a joint venture with Houston-based Baltic International. This was the first privatisation from Aeroflot, which contributed the fleet so that the new airline was not burdened by debts. It had thirty-seven aircraft, all Soviet-built, including eight Tu-154s, fourteen Tu-134s and fifteen An-24s. These would be refurbished and new aircraft would be bought in the West, or possibly leased. SAS and McDonnell Douglas cooperated to make DC-9s available. Services were offered from Riga to Copenhagen, Stockholm, Helsinki, Hamburg and Tel Aviv as well as forty daily flights to Moscow, St. Petersburg and other cities in Russia and the other republics of the former USSR.

Major reconstruction of Riga's Spilve airport is to be undertaken with American partners, involving both terminals and airfield facilities, notably an extension of the runway from 2,375 m to 3,350 m to accommodate new wide-body aircraft, new lighting and upgrading of the existing Category II instrument landing system (ILS).

4.4.8 Lithuania

This country has made progress with its airlines since independence in a number of ways. During autumn 1991 services operated under Soviet agreements to Germany, and Central and East European destinations were renegotiated while new agreements with, initially, Denmark and Sweden were sought. Finnair and Braathens SAFE (Norway) were approached regarding partnerships, and joint ventures were planned with North American interests. Both North American and European firms hoped to sell aircraft to replace the old fleet of Soviet aircraft. These comprised eight Tu-134s, twelve Yak-42s (120-seaters), five Yak-40s, four An-24s and three An-26s.

Finance was the problem with replacements, and there was no intention in 1991–2 to seek long-haul aircraft. Concentration on Europe and the Asian parts of the former Soviet Union was intended, at least for some years. A second airline, Lietuva Airlines, has operated between Kaunas, the second city, and Moscow as a separate Aeroflot department with five Yak-40s which were also used on charter flights.

It was intended that both airlines would remain in government ownership temporarily but privatisation is planned, with the smaller airline first in line. Private ownership of some airports is planned and Lithuania is anxious to attract Western investment to modernise and expand Vilnius airport, but air traffic control will remain a state service.

4.4.9 Estonia

In 1991 Estonia was linked with Moscow and eleven other cities in the European parts of the former USSR. Services to Helsinki, Stockholm, Frankfurt and Budapest were operating, with others to Copenhagen, London and Paris planned. A West European partner was sought. Long-haul flights were not contemplated. The fleet of twelve Tu-134s and four Yak-40s was inadequate and leasing of Western aircraft was viewed as a necessity (Endres, 1991).

4.5 Contemporary problems

4.5.1 The fuel problem

It will be clear from the foregoing that the former CMEA Central and East European airlines suffer from the necessity to continue operating Soviet-built aircraft which are extremely uneconomic owing in part to their high consumption of aviation fuel. This was not serious as long as the fuel was forthcoming from the Soviet Union at the special low prices which prevailed between the members of the CMEA, and as long as supplies were adequate.

Problems were beginning to become evident in the 1970s, however, as Soviet petroleum output failed to keep pace with rising demands. Long before the problem was admitted internationally, Aeroflot crews were set stiff tasks in fuel conservation. The pages of the professional aircrew newspaper *Vozdushniy Transport* constantly contained advice on how to achieve maximum fuel economy by methods ranging from not starting engines for pushback at airports (relying instead on tractor haulage) to choice of routes to benefit from the most favourable winds. There were many complaints from pilots about air traffic control allegedly keeping them circling prior to landing, and about unnecessary *en-route* diversions. As the 1980s progressed these complaints intensified. Pilots began to report having to divert to unscheduled stops solely to pick up fuel, so adding to the waste, and failure of airports to provide the refuelling required to maintain operations.

Inevitably, these problems spread to Central and East European airlines, which were almost entirely dependent on Soviet fuel, being not permitted to buy hard-currency fuel unless it was unavoidable. Payloads were cut in order to carry fuel for the return journey. By the 1990s flights were being curtailed and complaints mounted from passengers who were delayed for hours and even days at airports, leading to angry scenes and even violence in the Soviet Union and its successor states.

These problems were still in evidence in 1992. The independent countries were, of course, free to buy fuel anywhere but lacked the hard currency needed for adequate purchases.

4.5.2 The Gulf War and its aftermath

Airlines everywhere suffered from severe diminution of demand and therefore of revenue as a result of the Gulf War, which had catastrophic results on some Western airlines and also inevitably affected the struggling Central and East European carriers. Transition to profitability was delayed, old aircraft had to be kept in use, and improvements to airports and infrastructure were curtailed or postponed.

4.5.3 The fleet insurance problem

A problem not often considered outside the industry is that of insurance and re-insurance of fleets. This has been a major problem for the former CMEA countries. Surprisingly, perhaps, it has been argued that the insurance markets of Central and Eastern Europe under communism were models of stability, and that the prospect of finding hard currency cover for ageing fleets of Ilyushins was a relatively minor problem (Petch, 1991). But the pool for the reinsurance of hull risks of Soviet-built aircraft was wound up in October 1990, and, as has been seen, some airlines have lost no time in trying to dispose of Soviet-built airliners, although many were still in service in 1992. Finding and funding insurance for their operations is yet another area of great difficulty for the fledgling Central and East European airlines.

4.6 Conclusions

The former CMEA countries and the Baltic republics of the erstwhile Soviet Union have made good progress in the development of their own independent airlines in the relatively short period that has elapsed since they established their independence. By the spring of 1992 several of these airlines had succeeded in replacing at least part of their elderly and fuel-thirsty Soviet fleet with Western aircraft. Though handicapped by financial problems they had benefited from Western help. It varied in its effectiveness and was developing in several different forms, ranging from bank loans to technical help from Western aircraft manufacturers and the participation in investment by Western airlines. The fact that such assistance would be intended to result in, eventually, substantial gains for the Western investors does not reduce the value of the help.

The re-equipping of the fleets has been helped by a period of relatively weak demand for new airlines during the period of the Gulf War and the slow recovery that has followed. As a result, the major manufacturers – Boeing, McDonnell Douglas and Airbus – have been willing to negotiate terms favourable to the airlines. On the other hand, the weak market has hindered the disposal of the old Soviet types.

Privatisation has been clearly stated as the aim of virtually all the airlines of Central and Eastern Europe, but progress towards it has been uncertain in most cases. The unfamiliarity of all these countries with the operation of the market and the recognition of the importance of first creating a sound technical base for safe operations has led to some reduction of earlier over-enthusiasm, nevertheless, privatisation should be achieved in most cases before the year 2000.

On the whole, airline reconstruction within the region, partly due to the importance attached to it by the governments concerned, has made quite impressive progress in a relatively brief period of time.

5 Transport implications of German unification

Jan Kowalski

Plate 5.1 An immediate consequence of the fall of the Berlin Wall has been the opening up to public access of a large swathe of previously sterilised land through the middle and around the western periphery of the city. Here, just to the north of the city centre, where Prenzlauer Berg to the east had been separated from Wedding to the west, a Wall Park is being established, with the former Volkspolizei border patrol path and guard dog-run transformed into a footpath and bicycle-way. (Derek Hall).

Plate 5.2 An unflattering comparison of East and West German transport technology. On the left is the only bus type to have been manufactured in the former GDR. The 21-seat Robur LO 3000 is based upon a light truck chassis built at Zittau, but it has seen service as a bus both in Eastern Europe and in socialist developing countries such as Cuba and Mozambique. On the right, a Mercedes-Benz 0303 integral coach in the colours of LOT Polish Airlines. (Derek Hall)

5.1 Introduction

The fall of the Berlin Wall (Plates 5.1, 5.2) and the unification of Germany, coupled with the mostly non-violent deposing of the communist governments in Central and Eastern Europe led to dramatic adjustment processes in the heart of the European continent. This chapter offers some initial assessments of the probable consequences of these transformations in general and of German unification in particular, for the transport sector. The changes in infrastructure networks and flows, as well as in the functioning of transport companies therefore requires examination from at least two perspectives:

(a) that of a unified Germany, influenced by the regulations and financial transfers from the western to the eastern part of the country and by rapid legal, economic and social integration; and

(b) that of Central and Eastern Europe, where the transport flow patterns and the functioning of the transport sector are changing as a result of: (i) the transformation of formerly centrally-planned economies to market-oriented ones; and (ii) the intensification of interactions with Western Europe, through association with the European Community.

Chapter 2 pointed to the particular importance of developing adequate transport links between the transforming countries and the West, as well as within these countries themselves. Although several authors, especially those who devote themselves exclusively to transport research, maintain that the transport sector became the most backward sector of the former communist economies, the situation of transport was neither better nor worse than that of the other sectors of the economy (Funck and Kowalski, 1987, 1989). At present the short-term pressure on the transport sector has decreased as a result of a decline in the volume and share of investment compared with other sectors, and a considerable reduction in demand for transport services as a result of the hardening of budget constraints of enterprises, following reforms inaugurated in January 1990.

Optimistically, it is expected that by the year 2010 Central and East European countries will reach approximately the standard of living levels of the Federal Republic of Germany in 1988 (Kowalski 1991b; Kessel *et al.*, 1990). It is assumed that this development level will induce transport demand comparable to that characteristic of West Germany in 1988. This implies steep growth rates in individual mobility and private vehicle levels, and less pronounced increases in goods transport volumes, due to increased efficiency in the market economy conditions.

The political and economic upheavals in Central and Eastern Europe and the dissolution of the CMEA is resulting in significant geographical adjustments in the patterns of trade and flow of people. In the past, the geographical distribution of foreign trade of socialist countries could be described by the 'one-third rule', that is about one-third of the turnover was conducted with the Soviet Union, one-third with the rest of the CMEA and one-third with the rest of the world. The share of hard currency countries was kept artificially low because of doctrinal reasons, but also because of the insufficient availability of means of payment.

In the wake of transformation in Central and Eastern Europe, the share of trade with the rest of the world, in particular with Western Europe, is increasing considerably, reflecting the need for a more intense economic interaction with these highly developed countries. One possible barrier to the growth of East–West trade may be seen in the high degree of indebtedness of Central and Eastern Europe in recent years. It can be expected that the payments problem will to some extent be resolved in a way similar to the Polish debt reduction schemes agreed in 1991 (whereby Polish debt to public lenders was halved), thereby enabling an intensification of East–West trade flows.

The extent of the increase in trade with Western Europe which could be observed immediately after the disruption of the communist system is probably artificially high. This is, firstly, because of the breakdown of Central and East European markets due to the currency problems experienced in the phase of transition from rouble-based to convertible systems. Secondly, it is because of the inclination of most consumers to choose, in the early days of transition, Western rather than Eastern-produced goods.

This phenomenon, especially intense in East Germany in 1990, was also observed in Hungary, Poland and Czechoslovakia. But within two years consumers were starting to search for cheaper local goods again. It can be expected therefore, that within five to ten years the geographical proximity of the former communist countries will again play a considerable role in the determination of the spatial structure of commodity flows.

In addition, strong growth in intrasectoral, as opposed to intersectoral, trade is to be expected. In the past, the CMEA agreements enforced a high degree of sectoral specialisation in the foreign trade structures of Central and East European countries: for example, Bulgaria specialised in certain kinds of electronic data-processing products, Poland was responsible for most radio-location equipment, and the Soviet Union for certain kinds of raw materials. Under the conditions of free market relationships the patterns of trade will, most probably, move towards more intrasectoral specialisation and exchange, as is well known from Western experience.

Coupled with these changes in the pattern of commodity flows, considerable increases in the movements of people can be expected between West and East. As is well known, most of the Central and Eastern European countries, with the notable exception of Poland, restricted the free flow of people, especially the travel of their own citizens to the West. Since the opening of the region the number of private and business-related journeys have increased substantially, and will increase even further in the future. This evolution finds its strongest expression in the heart of the European continent, in the area of the unified Germany, but flows with all the Central and East European countries will grow too. Table 5.1 shows the range of the expected increase in the flows of people, and postulates the situation had the Berlin Wall and Iron Curtain not been breached (Rothengatter and Kowalski, 1991).

Table 5.1 Germany: patterns of international passenger traffic (million journeys per year)

Between	1985	2010 With opening of frontiers	2010 Without opening of frontiers
West Germany (excluding West Berlin) and 'CMEA' countries (other than East Germany)	8.4	39.2	9.5
West Berlin and 'CMEA' countries (other than East Germany)	0.2	6.1	0.2
West Berlin and West European countries	2.1	3.8	4.8
Western Europe and East Germany via transit	0.2	10.7	0.3
Western Europe and 'CMEA' countries (other than East Germany) via transit	0.9	7.3	1.7

Source: Rothengatter and Kowalski, 1991, p. 223.

5.2 Eastern Germany: economic impact

In contrast to the situation for the other former CMEA countries, economic reform and the necessary adjustment costs (such as large-scale unemployment following the closure of numerous unviable enterprises) in the former German Democratic Republic are supported financially and organisationally by West Germany. In 1990 about DM 140 billion, and in 1991 around DM 180 billion were transferred to eastern Germany through various programmes. It has been possible also to apply in the East most of the legal regulations pertinent to the functioning of the socio-economic system from the West. Therefore the systemic transition to the market economy has been completed very quickly in the territory of the former GDR. The monetary and economic union created almost overnight a single, although uneven, German economy.

This does not mean, of course, that the process of change is devoid of problems. The mass media have been filled with negative reports on the psychological, social and economic consequences of rapid change, in particular the high unemployment levels. Officially 14 per cent in mid-1992, levels of unemployment are in reality much higher, due to 'hidden' unemployment cloaked in various social support and retraining programmes.

Official statements promising the citizens of the new German Länder that their standard of living will equal that of their Western compatriots in three to five years are either wholly politically motivated or based on a complete ignorance of the impossibility of attaining the high GDP growth rates necessary to fulfil such visions of 15 per cent per year from 1992 to the year 2000 in order to equalise per capita GDP in both parts of Germany by that year. Within a period of about twenty years most of the transport sector issues arising from German unification should be resolved.

In an extensive study of the future demand for transport services conducted for the German Federal Ministry of Transport, and used as a basis for conceptual work on the future German transport network system (Kessel *et al.*, 1990) the following assumptions concerning changes in East Germany were formulated:

(a) by 2010 GDP per capita will be roughly on the same level in both parts of the country. This does not preclude persistence of inter-regional differentiation;

(b) the sectoral structure of the eastern German economy in the year 2010 will correspond approximately to that in western Germany; and

(c) trading relations of the eastern German territory will undergo a reorientation towards the West, in particular toward western Germany.

A rapid growth in the Greater Berlin area is particularly expected, due to the internationalisation of the service sector and its expansion towards the Central and East European markets as well as to the increased administrative functions of the city as a capital of the whole republic. The population of this area is likely to reach about 5.5 million in the year 2010 as compared to 4.3 million at present. More modest growth for the Baltic coastal area around Rostock, reflecting its tourist potential and its role as a gateway to Scandinavia, the Baltic states and to St. Petersburg, is anticipated. Such large cities in the south as Dresden (university and administrative centre) and Leipzig (fairs and conference centre) can be expected to remain as growth poles. A new international airport is likely to be constructed north of Dresden, strengthening that city's position as a possible location of corporate headquarters. Also, the south-west former GDR Thüringian region is expected to register above average growth rates, due mainly to its favourable economic structure dominated by increasingly innovative small and medium-sized enterprises.

On the other hand, the peripheral rural areas in the north and east are unlikely to show much dynamism and will experience relative or even absolute decline. The same applies to areas of single-sector industrial concentrations, specialising in metal extraction, brown coal, chemicals, heavy engineering and textile production. A very special problem faces the old industrial regions around Halle and Leipzig. Leipzig itself, as mentioned above, is in a relatively favourable position. But the areas around it and towards Halle will be blighted for decades by the closure of the old metal and chemical plants and by an exodus of labour. The catastrophic environmental situation of this area also constrains Western enterprises from taking over and restructuring production capacities. Another problem region is the lignite mining area around Cottbus in south-eastern Saxony.

5.3 Transport implications

The transport infrastructure network in eastern Germany is relatively dense but in a state of neglect. The railway system comprises around 14,000 km of lines, that of roads about 120,000 km. The density of the railway network is slightly higher than in western Germany, while that of the roads is lower. The inland waterway system is also relatively well developed (2,300 km).

It is to be expected that the preferences and travel behaviour of eastern Germans will follow the patterns known from the West. This means that both in goods and passenger traffic the share of the road traffic will increase to the high western levels at the expense of the railways, which, as in the other CMEA countries previously carried about seventy per cent of goods and passengers. It is estimated that the railways' share in long distance passenger traffic in 2010 will sink to about 8.5 per cent, that of air traffic to reach 4.0 per cent, and the share of the private road traffic in the modal split to rise to 87.5 per cent. It should be noted that even this very high figure is lower than that predicted for western Germany, expressing the past long-term preferential treatment accorded to the railways in the East.

This prediction is made on the assumption that no major change in transport policy in favour of railway transport will occur. It is of course possible to influence the modal split away from road transport. Experience in the Federal Republic of Germany in this respect shows that the pressure of the road and car lobby is hard to withstand.

By the year 2010 a seven- to ten-fold increase is expected in long-distance passenger trips between the Central and East European countries and the whole of Germany as well as in transit traffic through Germany, with a doubling in the tonnage of transported goods.

While within a united Germany the changes in total traffic volume are likely to be relatively limited, due to the unchanged time and money budgets of transport users in western Germany, some major geographical shifts, especially with respect of the areas close to the former inner-German border, are occurring already. If Germany as a whole is divided into a southern part comprising Baden-Württemberg and Bavaria, a northern part consisting of the rest of the territory of western Germany and the eastern part formed by its five new Länder, the spatial structure of future passenger flows predicted in the above mentioned forecast, on which the German general transportation infrastructure plan is based, is shown in Figure 5.1. The north–south flow decreases by eleven million journeys. On the other hand the east–north flow increases seven-fold by 67 million trips in both directions. An analysis at a more disaggregated spatial level shows that the heaviest flows will occur between the southern parts of eastern Germany together with Berlin to the federal states of Lower Saxony and North-Rhine-Westphalia.

Manifold growth of the flows of goods traffic is also expected, together with a geographical reorientation from the north–south axis dominant in West Germany in the past to a west–east axis in the united country.

It is obvious that the existing transport networks in eastern Germany cannot cope with the projected explosion of traffic flows. In western Germany, the projected changes in the spatial structure of flows calls for major extensions to the existing networks.

With this concern in mind the German government decided to act as quickly as possible within the context of the German legal and bureaucratic framework. On 9 April 1991 the programme 'Transport for German Unity' (Verkehrsprojekte Deutsche Einheit) was approved by the Federal Government in advance of the preparation of the overall German Transport Plan 1992 (Bundesverkehrswegeplan) which was presented to the public in August 1992 (the previous west German plan dated from 1985). The aim of the initial programme was to start elaboration, cost and benefit calculations and financial planning for transport measures of special importance for the social and economic integration of the two parts of the country. Its projects have now been taken over by the overall German Transport Plan.

As noted above, the density of the networks in eastern Germany is relatively high. Consequently, the problem of infrastructure in eastern Germany is not so much that of quantity but of quality. The main thrust of the investment activities in the programme therefore concerns upgrading and renovation of the existing infrastructure networks. Some additional links must of course be constructed. Seventeen investment projects of special importance have been forseen, of which nine concern railways, seven road connections and one water transport. The overall investment volume expected for the implementation of these projects is DM 57 billion, of which about 12 billion should be spent in the old Bundesländer (states). Most of the money will be assigned to the railway projects (about DM 30 billion) which is emphasised by the Federal Transport Ministry as a clear sign that the long-term preponderance of individual car transport in Germany is coming to an end. The road projects will cost approximately DM 23 billion. An inland waterway

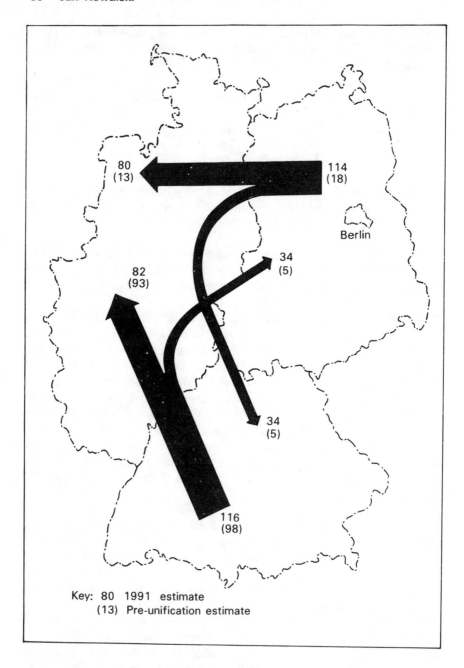

Key: 80 1991 estimate
      (13) Pre-unification estimate

Figure 5.1   Germany: projected long-distance passenger traffic flows, 2010
Source: (German) Ministry of Transport, 1992.

Table 5.2 Rail and road projects of the Transport for German Unity
Programme

Project No.	Project	Costs in Bill. DM
	Railways	30
1	Lübeck/Hagenow Land – Rostock – Stralsund	
2	Hamburg – Büchen – Berlin	
3	Uelzen – Salzwedel – Stendal	
4	Hannover – Stendal – Berlin	
5	Helmstedt – Magdeburg – Berlin	
6	Eichenberg – Halle	
7	Bebra – Erfurt	
8	Nürnberg – Erfurt – Halle/Leipzig – Berlin	
9	Leipzig – Dresden	
	Roads	23
10	A 20 Lübeck – Bundesgrenze D/PL	
11	A 2/A 10 Hannover – Berlin and Berliner Ring to Schwanebeck/Abzweig Prenzlau	
12	A 9 Berlin – Nürnberg	
13	A 82 Göttingen – Halle	
14	A 14 Halle – Magdeburg	
15	A 44/A 14 Kassel – Wommen and Bad Hersfeld – Görlitz	
16	A 73/A 81 Erfurt – Schweinfurt and Bamberg	
	Total	53

Source: (German) Ministry of Transport, 1992, p. 7.

project (Mittellandkanal–River Elbe–Havel Canal–Berliner-Wasser-strasse) is costed at DM 4 billion. A detailed enumeration of the road and railway projects is shown in Table 5.2.

One aspect of the proposals should be emphasised. For the first time in German transport planning, the economic consequences of resulting flows between Germany and Western Europe on the one hand and Eastern Europe and the territories of the former USSR on the other have been explicitly taken into account.

Already in the early stages of the preparation of the projects it has become obvious that a major barrier to the rapid implementation of these measures lies in the very complicated and time-consuming procedures for transport project approval found in German law. It takes ten to twenty years from the conceptual start of a project to its implementation, due mainly to environmental concern and land property rights disputes. Because of the special importance of the infrastructure improvements for the economic prospects of eastern Germany, the Federal Government has elaborated and accepted a simplification of these regulations, making it easier to implement transport investments. As might have been expected, these changes in legal regulations concerning ownership rights and environmental issues have raised substantial opposition. Actual implementation of the legal simplifications remained pending as this volume went to press.

5.4 Conclusions

The unification of Germany and the opening of Central and Eastern Europe has changed and will modify increasingly the transport map of the continent. Experiences of the last two to three years show that the task of providing an adequate infrastructure to accommodate these changes, while being enormous, remains feasible. The major and unresolved issue is the question as to whether it is desirable that eastern Germany and the rest of the former Soviet bloc repeat the patterns of transport development which have been experienced in Western Europe and have led to many negative consequences. Any reflection on the possibilities of policies aimed at reducing the transport intensity of economic growth patterns, and of encouraging more ecologically sensitive paths of development has been almost totally absent in the period of systemic transformation. The rapid growth of GNP has been the all-embracing motor. Under these circumstances in all probability the development of the transport sector in the former communist countries will follow fairly closely the Western European pattern.

6 Transport restructuring in Hungary

István Prileszky

6.1 Introduction

The decisive step in Hungarian economic reform came in the spring of 1990, with the first free post-war election. The people rejected the socialist regime in favour of a transition towards a market economy. Although some reforms had been made in 1968 and in the 1980s, Hungary's economy was typical of that of a socialist system. The transport sector was no exception; some creeping reforms were being made, although these were not significant enough to effect much structural change.

6.2 The structure of Hungary's transport system before political change

The Hungarian transport system prior to 1990 had the following characteristics:

6.2.1 Road haulage

The road haulage industry was composed of four main sectors:

6.2.1.1 Volán sector. This sector consisted of the Volán organisations, controlled by the Ministry of Transport. Each organisation served a specific county, with several depots coordinated by a central office located in the county town. They provided both freight and passenger transport, except in Budapest, where separate divisions were established due to the size of the city (containing one-fifth of the nation's population).

Table 6.1   Hungary: structural changes in freight transport, 1988–91

Mode of transport	1988	1989	1990	1991
	a) % of tonne-kilometres			
Railways	41.1	37.6	35.4	30.6
Road transport, of which:	30.8	33.6	33.7	38.1
transport organisations[1]	14.5	14.5	14.1	13.9
non transport organisations[2]	11.8	13.0	12.3	13.6
private	4.5	6.1	7.3	10.6
Water transport	28.1	28.8	30.9	31.3
Totals (%)	100.0	100.0	100.0	100.0
(in millions)	51,295.6	52,658.4	47,330.0	38,946.4
	b) % of tonnes carried			
Railways	13.9	13.1	12.8	10.6
Road transport, of which:	84.8	85.5	85.6	87.9
transport organisations[1]	27.2	25.3	19.8	18.1
non-transport organisations[2]	41.7	40.2	40.9	39.4
private	15.9	20.0	24.9	30.4
Water transport	1.3	1.4	1.6	1.5
Totals (%)	100.0	100.0	100.0	100.0
(in millions)	804.2	800.3	683.6	609.0

1 – Volán and Ministry-owned specialised hauliers
2 – Own-account transport

Source: Department of Economics and Privatisation of the Ministry of Transport, Telecommunications and Water Management, Budapest, unpublished data.

6.2.1.2 Specialised haulage.   Specialised haulage was state-controlled by individual ministries, providing transport dedicated to their own economic sector. For example, the Ministry of Construction had its haulier EPFU (Építöipari Szállítási Vállalat), which provided building materials transport for the construction companies under its control. These hauliers were permitted to use any free capacity to offer transport services to any other industry.

6.2.1.3 Own-account transport.   Due to the unsatisfactory service levels of the state-operated transport firms many companies exercised their right to establish own-account fleets. The vehicles of these fleets were also permitted to work on a hire and reward basis, although this did not form a significant proportion of their work.

The Volán companies opposed and often criticised these developments on the grounds that own-account fleets were under-utilised and lacked both the opportunities for scale economies and the responsibility of being profitable in themselves. To promote higher utilisation levels, a fines system was in operation on empty running over a distance threshold of 50 km. This was abandoned in 1988, in the first wave of liberalisation under the reformist government of Miklós Németh.

6.2.1.4 Private sector. In the original socialist model the only private sector element was the transport of goods for the general public, such as furniture removals and coal deliveries. It was served mainly by owner-drivers, with some government regulation. In 1988 operating restrictions were lifted, allowing private operations to enter the wider freight market. Many made the most of this opportunity, creating real competition for the state-controlled Volán and specialised haulage operators. Table 6.1 shows the relative importance of these sectors.

6.2.2 Road passenger transport

6.2.2.1 Suburban to city and inter-city transport. These services were provided solely by Volán companies. Low car-ownership levels, coupled with segregated urban industrial and residential development, produced high-density demands for public suburban transport. Accordingly, public transport had a high social priority. This resulted in a dense network and high service frequencies.

Labour shortages in manufacturing and construction in the 1970s and early 1980s drove employers to recruit from suburban and rural areas. The long commuting distances involved forced firms to establish their own bus fleets to serve their own employees exclusively. In this way a secondary bus network evolved, having almost the same density as the Volán network. A single firm might thus have a network parallel not only to the Volán public network, but also to those of other firms. Besides providing better travel for their employees, the firms benefited from sheltering their own workers from the temptation of other employment opportunities communicated by another company's employees during travel.

The existence and operation of own-account bus fleets was also often criticised by the Volán management, who pointed out that the poor utilisation of their own fleet was a waste of national resources.

The recession of the late 1980s reduced demand for labour, resulting in spare capacity in these 'employee-only' bus fleets. Tourism appeared to be the only opportunity to utilise these vehicles.

Long-distance inter-city coach services were discouraged by the government in the 1970s in favour of the railways, on the grounds of fuel efficiency. Although this pressure did not exist in the late 1980s, long-distance coach services played a role mainly where there was no

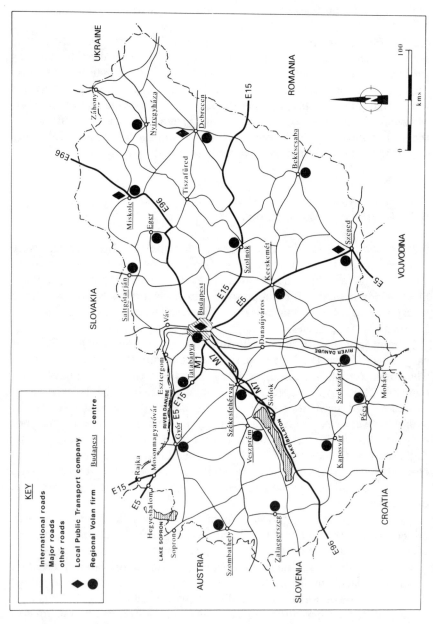

Figure 6.1 Hungary: road network and location of bus operators

railway connection. The railway network is basically radial; coach services provided tangential connections to the railway centres.

6.2.2.2 Urban public transport. The cities of Budapest, Szeged, Debrecen and Miskolc had their own public transport organisations, controlled by the Metropolitan Authority (Figure 6.1). These operated buses, tramways, trolleybuses and (in Budapest) metro lines. Volán also offered competing bus services in Szeged and Debrecen, and provided the only public transport in Hungary's other towns and cities.

6.2.3 Railways, air and shipping

In each of these modes there were state monopolies controlled by the Ministry of Transport. Air had no major significance in domestic transport, and shipping was limited to long-distance hauls of bulk cargoes of aggregates along the Danube.

6.2.4 Economic regulation of transport

As Hungary in 1990 was basically a socialist country, economic regulation followed socialist ideology. Its primary aim was to secure the survival and operations of state firms. Characteristically, this system was often organisation-based rather than activity-based: that is, the rules for one firm often differed from those applying to another engaged in the same activity. The idea of neutrality of regulation emerged only in the late 1980s.

6.2.4.1 Volán firms. The most problematical area of regulation concerned the Volán companies. Volán was a unique example as it offered both freight and passenger services, and in the framework of passenger transport, urban and inter-urban services. These operations were not separated in its organisational structure, therefore efficient cost allocation to each activity was not possible. This was compounded by the fact that in its public transport operations some resources were shared by the inter-urban and urban services. Cross-subsidisation was widespread and inextricable.

The legal status of Volán was termed 'state supervision': a means of control over state-owned firms which was introduced with the 1968 economic reforms. It means that the director of Volán was appointed by the Minister of Transport, but that the state could not intervene in management's decision making. The state did not take the financial responsibility for the firm, which should have been profitable. According to the law, the Minister could instruct the firm to undertake unprofitable

LIVERPOOL HOPE UNIVERSITY COLLEGE

activities only if the Ministry then assumed responsibility for the financial consequences. As the Ministry's budget had no money for such a purpose it was very rare for any conspicuous intervention to occur; however, informal influence over the Ministry-appointed director was quite common. It was widely expected that these firms should maintain those non-profitable services regarded as socially necessary.

The economic regulation of these firms was undertaken by the Ministry of Transport co-operating with the Ministry of Finance, through:

(a)   setting the tariffs both for freight and passenger transport including any concessionary schemes, and
(b)   determining taxes and subsidies.

These decisions were made in such a way that Volán passenger and freight operations together should have been profitable. It was less important to secure the profitability of each sector in itself.

Volán firms in a disadvantageous starting position (for example, operating in rural areas and therefore having higher cost levels) were given extra support which was determined annually. This support depended on the budget and did not create a consistent logical system.

A remarkable feature of Volán regulation was that suburban and inter-city bus transport never received any subsidy. High use levels with low car ownership, coupled with the state monopoly, enabled the Volán organisations to reap high profits, which were then extracted by the state imposing a special tax. For many years the curious situation existed whereby urban and inter-city bus services were burdened by extra tax levels on a par with luxury items such as jewellery, fur, and alcohol. This taxation was only lifted in 1989.

6.2.4.2 Urban public transport. Urban public transport presented a typical example of organisation-based regulation. There were two forms of organisation operating in this field: the Volán firms and the local public transport companies (in four towns) belonging to, and controlled by, the local authorities. The regulations applying to these two types of organisations were different, as was their legal status.

The local companies had 'public service company' status, which meant that they were not independent in their decision making. The owner (embodied in the city council) could intervene in their management. The service level, network and timetable were approved by the local authorities, as were the company's annual cost and financial plans.

These companies were not forced to be profitable, the financial responsibility for their activity being borne by the local authorities and in an indirect way partly by the Ministry of Finance, since the latter was responsible for the financial position of the local authorities. They received subsidies which were determined each year in the process of nationwide financial planning. Through subsidisation such companies could charge prices below their costs. The BKV (Budapest public transport company) in particular received significantly high levels of subsidy which sometimes amounted to half of the firm's costs.

On the other hand, the Volán organisations were forced to be profitable. Being independent, their network, service level and timetable were approved by the company director. It was not logical that public transport was regarded as a public service in one town and not in another. In one town the local authority had to control the service in order to enforce the public interest, yet in another it was not considered necessary. This duality did not cause serious problems under the communist system because, apart from the legal framework, everything was guided by the leading (communist) party, mainly through party channels. In a situation without this party control, however, such a system would not be viable.

6.2.4.3 Railways, air and shipping. The railways were regulated through the tariff and tax system like the Volán organisations. The railways received some state support for track development, but the amount of this money was limited by budget problems. The only airline (MALÉV) and the sole shipping company (MAHART) were observed continuously and the state could intervene if necessary to secure the competitiveness of these firms in the international market.

6.2.5 Contribution of transport to economic development

The level of transport development as a whole normally corresponds to the level of economic development of the country. In 1991 the Technical University of Budapest analysed the level of general economic development and of development across industrial sectors for a selection of Western and former Eastern bloc countries (Borotvás and Veroszta, 1992). Various development factors were quantified, allowing direct comparison between nations.

It was found that if transport development is compared with economic development then Hungary has levels proportionally similar to that of the USA and the UK. This reflects the view – which is generally accepted by domestic experts – that transport did not hinder Hungarian economic development. On the other hand, there persisted an under-development of Hungary's transport system in comparison with that of most developed countries in the world. The reason for this under-development is the performance of the economy, which is not sufficient to produce enough revenue for transport investment. As economic problems became more serious in the late 1980s the government saved money on infrastructure development to maintain the standard of living. Transport became the victim of the recession, and road investment in particular has been insufficient in relation to rising car ownership.

6.3 The transition to the market economy

The idea of the market economy was accepted by the last (reformist) communist government and some steps were made in this direction, several of them in transport. The most significant move was the full liberalisation of road freight and taxi operations in 1988. Establishing a framework for economic transition was, however, left to the post-election government. This government faced innumerable problems, not least a restructuring of the manufacturing base, such that transport did not receive a high priority. Consequently market reform in the transport sector progressed only slowly.

Appreciating the problems emerging from this *laissez-faire* approach to the market, the new government introduced some controls on the mechanical condition of road vehicles in 1991. In 1992 this was extended to include international vehicle conditions and driver training. Further quality regulation was being planned for taxi operation.

6.3.1 The new transport policy

Significant progress has been made in the formulation of a new transport policy, the details of which were completed in the first half of 1992 (Ministry of Transport, Telecommunications and Water Management, 1992). This new policy indicates the fields where privatisation or private participation is possible. Its main features are:

(a) railway freight and high speed inter-city trains should be operated under competition but they should remain in state ownership;
(b) road freight, taxis, tourist buses, passenger ferries, freight shipping, operation of non-public ports, maintenance and repair of both road and railway vehicles, and catering services for those two modes are to be competitive and can be privatised;
(c) private firms can participate in the framework of a concession system alongside the state companies in passenger and freight operation of low-traffic railway lines, local public railways (tram, metro), public bus transport (both urban and inter-urban), motorway building, and the operation of public ports and ferries.

A new transport policy emphasises the importance of transport development and highlights the fact that without comprehensive state investment programmes the transport system will be one of the major obstacles to the country's development. However, the source of financing is an open question as the method of privatisation is not yet known.

6.3.2 The transport system in 1992

The main features of the transport system in 1992 can be summarised as follows.

6.3.2.1 Road freight. The most important development was the dramatic rise in the number of firms in this sector. After liberalisation many people started a new career as private entrepreneurs offering road freight transport services. Initially, becoming a road haulier offered very good prospects since it was easy to compete with the state hauliers. Lacking the overheads, small, mainly owner-driver firms could easily offer lower prices and provide a better service level. The first newcomers made substantial profits, and this encouraged even more people to follow them.

The more competitive the private hauliers were, the more of their market share the state hauliers lost. As a result of this workers were made redundant in the state sector, releasing their vehicles for sale too. The only opportunity for such people was to buy these used vehicles themselves and start a business privately.

By 1991 30 per cent of the national lorry fleet was privately owned (Ministry of Transport, Telecommunications and Water Management, 1991), a level of privatisation far higher than that for any other industry. Parallel with this process, the economic recession accelerated and the amount of goods to be transported decreased sharply. These two effects resulted in an imbalance in the supply–demand equilibrium, and over-supply came into existence. In addition, the fall in industrial output meant that former specialised hauliers became virtually redundant in their own sectors and wanted to earn their living in the general market. At the time of writing, business is hard to find and many road hauliers are in dire financial straits.

In the meantime the state hauliers (both Volán and the specialist hauliers) have changed their organisational structure, creating several smaller independent limited companies, in a few cases involving private capital. By separating the freight sector from the rest of the firm, ease of privatisation was envisaged. However, because of the recession and competition from the private sector, these units are often unprofitable and are unattractive to any potential buyer.

The main structural changes in freight transport can be seen in Table 6.1. Railway's share of the freight transport market declined between

1988 and 1991, both in terms of tonne-kilometres and tonnes carried. This was due mainly to the collapse of trade with the former Soviet Union and the decline of the industrial base. The total tonnage carried over this period fell by 24.3 per cent.

The road transport industry has continued growing: in 1991 it accounted for 38.1 per cent of total tonne-kilometres, but 87.9 per cent of total tonnage transported. The growth of the private sector has been dramatic: between 1988 and 1991 its share of both tonne-kilometres and tonnage carried approximately doubled. Noticeably, road transport organisations have seen a decline in their share of the freight market in terms of total tonnes carried, but the strength of Hungaro-Camion in international transport has maintained their proportion of tonne-kilometres.

Water transport has little significance in terms of tonnes carried, but the long distances involved, along the Danube, elevate its importance in international trade when measured in tonne-kilometres.

6.3.2.2 Rail and road passenger transport. Development in these fields has been very similar, therefore it is practical to discuss them together.

One of the main issues is that the idea of introducing market conditions was explicitly rejected in favour of continuing state control. Only one new measure was introduced: the concession system. This is the same in both rail and road transport, and these modes' legal frameworks were modified accordingly in 1992. The law states that railway and road passenger transport services may be offered by companies founded for this purpose and owned by the state or local authority or by a 'concession company'. Local transport should be supervised by the local authorities, and inter-urban and suburban transport by the Ministry of Transport. The latter will exercise this right through its state agency 'Transport Supervision'. These supervisory authorities should evaluate transport service levels. If they come to the conclusion that some improvement is necessary they should call upon the transport operating firms (including the railways) to improve their services. The operators then have three months' reaction time. In the case of their demands being rejected by the operators, the supervisory authorities should conduct a concessionary tender, in which all the conditions should be identified exactly. Any entrepreneur may compete in the tendering process, including the current operator of the service. The winner should form a 'concession company' unless it is a specialised transport company owned by the state or by the local authority. The authorities enter into a contract with the winner, in which the responsibility and the rights of the contractor, including the potential subsidy, should be fixed.

This system assumes that the state operators will remain in business and keep their operations in the future, the difference being that they will be under pressure of probable tendering if the authorities are unsatisfied with their services. It is assumed that this will force them to improve their services and maintain service quality.

As to the logic of the system, existing operators would stop their non-profitable services, which would be won on tendering, occasionally combined with subsidy. In this case subsidy would only be given through tendering; however, this is not fixed in any document.

It is too early to evaluate the system's operation, but some reflection can be allowed. It seems to be problematical that inter-city, and especially suburban, transport will be supervised by the Ministry Agency. The first problem is that this centralised form of supervision is potentially incompatible with suburban traffic, which has an essentially local character. The second problem is that this authority is not an elected body, has no direct links with the public and seems to be even less competent than the present operators to protect the public interest.

In this solution the present administrative form is re-enforced. After the 1990 election the new regime reorganised the administrative structure of the country, weakening local government. The reason for this was the fact that the local elections were mainly won by the opposition, and the government did not want to give large spheres of authority to countries dominated by their opponents. Regional offices of central ministries were created and authorised instead.

The introduction of this concession system provides a partial solution to the problem of towns where public transport is operated by Volán firms. As to the new regulation, local authorities have the right to approve the timetable, and to determine the tariffs, as they are responsible for levels of subsidy if it is found to be necessary. This is a very clear situation when the operator is owned by the town (in these cases the local authorities can use the owner's power to influence services), but in more than two hundred towns public transport is operated by firms controlled by the Ministry. In these cases the problem was that local authorities did not have the legal power to influence the services offered by the Volán firms. In the new concession system they now have the opportunity to involve new operators, including private firms, through tendering out some services if they are unsatisfied with the operation of Volán. In this way regulation is the same for both Volán and local public transport firms, so that the duality of regulation is removed.

6.3.2.3 Taxis. The development of the taxi market was similar to that of road freight. After liberalisation this industry seemed to be a good business and many people became taxi entrepreneurs. It was common for the unemployed to be advised by the Labour Office to start a taxi business. It was very easy to enter this market, as the only condition to be satisfied was possession of a professional licence and a four-cylinder motor car not over ten years old. But with the rise in the number of taxis, the demand for them decreased because of the recession and falling living standards. A huge over-supply came into existence: for example in Budapest, which has two million inhabitants, there are more than 13,000 taxis. This led to a dramatic income reduction for the taxi drivers, with the consequence that they attempted to overcharge. In particular Budapest became notorious for its 'cheating' taxi drivers, thereby damaging the country's reputation.

A dissatisfied social group was thus created, containing the first victims of the market economy. It was not by chance that the large demonstration against the government in the autumn of 1991 was started by taxi drivers, causing the deepest crisis since the election.

The government plans to re-introduce restrictions in this market. The problem is that the number of operators can not be limited legally, therefore new conditions are to be imposed on vehicles. The plans are rigorous: all taxis should be painted in a special colour, not be allowed to be used for private purposes, should be numbered strikingly, and be no older than four years.

Taxis will also be obliged to have taximeters of the type which stores the revenue in an irremovable way. This will prevent the drivers hiding their income from the Tax Office.

6.3.3 The state–railways relationship

One of the most important issues in the transition to a market economy is to reorganise the relationship between the state and the railways (Figure 6.2). The railways should become a consumer-oriented, commercial organisation responsible for its own profitability and development.

The state will be responsible for the track and for equipment belonging directly to the track. Vehicle fleet operation, maintenance and investment will be the responsibility of the railways. The railways will pay a fee for using the track and other entrepreneurs will be allowed to run trains under the same conditions. In this way track maintenance and development will be separated from railway operation. Hungary will thereby adopt the West European model. However, in the initial stages no unique state agency will be founded for taking care of the track; this will be entrusted to the railways on a contract basis. This seems to be an incomplete solution, but represents very significant progress from the past.

The railway network density is higher in Hungary than in the West. The average network density of eighteen European states is 51 km/1,000 sq. km, in Hungary it is 80.6 km/1,000 sq. km. In spite of this fact there is no aim to reduce the network: it is estimated that the state is able to take care of about 80 per cent of it. The remaining 20 per cent of lines support only light traffic, and should be operated in concession form, with contributions from local authorities and interested economic organisations.

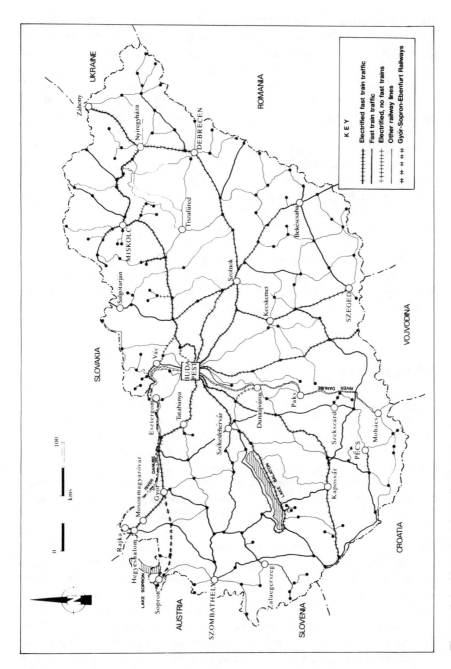

Figure 6.2 Hungary: the rail network

6.3.4 Other problems

The restructuring of the Volán organisations, which was continuing at the time of writing, represented an important step in the transition process, since the traditional Volán structure is incompatible with a market economy. It is obvious that freight operations should be separated and privatised. The problem is the means of privatisation. There are so many hauliers that there is over-supply in the market; purchase of these firms would therefore not offer good business prospects.

One of the present problems is that the state statistical system for transport has collapsed. This was based on the state companies' obligation to give statistical data regularly to the Ministry and to the State Office of Statistics. Private firms and small entrepreneurs are not burdened with the same obligation. It is not known exactly, for example, what proportion of the transport market is held by the private sector, or how many vehicles they have. Even the number of private hauliers is unknown. To establish a good sample system would be beneficial.

It is necessary to find a method for privatising the Hungarian shipping firm (MAHART) and the airline (MALÉV). Relatively little progress has been made in this field.

6.4 Conclusions

In assessing the progress made in reforming the economy as a whole, and the transport sector in particular, it must be emphasised that a process has been initiated which has no precedents. There is no experience at all for converting a planned economy into a market-oriented one. In the absence of any blueprint the transition will take a long time.

In restructuring the transport industry, a major problem has been determining the most appropriate type of market. In freight transport, full liberalisation (in some aspects an over-liberalisation) has taken place. In public transport a centralised model with state ownership and control has been chosen, at least for the short- to medium-term.

Underdevelopment of infrastructure is now the most serious problem facing the Hungarian transport system. The bus fleet is out-dated, and in some firms more than half of the buses are fully depreciated. The railways are suffering from the poor condition of track and rolling stock. The road network is insufficient and is falling increasingly behind rising car ownership levels. The whole transport infrastructure is afflicted by the money-saving policy of the 1980s when attempts were made to hide the problems of the country by reducing 'public' investment. It seems that railways, bus transport and urban public transport will not be able to operate without a larger investment programme. But the state budget of a country with a declining economy does not have the resources for such investments. The only solution would appear to be a higher proportion of foreign investment. The means whereby Hungary can attract more foreign investors in the transport infrastructure sector is now, therefore, the crucial question facing the industry.

7 Recent transport development and economic change in Poland

Zbigniew Taylor

7.1 Introduction

The purpose of this chapter is to provide some insight into: (1) the nature of the transport system in Poland and its previous contribution to economic development; (2) current processes of restructuring and privatisation; (3) the impact on Poland of change in neighbouring countries; and (4) the likely nature and role of Polish transport in the 1990s. As the situation in maritime transport is addressed in Chapter 8 and in previous publications by the present author (Potrykowski and Taylor, 1986; Taylor, 1984a, 1987), and Polish air transport was discussed in Chapter 4, this chapter concentrates mainly on land-based transport forms.

The Polish transport system is marked by some specific features which will be examined at the national level within the context of socio-economic change. Not all transport modes are well documented and understood. For example, very little is known about road transport, dispersed in tens of thousands of firms and enterprises subordinated to many departments, organisations and central offices, or owned by private, usually smaller, firms. Only part of this sector is reported in statistics: there are no data for road freight in terms of commodities carried.

7.2 Volume and structure of traffic

Haulages in Poland rank among the greatest in the world, especially when compared with the size of the nation, its output, or level of economic development. Railways are particularly burdened due to the raw-material nature of most goods carried and the underdevelopment of other modes of transport. An especially undeveloped area is inland shipping, which could take over a significant share of bulk commodities traffic. For most of the post-war period transport capability has been a bottleneck constraint on the development of the national economy; but today's situation seems to be slightly different.

Polish railways rank very high in terms of the volume of traffic. In absolute measures of freight tonne-kilometres Poland is placed just behind much larger countries such as the former Soviet Union, the United States, China, Canada and India. In passenger-kilometres the Polish State Railways rank seventh in the world – after the ex-USSR, Japan, China, India, Germany and France. The Polish railways rank even higher in relative measures of traffic *per capita*, and eleventh in the world according to the length of routes (around 27,000 km in 1990, including nearly 11,400 km electrified). At present some 80 per cent of all freight and above 55 per cent of passenger traffic is hauled electrically.

Much lower is Poland's position in relation to road traffic, although comparative data are incomplete. We know, however, that the structure of traffic is diversified. In Poland it is public transport that still plays the predominant role, while in the most developed countries the share of private transport, especially in passenger traffic, is much greater. Nevertheless, in terms of passenger-kilometres, Polish buses and coaches carry more people than their British equivalents, for example. Compared with other countries, the role of road freight traffic in Poland is minimal.

7.2.1 Freight traffic, 1955–1990

To explain the expansion of public freight traffic of today, one needs to examine its growth rate over specific periods (Figures 7.1, 7.2). In the first period, 1955–1978/9, the increase of traffic by weight was nearly five-fold, and on the basis of tonne–km nearly seven-fold. Then, the increment of traffic save for maritime shipping was also twice as fast as the relevant volume of material production (Lijewski, 1980). An especially intensive rise was noted in the mid-1970s as a result of the more accelerated economic growth of the country. The 2,705 million tonnes carried in 1978 have not been exceeded since. As the national situation was drawing towards a crisis, initially there was a slower rate and subsequently a sudden drop in absolute freight traffic. The post-war trend of growing demand for transport thus experienced a setback for the first time. The slump of 1980–82 caused a sharp decrease in traffic, accounting for about 37 per cent on a tonnage basis (and slightly less on the basis of tonne-km) – to the level of a decade previously. In terms

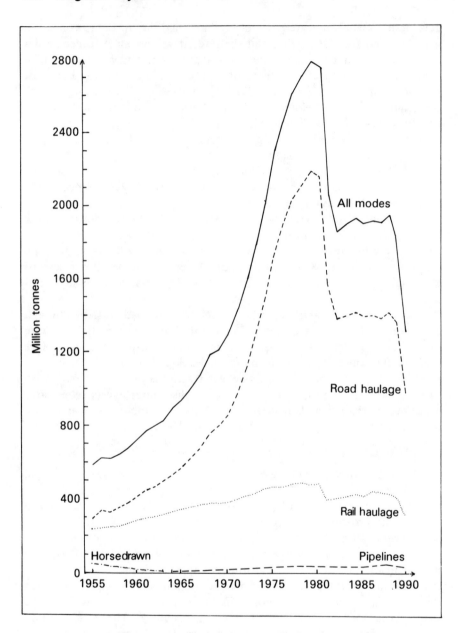

Figure 7.1   Poland: freight traffic by mode of socialised transport (in tonnes)
Source: GUS, various.

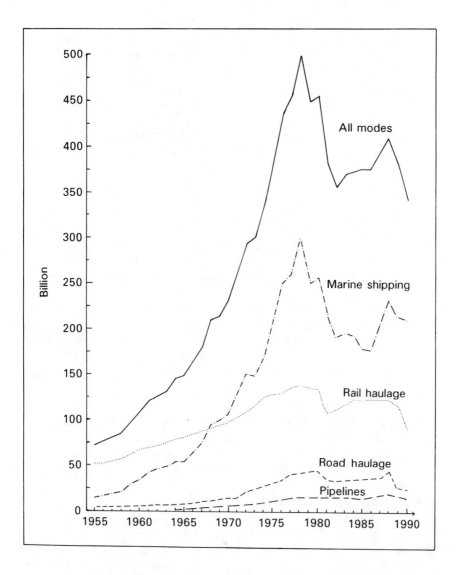

Figure 7.2 Poland: freight traffic by mode of socialised transport (in tonne-kilometres)

Source: GUS, various.

of freight traffic carried between 1980 and 1982, rail-borne tonnage decreased by 16.6 per cent and that of road-borne by about 43 per cent. The slump in the Polish economy reduced pressures on the country's transport system but previous insufficient investment levels continued to affect costs and have contributed to the congestion problems of today.

In the early 1980s the total cargo carried increased slightly: by 4 per cent in tonnage and 4.5 per cent in tonne-km. The absolute traffic increment, however, was a result of in-built inertia: no radical changes took place in the Polish economic structure under communism. As in the previous period, coal formed 39 per cent of rail-borne freight tonnage overall. In the 1980s carriers had many problems even with much smaller freight. But at the beginning of the 1990s the situation changed rapidly. Due to the collapse of the so-called centrally planned economy and a slump in production, demand for transport and freight traffic decreased radically.

In terms of tonnage (Figure 7.1), road-borne freight increased five-fold between 1955 and the mid-1980s, and accounted for up to 70 per cent of total flows. Its average annual increase of 126 million tonnes in 1970–79 rose dramatically to over 200 million tonnes in 1974 and 1975! The railways were not able to take full advantage of the growing freight market, and the tonnage they carried only doubled between 1955 and mid-1980s, with their share falling from more than 40 to some 20 per cent.

In terms of tonne-kilometres, the situation is very different (Figure 7.2). Generally, the rates are on the increase save for the rapid falls noticeable in the early and late 1980s. The expansion of maritime shipping was to accommodate rapid economic growth and to facilitate the export of minerals, especially in the mid-1970s. Maritime shipping cargoes increased twelve-fold between 1955 and the mid-1980s to capture a majority of traffic share, mainly at the expense of the railways. Other modes reflect the evolution of the transport system. Taken overall, road-borne freight traffic increased nine-fold, while rail-borne traffic rose just over two-fold at maximum but has recently dropped radically.

In terms of freight carried, the railways have sustained their position reasonably well in tonne-km with a marked drop in the total tonnage carried. Road haulage has expanded to capture the major share of tonnage carried (from 50 to 75 per cent) from the railways but in tonne-km has only risen from 7 to 20 per cent. This is due to the fact that the railways carried most bulk commodities on long hauls: 300 km on average in 1990, while on the roads the average haul was about 20 kilometres. The temporary shift from rail to road as a means of transport in the 1970s was a result of several factors. The carrying capacity of railways had been much more constrained and difficult to expand – as was also the case with inland shipping – than that of road transport. Moreover, road-borne haulages were more suitable for the then expanding construction and building materials industry. Despite these temporary changes, the share of national freight carried by rail increased in the early 1980s and by 1990 the railways were dealing with predominantly freight traffic: nearly 69 per cent of all tonne-km but only 22 per cent of overall tonnage. The situation in Poland in this respect resembles that in Czechoslovakia and the former East Germany, but is diametrically different from that in developed Western countries.

Eighty per cent of road freight haulages are found to be confined within a 30-km radius from their origin, emphasising the significance of local goods flows. By contrast, in rail haulage, trends towards long distances were identified as the majority: more than 50 per cent of traffic is carried over 150 km and another 30 per cent from 50 to 150 km. There is also a 'substitution zone' of both modes between 30 and 75 km.

Specialisation on the railways consists in carrying raw materials such as ores, coal and fertilisers, while road-borne transport specialises in processed goods including perishables. These specialisations are connected with the concentration of origin and destination points in rail-haulage and their dispersion in road-haulage.

The cost of one tonne-km in road haulage is estimated as being nearly six times higher than on the railways. Certainly, the reduction in railways' share of freight traffic in the 1970s was disadvantageous, since the unit transport cost in all modes increased by 33 per cent (Kuziemkowski, 1981, 1984). In the early 1980s, a trend towards more economical consumption of fuels was favouring the further development of rail-borne traffic which consumes four times less fuel than comparable road haulage.

The share of national freight carried by the pipeline network increased substantially after 1964, when the Friendship pipeline was constructed; but it has recently declined: in 1984 it accounted for 10 per cent but by 1990 carried only 4.1 per cent of traffic on the basis of tonne-km. This is disadvantageous to the economy since pipeline unit transport costs are the lowest of all land freight, partly as a result of having the longest distance hauls (420 km).

Freight volumes carried by other modes of transport – horses, air transport and inland shipping – are minimal. Especially disadvantageous is the small and diminishing role of inland shipping, a much-neglected area of freight transport. Its operating conditions have deteriorated in the last twenty years as a result of the unmet need for renovation and re-equipment of transport facilities, mainly on the Odra waterway (Taylor, 1987); in effect the average distance of freight carried decreased from 261 to 106 km between 1970 and 1990, thus emphasising flows of local goods such as sand and gravel. By 1990 the inland waterway share of freight traffic fell to 0.3 per cent. Only countries with very unfavourable natural conditions for navigation such as Italy have a similar low share.

LIVERPOOL HOPE UNIVERSITY COLLEGE

7.2.2 Transport intensity and national economy

The Polish national economy is highly transport-intensive: a unit of finished product involves more freight traffic than in other comparable countries. Referred to as *transport absorptiveness*, this phenomenon appeared strongly in the early 1970s when the growing demand for transport was becoming increasingly a bottleneck constraint on the economic growth of the country. It is a common feeling that transport intensity in the Polish economy is excessive and the volume of freight traffic should be decreased. The share of irrational freight carried has been estimated at between 20 and 30 per cent (Kuziemkowski, 1981). Although the centrally planned economy is withering away, transport intensity remains as one of the obstacles to conversion to the market economy.

The factors influencing this transport intensity can be divided into objective and subjective groups (Taylor, 1989). The first includes the natural conditions for socio-economic activity, being a result of:

(a)   the uneven location of natural resources, concentrated mainly in the southern part of the country;
(b)   the development of the mining industry and the material- and energy-intensive processing industry;
(c)   primary energy production based on heaviest fuels: coal and lignite;
(d)   the export of most mineral products through distant Polish seaports;
(e)   the import of most heavy minerals in large quantities;
(f)   agricultural specialisation in heavy goods (potatoes, sugar beets, milk), and the past mal-location of agriculture processing plants, requiring bulk commodity flows between regions;
(g)   a transport pattern unsuited to present-day needs (built mostly within different state boundaries).

Taken overall, the combination of these factors seems less favourable in Poland than in other developed countries.

The second group is composed of subjective factors arising from the centrally planned economy (Lijewski, 1980; Morawski, 1980):

(a)   specialisation of production and services, based on co-operation between plants, and the increment of freight flows, frequently between distant places. Too large-scale cooperation and over specialisation can contribute to the overloading of transport, as has been experienced in, for example, the cement industry;
(b)   overconcentration: an increase in the scale of production and its concentration in a smaller number of places leads to the excessive elongation of the supply routes of raw materials and semi-finished

products and the delivery of goods, as in the iron and steel industry, engineering, electronics, chemical, and food industries. This not only leads to increases in the average distance of freight carried but also to the deterioration of products – a classic example here is the food industry;

(c) Mal-location of production in relation to raw materials and/or consumption;

(d) technology of output frequently does not minimise labour inputs in production and haulage, but maximises the quantity effects, as in the Polish building industry. The volume of cement, steel, fertilisers or sugar beet carried could be much smaller if the product was of better quality;

(e) defective management and administration barriers are the most irrational factors influencing transport intensity, as seen in interregional flows of sand and gravel, or simple products of great weight such as prefabricated concrete elements, timber, glass containers, sugar and flour;

(f) disruption of the transport chain, bringing about an excessive number of intermediate links between producer and consumer;

(g) apparent cheapness of transport costs: this situation has changed recently, and freight traffic is no longer subsidised from the central budget.

All these factors have contributed to unreasonable production costs, with transport costs undoubtedly constituting one of the major elements.

7.2.3 Passenger traffic, 1955–1990

Public passenger traffic (excluding urban transport) differs from freight traffic in that the rates of movement have been generally increasing, except for the troughs apparent in 1960, the late 1970s to early 1980s, and a sudden drop at the beginning of the 1990s (Figures 7.3, 7.4). From 1955 to 1989 a consistently upward sloping curve is apparent, which is steeper for road-borne traffic, especially for the period from 1960 to the late 1970s.

Since 1989, the situation has changed radically. Economic activity diminished substantially and – as a result – so did commuting to work. Unemployment rates increased monthly (to over 12 per cent in mid-1992). On the other hand, the number of private cars is increasing as a result of easier access and widening income disparities within society.

A shift from rail to road as a means of transporting people has been persistent in terms of the number of passenger journeys and, in the short term, on the basis of passenger-km. The journeys of road-borne transport increased sixteen-fold between 1955 and the late 1980s, with an average

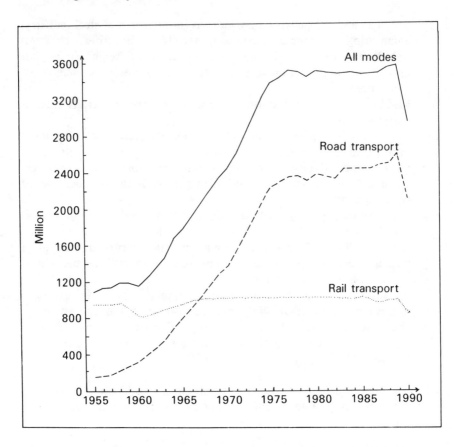

Figure 7.3 Poland: passenger journeys by mode of public socialised transport

Source: GUS, various.

annual growth rate of 11 per cent in the middle of that period (Figure 7.3). This sharp rise in travel stands in contrast to the number of rail passengers carried. The latter reached a plateau by 1967 when both modes were equal, but the ascendancy of road over rail continued to a point where it counted for up to 70 per cent of all journeys.

The railways have sustained their position reasonably well in total passenger-km with a relatively small drop between 1973 and 1990 (Figure 7.4). The share of both transport modes is now roughly balanced.

In summary, therefore, rail has maintained its dominant position in the total mileage of freight carried (69 per cent) while since 1973 buses and coaches have become equal partners with rail in passenger mileage.

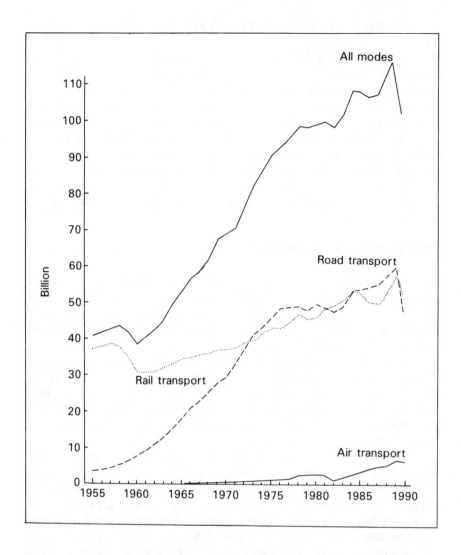

Figure 7.4 Poland: passenger–kilometres by mode of public socialised transport

Source: GUS, various.

7.3 Investment policy in the 1970s and 1980s

A major reason for relatively poor transport services is connected with the general economic crisis in Poland. The development of transport as a basic element of the infrastructure should be given priority before other sectors of the national economy. To achieve this, transport should not be as neglected a field of economic activity as it has been in the past.

The permanent growth in demand for transport, coupled with technological insufficiency, produced increasing bottlenecks in meeting the transport needs of the national economy. In particular, any transport projects initiated in the 1970s were not completed, resulting in serious shortages of carrying capacity in the 1980s in all transport modes.

7.3.1 Allocation of expenditures for transport, 1970–1990

Poland enjoyed a relatively low level of public transport expenditure, ranging between 6.7 per cent of the socialised sector in 1982 and 11.3 per cent in 1975 (Figure 7.5). Additionally, measures such as tariffs, subsidies and taxes have played a much smaller role in the modal split of a centrally planned economy.

The main aim of investment policy in rail and in other modes has been to increase carrying capacity and satisfy growing traffic demand, rather than to improve quality and productivity. Indeed, while railways have received about 35–40 per cent of total expenditures (Figure 7.5), they have become, nevertheless, a bottleneck constraint in the national transport system.

The main attainment not only of railways but of the whole transport sector in the post-war period was the progress achieved in the electrification of routes (Table 7.1). Although the annual rate of electrification decreased in the late 1970s considerable progress was achieved in the 1980s, peaking at an extra 595 km in 1985. Modernisation was concentrated on routes connecting the Upper Silesian coal basin and seaports. For example, the route along the Odra river from Opole to Szczecin and Świnoujście was upgraded by double-tracking and electrification. But such projects were not able to be completed in the 1970s, and shortages of funds caused delays in the modernisation of stations, marshalling yards and repair workshops.

Up to 30 per cent of total inputs was allocated to road transport, in addition to an extra 10–15 per cent on the roads themselves (Figure 7.5). Road maintenance, rather than new construction, tended to dominate investment (Berman and Alvstam, 1985). Vehicle purchases were selective, with a concentration on small lorries (2.6 to five tonnes) and vans (0.6 to one tonne) at the expense of heavy lorries. The shortage of the latter was partly alleviated by imports, but there remained a shortage of

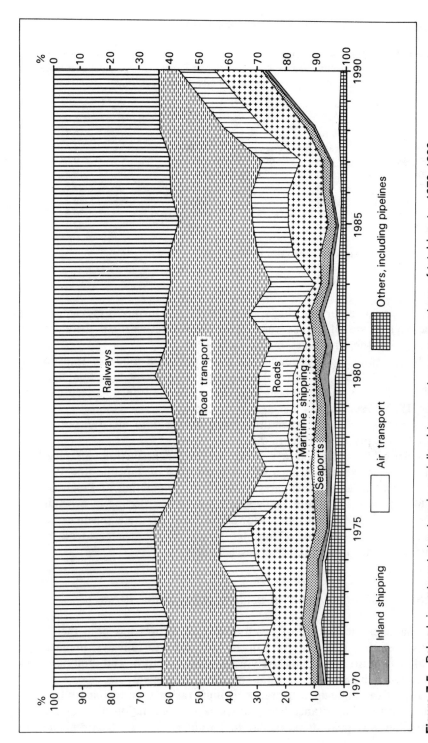

Figure 7.5 Poland: investment structure in socialised transport as a percentage of total inputs, 1970–1990

Source: GUS, various, author's calculations.

Table 7.1 Poland: post-war electrification of railways

Years	Mean annual rate of electrification (km)	Length of electrified routes at the end of period (km)	% share of electrified routes
1950	–	156	0.7
1951–55	64	477	2.1
1956–60	110	1,026	4.4
1961–65	240	2,227	9.5
1966–70	329	3,872	16.6
1971–75	343	5,588	23.5
1976–80	256	6,868	28.2
1981–85	407	8,902	36.6
1986–90	497	11,387	47.5

Sources: GUS (various); Nasiłowski (1986, p. 53).

trucks designed for carrying special freights. A further disadvantage was the high share of trucks running on petrol rather than diesel, which intensified fuel shortages in the early 1980s.

Inland shipping is probably the most neglected mode of transport in post-war Poland. Its share of expenditures was kept at a minimal level of between 0.3 and 2.3 per cent of inputs in the transport sector during the 1970–1990 period.

A similar share of expenditures was allocated to air transport (from 0.1 to 4.8 per cent) (Figure 7.5).

Relatively higher outlays went on the construction of pipelines, including the second branch of the Friendship oil pipeline (the Pomeranian), and three product-carrying pipelines originating at Płock (Figure 7.6). The late 1970s and 1980s saw a substantial decline in expenditures for this mode of transport. Nowadays most of these pipelines remain underused as a result of oil and natural gas supply problems from Russia and other neighbouring countries (Chapter 3).

7.3.2 Specific features of investment policy in the 1970s

A characteristic feature of investment expenditures has been their evenness over time (Figure 7.5). Priority was given to railways: maintenance and renovation of intensively-used infrastructure and rolling stock obtained a high share of total transport investment.

Inputs were allocated to transport units rather than to fixed infrastructure, with no importance being attached to coordination of efforts. Little attention was paid in particular to terminals and the technical base of

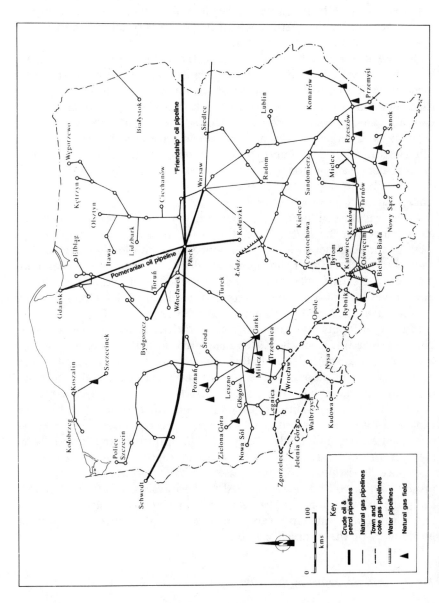

Figure 7.6 Poland: the pipeline network

transport. Over 60 per cent of railway expenditures were spent on rolling stock – a large share, considering the need for investment in the infrastructure. A huge amount of funds was spent on road vehicles, but much less on an improvement of the road network. In air transport priority was given to purchases of (Soviet-built) planes instead of airport modernisation. By the 1980s, a significant segment of all transport modes was either redundant or uneconomic.

Because investment funds available in the 1970s were generally bigger than in the previous periods, a trend towards preference for larger investment projects appeared as a means of solving economic problems, rather than modernisation projects which would have brought an increase in carrying capacity and improved efficiency. Instead of constructing new expensive rail routes, for example, it would have been better to increase rail electrification and improve the standard of track and the signal system. For example, on congested routes an automated block system can provide the same additional capacity as the construction of a third track, but at a tenth of its cost.

There was no continuity or sequence in the implementation of investment projects in the 1970s. Expenditures for modernisation and development of the road network were not concordant with long-term goals but seemed to result from urgent immediate demands; even those needs were not met to a satisfactory degree. The introduction of a container system exemplified lack of logic and continuity: despite considerable inputs, the effects, save for maritime shipping, were extremely modest.

Priority in inputs was given to freight traffic. It was anticipated that doubling investment in the 1970s compared with the preceding decade would meet transport demand. But this was not the case. Despite some positive results in modernising a part of the fixed assets and a development of rolling stock, the overall effects were not satisfactory in comparison with expenditures. Low efficiency of invested capital can be explained by its concentration on large new projects instead of on selective maintenance and modernisation of the infrastructure, especially in the case of railways. Such a policy led to capital being locked up in suspended investments. Similar losses of capital continue to occur in projects which will not be completed in the foreseeable future. Paradoxically the growth of the investment rate was simultaneously too slow in terms of needs, and too rapid in terms of the current investment possibilities of the national economy.

7.3.3 Polish transport in the 1980s

In the 1970s there was no general concept of coherent and long-term development of the transport system. Structural disproportions in the national economy were caused, to at least some extent, by underestimation

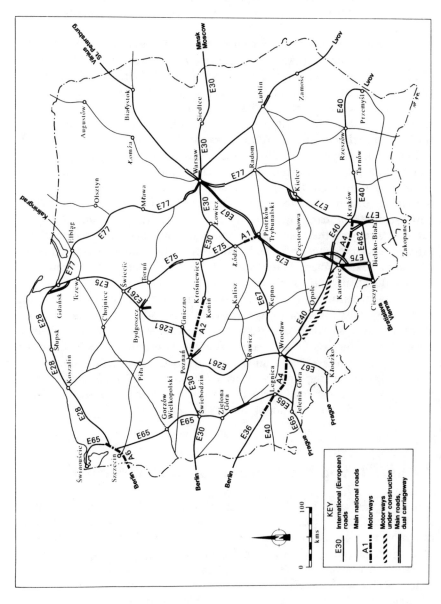

Figure 7.7 Poland: the main road network

of the transport factor in the harmonious economic development of the country.

The influence of the deep socio-economic crisis of the 1980s had many facets. It diminished the volume of output and investment rate, such that transport was no longer viewed as a bottleneck for the economy to such a great degree.

Investment expenditures for transport fell to below 7 per cent of total inputs while in neighbouring countries they were well above 11 per cent. This resulted in an accelerated decapitalisation of the technical infrastructure and lack of modernisation. As a consequence, the rail system is ill-suited for intensive traffic. There are arrears in overhaul repairs on routes, at depots and stations. The investment effort is concentrated on further electrification of routes, expansion and modernisation of technical maintenance facilities and renovation and re-equipment of marshalling yards. An extension of electrification is prompted mainly by liquid fuel shortages. The negative side of the electrification programme is that there is no parallel improvement of the signalling system. Thus, improvements in carrying capacity are limited (Berman and Alvstam, 1985). Moreover, there are delays in the maintenance and repair of the existing electrified network, and deliveries of new stock are insufficient. Although several marshalling yards have been modernised recently, a further dozen urgently need reconstruction.

The construction of higher standard roads has almost ceased save for small fragments of motorways between Kraków and Katowice (A4), Wrzesnia and Konin (A2), dual carriageway running through Upper Silesia from the East, and some smaller stretches of express routes (Figure 7.7). An average annual rate of road construction diminished from 2,000 km in the mid-1970s to 1,000 km in the 1980s and to even less nowadays. Most road surfaces are not suited to heavy traffic. There are bottlenecks in the national road network.

7.4 Introducing the market economy in transport

Transport, as well as the whole national economy, is undergoing intensive transformation from a centrally planned economy towards a market economy with adjustment to international cooperation. Since it is taking place in a period of economic difficulty with serious budgetary limitations, transformation faces significant obstacles and potentially unfavourable social responses.

Changes in the legal system for adjustment to the market economy are in train. The main problem here is to de-monopolise some fragments of the transport market and to establish new forms of ownership. In the new Constitution (1990) all forms of ownership are equal according to the law (state, private, communal, cooperative). A lot of former state property has become communal property, and, for example, urban transport has been taken over by communal enterprises. Small-scale privatisation and the deregulation of freight road transport has been undertaken already. As a result, there is strong competition in the market and a surplus of rolling stock. Some regulations protecting good firms against dishonest competition are under investigation. A model to be emulated is EC legislation, ensuring professionalism, good trading standards, the financial competence of firms and appropriate technical conditions for lorries and trucks. New legislation for rail transport and civil aviation is under preparation at the time of writing. Not all firms and enterprises will be privatised; more important is the commercialisation of their activities, rather than introducing privatisation as the only reform option. Thus far, larger firms seem to have been little affected by deregulation, and developments appear largely *ad hoc* and uncoordinated.

7.5 Impact of the market economy on road transport

7.5.1 Road construction and maintenance

In 1991, all units executing road construction and maintenance works were excluded from Road Administration supervision. They became independent state or private enterprises. Only small teams for simple intervention works remained within the central administration. Presently, an obligation of tendering for works ordered by Road Administration is being implemented. This requires preparation of bidding procedures, updating of standards and recommendations, development of technical specifications and training of the respective work force in all levels of Road Administration. Even though the tendering system is commonplace elsewhere, its full implementation in the current Polish situation requires careful preparation and monitoring.

7.5.2 The road management system

Substantial decentralisation in the management of rural and urban roads has now taken place. Only 12.5 per cent of road length remains supervised by central government, compared with 34.5 per cent by regional (voivodship) administration, and the remaining 53 per cent by local (urban and communal) authorities.

The road system requires a modern data bank. International cooperation is very important in this area, with Denmark, France and the World Bank all playing a role in this field.

7.5.3 Setting up a legal framework for operating toll motorways and a concession system

The absence of appropriate legislation has meant that the Road Administration, which already has very limited budgetary resources, cannot take full advantage of potential local and foreign investors' initiatives to upgrade road service standards through building motorways and service areas. It was intended to set up adequate legislation by the end of 1992.

In the present economic situation in Poland, one cannot expect a significant hastening of motorway construction. The financing of motorway construction and operation from tolls has been discussed by the Ministry of Transport and Maritime Economy, which has studied such approaches taken in France, Italy and Spain. Certainly, the only chance for such project implementation in the foreseeable future is through cooperation with foreign capital.

Revenues from tolls, enlarged by income from granted concessions (services and other economic activities) along the motorway could enable a long-term recovery of costs. Two basic ways of financing construction of the motorway are thus under examination: (1) through a special-purpose unit, such as a motorways agency, which would carry on construction using foreign loans, guaranteed by the state; and (2) through concessionaires by way of tenders and concessionary agreements. In this system a sizeable part of revenues from operating of the motorways (toll charges) would go to the concessionaires.

7.6 The international context

7.6.1 Poland's transit location

The situation of Poland mainly on lowlands between the Baltic Sea and the Carpathian Mountains presents favourable conditions for developing east–west transit routes, while ports along the country's 524-km Baltic coastline facilitate north–south transit traffic by providing freight services for land-locked Central European countries and convenient sea-land connections between Scandinavia and the Balkans.

However, route alignment is far from being the only factor in such developments: technical standards, border crossing facilities, passenger and transport services along the transit route are all important.

Table 7.2 Poland: status and development of road network (in kilometres)

Total: 364,200

1. Nature
Rural 313,000
            of which 187,600 improved
                         of which 152,000 paved
Urban 51,000

2. 1985 Public Road Act categories
National   45,500
               of which 4,280 improved

of which motorways	257
expressways	390
dual all-purpose	650

Regional (voidvodships)	128,900
Communal	170,000
Industrial	19,800

3. Density of paved roads per 100 sq km

1946	29 km
1990	60 km

Source: General Directorate of Public Roads, 1992.

7.6.2 The road network: its status and development trends

In 1983 Poland ratified the European Agreement on Main International Traffic Arteries (AGR): eleven international roads of about 4,800 km in length cross Poland. These are shown in Figure 7.7.

Road network development trends were the subject of intensive studies in the 1970s within the framework of the UNDP project *Development of the road network in Poland*. The resulting model envisaged the construction of three motorways of 1,900 km total length, and a system of expressways (one or two carriageway) of 5,100 km. So far, however, implementation of that system has been very slow.

Maintaining even the minimum standards required modernisation works on selected sections of inter-regional, and especially international roads. During the 1983–1992 period modernisation works were carried out on nine sections with the heaviest traffic volume, totalling 3,770 km in length (General Directorate of Public Roads, 1992).

One of the planned motorways (A1) has been an object of particular interest for nearly twenty years. Due to a Polish–Hungarian initiative, this motorway became the subject of an international project. It was implemented under the auspices of the Economic European Commission of the United Nations (EEC–UN) and UNDP and known as the

Table 7.3   Poland: planned motorway system

A1*   (Helsinki) – Gdańsk – Toruń – Łódź – Katowice – Gorzyce – (Ostrava):
representing the Polish section of the TEM

A2*   (Berlin) – Świecko – Poznań – Łodź – Warsaw – Terespol – (Moscow)

A3   Szczecin – Zielona Góra – Legnica – Lubawka – (Prague)

A4*   (Dresden) – Zgorzelec – Legnica – Wrocław – Opole – Katowice – Kraków –
Rzeszów – Przemyśl – Medyka – (Lvov)

A8   (Prague) – Wrocław – Łódź – Warsaw

A12   (Berlin) – Olszyn – Legnica – Wrocław

---

* receiving highest priority

Source: General Directorate of Public Roads, 1992.

North–South Trans-European Motorway (TEM). With ten countries participating, the project will see a system of motorways, over 10,000 km in length, connecting Gdańsk via Czechoslovakia, Hungary and Austria with Italy, former Yugoslavia, Greece and Turkey. In most of the countries involved, the implementation rate is lower than had been initially anticipated, and it is almost certain that the plans to start the operation of the whole system in the year 2000 will be not met. Lying behind the decision taken by the previous state authorities and by the EEC–UN regarding TEM as high priority was the lack of belief in the possibility of a fast growth in international traffic, especially road traffic, in an east–west direction. More was expected from the north–south orientation.

The new political situation and subsequent economic change requires a fresh look to be taken into the issues of transport development in Central and Eastern Europe, not least in Poland. Land transport requires especial attention since fundamental changes in the development of transport systems in neighbouring countries are to be expected.

As a result of liberalised economies and open borders, high rates of transport growth are likely to be maintained in both freight and passenger sectors, in the latter case particularly in relation to transit functions. New spatial alignments are also emerging, most notably the formerly inactive north–east – south–west axis. For the Baltic states, Kaliningrad, St. Petersburg and Finland, the shortest transit link with Western and South-Western Europe is offered by Poland.

Within this context, the future of the country's motor- and expressways was subject to critical analysis during 1990–91. As a result, the development of 6,000 km of expressways (3,500 km) and motorways (2,500 km)

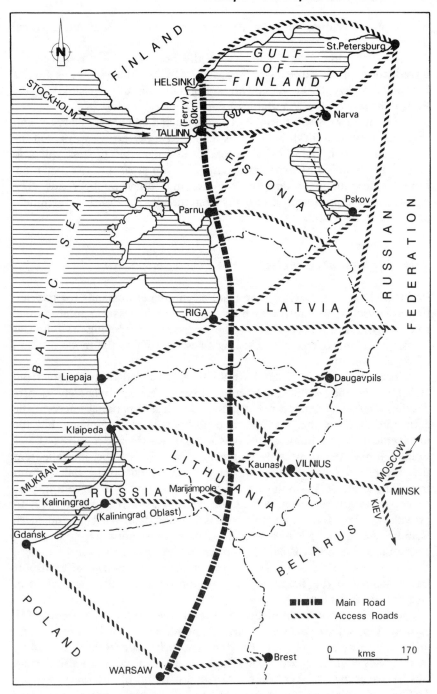

Figure 7.8 Poland: the Via Baltica route

Source: Miettinen, 1992.

LIVERPOOL HOPE UNIVERSITY COLLEGE

will be given priority in order to meet both national and international demands (Table 7.3).

One of the important elements of the new alignment is to be the introduction of an expressway Warsaw – Ostrów Mazowiecka – Łomża – Suwałki – Szypliszki – (Kowno – Riga – Tallinn – Helsinki) as the Polish section of the Via Baltica route (Figure 7.8).

While motorways will normally be constructed completely new, to limit encroachment on rural land, it is expected that expressways will be developed by converting existing roads, although this process will also require the building of bypasses around built-up areas and two-tier junctions to accommodate railway crossings and other public roads. The details of these proposals were being examined by the Polish Government at the time of writing.

7.6.3 The Via Baltica project from a Polish perspective

Political changes in Europe have resulted in greater demands for international transport, as illustrated by a significant increase in international road traffic flows. This creates the necessity of opening new border crossings or improvement of existing ones, as well as the modernisation of some road links.

Before 1989, few in Poland would have predicted that a route from Helsinki via the Baltic states and passing through relatively poorly developed areas of Poland would attract much international interest. The early initiative for the Via Baltica project came from Finland, but the involvement of the Baltic states was quickly sought and received. Later Poland joined the project development team. Soon it became apparent that the primary beneficiaries of the project would be the Baltic countries. The goals of Via Baltica have been stated as: (1) to serve transport needs within and between each Baltic country as well as Poland; (2) to provide a direct route to transit traffic to and from Finland, northern Scandinavia, parts of Russia (notably the St. Petersburg area), Germany, and countries south of Poland; (3) to create a tourist route on the eastern shores of the Baltic Sea; (4) to form a basic component of transport infrastructure in the Baltic states to support the establishment of local and foreign businesses (Miettinen, 1992).

The Baltic states traditionally have had adequate road systems. The existing Via Baltica route was part of the all-union road system mostly under the route number M12. For this reason it has been built according to relatively high standards. Therefore, in practice the Via Baltica route can be driven by car even today. At the north end of the route between Tallinn and Riga (270 km) it is at its best. The middle section from Riga to Kaunas via Panevesys (220 km) is of a lower quality. From Kaunas to the Polish border the road is partly in decent shape, but towards the border its standard becomes poor. The Polish section via Suwałki and Ostrów Mazowiecka consists of roads of secondary quality.

With the Baltic countries' changing trade relationships with the rest of the world, new transport routes will emerge, among them most importantly the Via Baltica. Although local traffic will dominate the volumes using the route, international traffic growth is likely to be greatest between neighbouring countries which previously had tightly constrained movement, notably between Finland and Estonia, Poland and Lithuania. Already, the number of vehicles crossing the Polish–Lithuanian border has grown from almost nothing in 1987 to 320,000 in 1991 (Miettinen, 1992).

The importance of this route development can be summarised as:

(1) intensifying the transport cooperation between the countries of the east and south sides of the Baltic Sea. Poland has already undertaken new road transport agreements with Lithuania, Latvia and Estonia. There are now also more frequent contacts between Polish and Finnish experts concerning the development of road-side services;

(2) opening the route for international traffic via the Szypliszki/Kalvarija border crossing will transfer freight and parts of passenger traffic from the previously used crossing at Ogrodniki/Lardijai. The change of traffic pattern will be a very important environmental factor, since the current traffic from the border uses roads cutting through the middle of Augustów Forest. The new route will bypass environmentally protected areas. In the proposed corridor of Via Baltica there is also a railway line, which following the opening of the Takiszki/Sestokai railway border crossing (after nearly 50 years!) will facilitate Lithuanian and Polish transport needs;

(3) aiding the economic development of north-eastern Poland. The local authorities hope to develop intensive international trade and joint ventures to improve the economic situation of the region.

7.6.4 Polish–German border transport cooperation

Germany has become the most important trade partner for post-communist Poland, taking the place formerly occupied by the Soviet Union.

Cross-border traffic has increased tremendously in recent years, especially after the cancellation of obligatory visas for Polish citizens by the countries of the so-called Schengen group. In 1991 60.6 million people and 14.9 million vehicles crossed the border, a four- and eight-fold increase respectively over 1980, the last year of no-passport movement with the former East Germany. Now there are eleven road crossings along the 460-km border. A further thirteen, including several adjusted for local traffic, are planned for opening before 1994.

There are also eight rail border crossings for freight traffic. Currently only four of these carry passenger trains, but it is envisaged that this will be extended to at least three of the remainder. In 1992 the first EuroCity train, *Berolina*, was introduced. It takes just five hours for the journey between Warsaw and Berlin.

But the development of Poland's road network, and especially motorways appears now most important. The Germans plan three east–west corridors to aid the development of infrastructure in eastern Germany, which will better link Poland with western Germany, and thereby the rest of Western Europe. These will be: (1) Szczecin via Rostock to Lübeck, Hamburg and Bremen; (2) Berlin to Hannover and the Ruhr area, to Leipzig and Southern Germany, respectively; and (3) Dresden to Kassel and southern Germany. Motorway construction especially from Berlin to Warsaw (A2), and from Berlin and Dresden to Upper Silesia and Kraków (A4) is thus of primary importance.

One should remember that Germany, along with the United States and Holland, is the most important foreign investor in Poland. To realise effective economic development in Poland from such investment, an appropriate traffic and transport infrastructure is essential. Most foreign investment has in fact located along the route from Berlin via Poznań to Warsaw.

7.6.5 Cooperation with other neighbours

During the last three years Poland has gained 'new' neighbouring countries (Germany, Russia, Lithuania, Belarus, Slovakia). In addition to stronger links with Germany, new dimensions of cooperation with other neighbours are also developing. There is a joint plan with Belarus and Ukraine for the modernisation of the Berlin – Kunowice – Warsaw – Brest – Minsk (E20) trunk rail line and its upgrading for high-speed passenger trains of up to 160 kph. Belarus is interested in the possible rail transit of her goods through the seaport of Gdynia. Polish State Railways, port authorities and shipowners are very keen for the further development of other transit routes, particularly as the volume of transit freight between Germany and the former Soviet Union decreased by 50 per cent during 1991 alone.

Recently passenger traffic between Poland and Ukraine has increased rapidly, and train capacity from Lvov, Kiev and Odessa is insufficient: over four thousand people daily use the rail border crossing at Medyka/Mostiska. Journey times are long. For example, the Legnica – Kiev service takes over 27 hours to cover a distance of only 1,298 km.

Much time is lost in changing bogies between the standard and broad-gauge systems. To avoid this, both countries are considering introducing the Spanish system of Talgo trains, applied with success by RENFE. If the technical studies are positive, Polish State Railways will be able to apply for financial assistance from the World Bank.

At the end of 1991 Poland became an associate member of the EC and a member of the Council of Europe. These developments have opened opportunities for receiving some assistance for transport modernisation and restructuring, such as the EC's PHARE programme (Poland/Hungary Assistance for Restructuring Economies). Such international financial organisations as the International Monetary Fund and the World Bank provide opportunities for assistance and the provision of expertise in areas such as privatisation.

In mid-1990 the first large credit, of $153 million, was provided for the modernisation of Polish Railways by the World Bank. In Warsaw, a new air terminal for three million passengers a year, a cargo airport and catering facilities for Polish Airlines LOT have been constructed by German firm Hochtief Ltd, and financed by a German bank with a credit of DM 300 million. Three Boeing 767s and ten French–Italian ATR-72s for LOT have been financed by foreign credits as part of a programme of fleet replacement and reorientation towards Western and away from Soviet technology: Soviet TU-134s have been sold on to Ukraine. As elsewhere in the region, however, the demand for assistance far exceeds the supply of funds available.

7.7 Conclusions

To understand the present-day situation of the Polish transport system one needs to undertake a thorough study of the post-war period. The system, and especially land-based forms of transport, is similar to those in other post-communist countries and very different from Western Europe, most notably in the predominant role of railways and the high transport intensity. Changes in the system have been introduced in response to the needs of freight rather than passenger movement. For many years the transport system suffered from a serious shortage of carrying capacity; paradoxically for a supposed centrally-planned economy, the need to construct a properly modelled system was treated as a matter of secondary importance.

Hitherto, processes of restructuring and privatisation have been slower for transport than in other branches of the national economy, such as retail and wholesale trade and even manufacturing industry. The fragmentary de-monopolisation of transport is not an easy task. Changes in road transport, for example, have taken place more rapidly than on the railways, with the introduction of market principles, changes in management, deregulation and modifications to the legal framework. On the other hand, motorway construction lags far behind that of Czechoslovakia and Hungary, not to mention the former East Germany. Rapid changes occurring in neighbouring countries are exerting a direct impact on the Polish transport infrastructure, however, as witnessed in the Via Baltica project and in cooperation with Germany, Belarus, Ukraine and other neighbouring countries.

8 The impact of economic and political change on Polish sea transport

Zofia Sawiczewska

8.1 Introduction

The Second World War and forty-five years of communist rule left Poland in a state of bankruptcy, misery and isolation. The country's debt interest payments alone exceeded total export income. Between 1986 and 1991 inflation reached a thousand per cent, but the average citizen did not have access to a bank account. Bills were settled in person and quite often cash was exchanged into dollars to combat inflation. Even cars and houses were paid for in cash. The first attempts to create a proper banking and currency system have now been taken, but any beneficial effects may not be expected until the Polish złoty is fully convertible, inflation is tamed and a dependable telephone system is in operation. Inflation and the hopelessly antiquated telephone network are slowing down the national bank's efforts to introduce cashless instruments for domestic transactions.

Early post-communist priorities were to stabilise inflation and hold firmly to an exchange rate set after a massive devaluation of the currency in 1990. The government managed to cut inflation to about 5 per cent by mid-1991. But the battle against inflation has been waged at the cost of workers' dissatisfaction, as incomes have been held down and consumer prices have risen. The signs of recession, with state-owned factories on the edge of bankruptcy and decreasing production, led to government changes.

New very complicated tasks needed to be solved: industrial production dropped by 40 per cent in the first quarter of 1991 compared with the year before and real wages were falling. Unemployment was rising, reaching 2.5 million or over 12 per cent of the labour force with up to 17 per cent in some rural districts of South-Eastern Poland by 1992 (compared to a rate for Warsaw of around 3 per cent). Political changes in the former Soviet Union brought political joy, but at the same time ruined numerous branches of industry which had based their exports on Soviet orders and which subsequently did not even receive payment for goods already delivered.

Unemployment figures are inflated by the large number of casual labourers who queue up outside employment offices and work only for a few days at a time to earn enough to pay for their minimal needs. Some obviously earn their money travelling, carrying goods from Western Europe and selling them on the streets. Nevertheless the unemployment problem is serious and where there is an absence of personal savings it can be dramatic.

The new government had to take the first serious steps towards reprivatisation of the economy in order to improve its structure, to modernise, to improve labour efficiency and managerial techniques.

Despite the image of industrial workers striking for freedom, Poland is also an agricultural country, full of small villages with about 30 per cent of the population tied up in agriculture. Farming escaped communist collectivisation and private fields make up 80 per cent of Polish farmland. However, the communist system required the obligatory delivery of farm products at low fixed prices. Today 70 per cent of goods in the stores are imported, while the country's own farming system is only beginning to improve its productivity. Another problem which Poland inherited from the communist regime is that of the work ethic: people who have not been working properly for many years find it hard to change their habits. For more than a generation it was common in the Polish workers' world to say: 'we pretend to work, and they pretend to pay us'. Wages were very low, fixed and not related to real effort. There was no cooperation with managers, who generally represented the regime and whose role was to cover up unfulfilled quotas. Although workers had poor pay, they had easy access to summer holidays in the factories' own rest houses, kindergarten, generous sick-leave and free medical care together with free education for their children.

Introducing free market forces cannot be performed in a year or two: reconstruction of all the country's economy is necessary and this is obviously a hard and painful operation. According to opinion surveys many Poles in 1992 considered themselves worse off than under communism. Many thought corruption a serious problem and economic scandals flourished. Many fortunes have been built on currency speculation, smuggling and a lack of clear rules and regulations concerning customs, taxes, credits, and the buying and selling of property. With such a tremendous transition and transformation of the economic, legal and political system, some fraud, bribery, theft and incompetence was inevitable. The conflicts of interest of individuals claiming property rights is causing delay in decision-making. The problem for Poland is that what is economically sound may be socially unacceptable, and what is socially acceptable can be economically harmful. The danger is that

Poles, seeing some of the less attractive sides of capitalism in its early stages, will lose patience and may be tempted by the populism of politicians trying to achieve their political goals and destroy a newborn democracy. Yet, for the first time in half a century, there are colours in generally grey cities, the shops are full, shop windows are clean, storefronts are newly painted, and service has become polite. There are no queues for food, no shortages, no under-the-counter sales. People are beginning to understand that they can relate this situation to the existence and prosperity of their employers.

8.2 Concepts and strategies for privatising the Polish economy

Post-communist Poland's new economists want to create a West European-style ownership structure and to put more than half of the state's assets into private hands. It is a task of great complexity. After forty-five years of centralised economy, it is no longer clear who owns what, what anything's value is, how it can be sold and to whom. There is a shortage of capital, expertise, proper management, motivation, productivity and efficiency. The government has been deluged recently with thousands of claims from pre-war shop owners, businessmen house owners and land owners for the return of property taken from them without compensation after the Second World War. At the same time people employed in factories and institutions and who have lived for years in labour-camp conditions claim their rights to participate in ownership.

Various concepts of getting Poland's economy into the hands of private owners have been discussed. One of them was the concept of granting the ownership of the state-owned companies to the employees, another was based on the idea of selling them to those who have the money to invest in business. In both cases the companies concerned needed to be converted into share-holding companies first.

Selling shares to those who are interested seems a good idea, but there are very few people in Poland who have the money, which is the obvious result of forty years of communist centrally-planned rules and regulations. The average Polish employee would not be able to purchase the shares of his enterprises for another fifteen to twenty years; the only people to be in the position to be buyers today are foreigners, former top party activists and black-marketeers.

One proposal which seemed to gain general support was the idea of distributing bonds to all adult citizens of the country. These bonds could either be sold freely or used for buying shares on the stock exchange. There were arguments, however, that this policy was moving too quickly and haphazardly and that the state-owned enterprises' management should be improved before they are privatised, in order to increase their value.

A second approach was that of issuing stock in the companies, which would be turned into a mutual funds programme in which every adult Pole who wished to start individual economic activities would be able to participate, in the form of twenty-years' low-interest loans. The government would create a stock company wholly held by the Treasury, giving 10 per cent of the shares to the workers in the hope of creating immediate political support.

With enterprises generally in fragile shape and with little financial data available, most people were expected to avoid the risk of buying a particular stock and to put their vouchers into the mutual funds. In practice, there are enterprises where the legal status of ownership of the buildings, the lands and infrastructure needs to be resolved first. The private, municipal and state owners, together with the employees, claim their rights; however, neither proper documents nor other evidence to support their rights are available. The government, namely the Privatisation Ministry, has often failed properly to solve individual cases, and is being accused of acting too slowly, inefficiently and of showing bias.

8.3 Poland as a maritime nation

The ownership, structure and organisation of Polish ports and shipping which have been maintained for over forty years now require changes which are not only desirable but absolutely necessary (Misztal, 1990). Their former status and organisation caused a lack of progress and prevented innovation, leaving Polish maritime transport behind the rapid technological progress of the Western world.

In contrast to many comparable countries which have had a history of international trade and maritime commerce, the history of the Polish merchant fleet began only in the 1920s following two centuries in which Polish independence had been extinguished. Poland thus does not have a long-standing history as an independent maritime nation. Initially, shipping lines serving Poland's passenger traffic and limited foreign trade operated with the help of other countries (Borowicz, 1988). In 1930, for example, as a result of an agreement between the small Polish Shipping Company and the Danish East Asiatic Company Ltd, a limited company was formed, called Polish Transatlantic Shipping Company, Limited: Gdynia-America Line (GAL). Its purpose was the operation of a regular passenger and cargo service to North American ports. Initially, 52.2 per cent of the company's stock capital was held by the Polish partner, but by 1938 the Polish share was 98.65 per cent. At the same time Polish–

British co-operation saw the inauguration of a deep-sea bulk-cargo service. During the Second World War the majority of Polish ships were chartered by the British Government. GAL's vessels, with their base in London, took part in all the major operations which required merchant ships. During the Blitz, for example, the ms *Batory* carried English children from the UK to the relative safety of Australia, gaining much popularity and respect in the process. Losses incurred by Polish shipping companies amounted to nineteen ships (63,345 GRT) of which GAL incurred the greatest losses.

During the years between 1945 and 1950 GAL endeavoured to replace this tonnage, but fulfilling its tasks for the modernisation of a merchant fleet became increasingly difficult in the changing political, social and economic circumstances.

In 1951 two nationalised and centrally controlled shipping companies were established by the communist authorities – Polish Ocean Lines and Polish Steamship Company, By 1967 the Polish merchant fleet amounted to a total of 228 ships, with 1,618,000 dwt. The fleet operated on thirty-two regular lines, and in ocean tramping Polish ships sailed practically to every port in the world. In 1970 the fleet consisted of 259 vessels of 1,926,000 dwt. By the mid-1970s, which were the best years for the Polish shipping industry, the fleet had reached 315 vessels totalling almost four million dwt. In the post-war decades, and notably in the 1960s, much attention was paid to the expansion of the fleet of the Soviet Union and its satellite states. Shipping came to be seen as an extension of ideological policy. But although it may be tempting to see the maritime policy of Poland in this light, the Polish approach was in practice, more pragmatic. It was based on economic rather than political nationalism, and efforts were made to minimise Soviet influence. In addition to the party activists who were appointed to the top positions in all companies, there was always the need to maintain professionals with a knowledge of the changing world market environment and who could read English documents.

Polish sea ports and shipping played, and still play, and important role in the country's economy and foreign trade (Zurek, 1991). About 90 per cent of the total ports turnover are goods of the Polish foreign exchange of which about 90 per cent is bulk cargo such as coal and sulphur exports, and iron ore, grain, fertiliser and oil imports. General cargo accounts for about 10 per cent of the ports' tonnage trade, and a proportion much greater in terms of value.

Poland has traditionally considered foreign trade a key element in its national development strategy. In particular, foreign trade is viewed as necessary in order to promote exports and the adoption of new technology. Poland's economic health depends upon the vitality of its export sectors. The continued growth of the country's foreign trade requires unimpeded access for shippers to an efficient and competitive transportation system of which international shipping is an integral part. This objective is being underlined by the open-door policy introduced after the dramatic political changes in 1990. The importance to shipping of this policy lies in the fact that, shipping being a subset of foreign trade, it should be considered as a crucial element in the national development strategy.

Poland is a country with an uneven distribution of raw material sources. A surplus of coal, sulphur and copper contrasts with a shortage of crude oil and metal ores. Over 50 per cent of the country's coal and sulphur goes through Polish ports, in addition to 52–62 per cent of fertilisers, 73–92 per cent of grain, 75 per cent of sugar and 99.9 per cent of cement. All this created favourable conditions for the development of the bulk cargo fleet. Participation in the exchange of manufactured goods also brought the necessity to maintain the existence and the development of general cargo transport. Thus, Poland relies on maritime transport for a substantial proportion of her foreign trade, the efficiency of which therefore becomes a key issue.

At present about 30 per cent of Polish sea-borne trade goes to Western Europe and about 20 per cent to the Baltic region. The remaining 50 per cent is long-distance traffic: to North and South America, the Far East, Australia and Africa. About 17 per cent of total cargo is in transit to and from Czechoslovakia, Hungary and Austria across Polish territory. In the years 1960–1981 transit trade through Polish ports averaged 4–5 million tonnes. Since 1983, a considerable increase in transit traffic brought the amount to a peak of 7.7 million tonnes, largely as the result of Soviet oil shipments through the North Port of Gdańsk. There could have been much more transit cargo, had the country's infrastructure been better and the port's services more efficient.

Polish ports are located away from the main world routes, which focus on the great European ports further west: Rotterdam, Antwerp, Hamburg, Bremen, London. They are nevertheless vital in serving South–North European transit traffic, as well as meeting the needs of Polish seaborne trade. Deep water accessibility of Polish seaports varies from a capacity to berth 150,000 dwt ships in Gdańsk North Port to 60,000 dwt ships in Świnoujście, 25,000 dwt ships in Gdańsk and Gdynia terminals and 15,000 dwt in Szczecin harbour, along the Odra river.

The seaports provide employment for a large number of people. It has been estimated that up to half the total labour force of Gdańsk, Gdynia and Szczecin have been involved with the maritime economy. The inadequacy of port mechanisation is one of the reasons for the relatively large labour force employed in the ports. There is a pressing need for improved infrastructure, both within the ports and at the interface with an already overloaded inland transport system. As a result of such shortcomings serious delays are encountered in the loading and unloading of cargo and its onward distribution, both domestically and internationally (Sawiczewska, 1992).

The rail system, traditionally the cheapest and the most popular means of transport, still plays its dominant role in delivering bulk cargo to the ports (up to 85 per cent), but will be further strained by an expected increase in coal production. The system is totally inadequate for container traffic. In 1973 the government started to establish and coordinate the country's domestic and international container traffic. Despite the establishment of some necessary institutions, mostly in the port of Gdynia and in the Polish Ocean Lines shipping company (Plates 8.1 and 8.2), container movements continue to suffer from inadequate coordination in port handling, cargo dispersion and container collection. As container traffic is expected to continue to grow during the 1990s, it will continue to outpace capacity and the rail system bottleneck will persist.

Two large Polish rivers, the Vistula and the Odra, which theoretically could provide ideal connections across the country, have been prevented from providing a means of convenient and cheap water transport. The communist regime forbade the ownership of private boats and small river ships (to prevent the people from escaping from the People's Republic), such that the river fleets and small harbours which survived into the late 1940s disappeared slowly in the 1950s. Between 1970 and 1990 the share of expenditure on inland shipping ranged from 0.3 to 2.2 per cent of that for the transport sector as a whole (Figure 8.1). Heavy pollution and lack of necessary works to regulate the rivers for navigation further exacerbated a situation whereby only about one per cent of cargoes to Gdańsk and Gdynia are carried by river transport, and to Szczecin about 3 per cent. Neither does the country's road transport network serve sea-borne cargo effectively, transporting only about one per cent of deliveries of goods to the sea-ports. Heavy trucks and container vehicles have limited access to the ports due to the lack of motorways. Roads in Poland are insufficient either to serve the rapidly growing traffic or to connect international transit across the country. A large proportion of rural roads is unsuitable for heavy trucks, and many are still mud tracks.

Further Polish economic development depends to a critical extent on the improvement of its transport infrastructure. Currently the transport sector is strained by congested short-haul services, inadequate long-haul capacity, and insufficient inter-modal connections. Therefore it is necessary to develop an adequate programme and clear perspective of the future shape of the country's transport system. It must not be simply a reconstruction or maintenance of the existing infrastructure, but a totally new system of motorways and terminals is required. There will be a need to demolish numerous old warehouses and buildings, both in the ports and in the cities nearby, in order to open the large areas of clear access to the seaports for direct door-to-door multi-modal connections. This will require large investments and a totally new way of thinking, but it is the only way to improve the existing transport system. The degree of

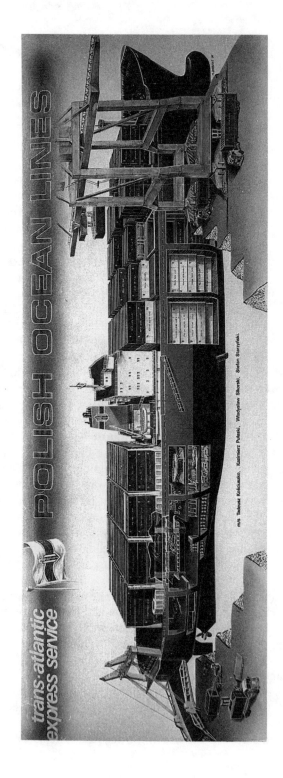

Plate 8.1 Model of Polish Ocean Lines container ship

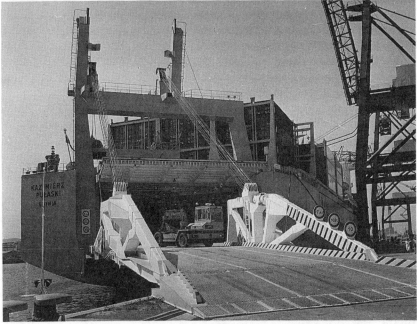

Plate 8.2 Polish Ocean Lines container ship ms *Kazimierz Pułaski* at Gdynia: (a) front view in harbour; (b) rear view showing ro-ro facility.

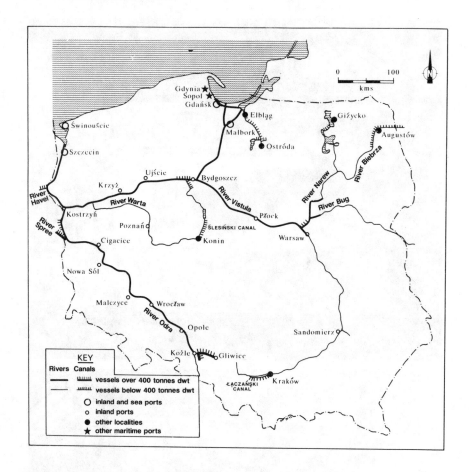

Figure 8.1 Poland: ports and inland waterways

deterioration of ports' technical equipment is estimated as about 35–55 per cent: half of all cargo handling facilities need replacement and almost half of all storage capacity requires major repairs. Ports such as Gdynia or the North Port of Gdańsk were expanded and developed to relatively high technical standards but traffic remained low because of landside problems, notably inland transport bottlenecks.

The organisational structure and the division of labour in Polish ports is a result of some pre-war traditions but mostly is a result of the central state's regulations in the early 1950s. In the first years after the Second World War the ports' infrastructure belonged to the state, but all the services were performed by private companies of various sizes and profiles.

In the early 1950s a highly centralised system was introduced with the total monopolisation of executive services in one large state-owned enterprise, with other supplementing services provided from a limited number of large centrally controlled units. Each of the three Polish ports' activities in trade, services and maintenance were monopolised by a very few centrally-controlled units. All the income which the ports earned went into the state's budget and very seldom came back in the form of new investments. It was estimated that the ports could have covered at least 25 per cent of their investment needs from their own profits, however the government in Warsaw always had more important demands on its exchequer and neither let the ports accumulate nor distribute their own profits. Attempts to create 'free port' zones were for many years considered a political offence and publications on the subject were rejected by the censors.

8.4 Re-privatisation and reconstruction of the Polish maritime economy

The process of re-privatising Polish ports has advanced with some individual services returning to private hands. In spite of various unsolved problems of the ownership of land and buildings, it is considered that the country's ports can be reconstructed relatively rapidly with improved organisation and better efficiency of their operations achieved.

It should be remembered that the specific situation of Polish ports and shipping is different from most other branches of economy in that the management, port employees and outgoing crews are generally better prepared to enter into cooperation or common ownership with foreign partners. This reflects their relatively closer contacts with international foreign trade, exchange and international market conditions. Polish shipping management has a good knowledge of the English language together with expertise on international maritime cooperation, law, customs and documents.

This should be taken into consideration when new ideas and concepts of future changes are developed. The whole process may take time but the first to change are small forwarding firms, shipbrokers, agencies and all the smaller specialised port and ship services. The three large Polish shipping companies that were amongst the largest in the world are also facing the necessity of profound change. Polish shipping tonnage in 1990 was 3,360,000 shared between Polish Ocean Lines, a shipping enterprise specialising in general cargo transport and door-to-door container services; the Polish Steamship Company, specialising in tankers and bulk carriers; and the Polish Baltic Corporation, established in Kolobrzeg in

1976, operating mainly ferry-boats and conventional liners. All of these were large, specialised units apparently too big to manage and too specialised to maintain security against market fluctuations.

Under the communists they were not able to enter into any other field or economic activity, unlike shipping companies elsewhere. However, they are now undertaking a diversification of their activities into other branches of the economy and services such as trade and wholesaling, tourism and accommodation, inland transport and the exploitation of maritime resources. This is believed to be an appropriate way of generating capital for further investment and creating jobs. Shipping companies are determined to extend their present economic independence and press for full freedom in decision-making. Early effects of this have seen the proportion of cargo carried by Polish ships between foreign ports (cross-trade) increase from thirty per cent to about two-thirds of the total.

An open-door policy now seeks to attract foreign capital and technology promoting joint ventures while at the same time trying to find domestic investment and support. Joint ventures are being actively encouraged for port development and container services. However, it would seem that foreign participation is still carefully circumscribed and geographically limited.

The Polish merchant fleet is facing numerous problems connected with the long-term freight market recession and the continued world tonnage surplus. But the most difficult problems to be solved are internal ones.

Shipping companies have already employed their newly flexible roles to sell or lease their spare land and buildings, sell or charter ships and establish their own budgets. They are changing their internal structures to create several small financially independent units which are more efficient and flexible in day-to-day operations. They are also trying to obtain credits to cover the costs of previous ship orders and to eventually supplement other shortages by purchasing second-hand tonnage or chartering. At present, however, such companies' financial situation is so bad that they face possible bankruptcy. The government is not able to offer any financial help, but places a heavy taxation burden on the shipping industry. There is a serious danger of losing goodwill, traditional connections and established services to foreign interests who could easily see Polish shipping eliminated. This is perhaps a more emotional than real fear but such emotions and patriotism play a very important role in Poland. Given the importance of shipping to the national economy, therefore, shipping could be viewed as a public service and as such should not be left totally in private hands and to the mercies of world market forces. Eventually the government's presence in shipping may be quite important. Thus in spite of the current difficult national financial situation, in developing a new programme of re-privatising Polish shipping, forms of mixed ownership must also be considered, with the state taking a majority share.

This does not exclude the possibility of putting some Polish ships under flags of convenience or chartering some part of the fleet to foreign operators. The goal must be maximum flexibility, efficiency and adaptation to changing market conditions. This may mean a somewhat smaller fleet in terms of tonnage, but it does not imply any reduction in transport or earning capacity. After a short- to medium-term period of difficulties and adaptations, one may hope to expect another period of positive achievement in the Polish maritime industry. Polish shipping does possess certain advantages which should play their role in any future development of the industry. Polish ships are currently able to carry cargo at lower rates than other nations due to real cost differences, especially lower labour costs, and not deliberate dumping or any special non-commercial advantages, as in the past. Polish crews are generally well trained and their labour is still very cheap in world terms.

Although it has been argued that the maintenance of a Polish fleet would create employment opportunities for Polish seamen and officers, it is clear that the total number of positions created would be limited as shipping is no longer a labour-intensive industry. Poland also has its own well-developed ship-building and ship-repair industry, experienced ship-broking and forwarding agents, nautical and shipping economics education facilities together with well developed research institutes. Additionally, the sea-fishing industry has seven fishery and fish-processing enterprises and numerous plants producing pumps, hydraulic drives and other ship equipment, further elaborating the structure of the country's maritime economy.

8.5 Conclusions

Polish liner shipping has had long-standing connections with the liner conference system, ship-owners and shippers from various countries (Sawiczewska, 1986). The Polish shipping industry should build on this experience and concentrate on those sectors of the market which require high standards of organisation, quality, reliability and efficiency. This means that the industry must be constantly on the lookout for new ways of improving its services and management. These may be found in the vessels themselves, as well as in on-board management systems and in the professional skills of crews and staff ashore. Advantage must be taken of the possibilities offered by electronics and modern communications systems. These factors, together with the reconstruction of ownership of the shipping companies and changes in their management, bring new hope for future development of Polish shipping.

In general, Poland has come a long way towards opening her economy to foreign trade and, to a lesser extent, to foreign investment. Although

past political and military barriers have been removed, bureaucratic practices and conventional thinking, including fear of potential dominance of
foreign firms, remain. Poland's long history has been characterised by
harmful foreign domination, and it will take some time before there can
be a profound change in attitudes at all levels of Polish society. While
the open door principle appears to have been accepted, there is still
disagreement and considerable uncertainty about the speed and extent at
which to proceed. Nonetheless, the role of foreign trade and the
maritime economy which directly effects Poland's development will be
considerably enhanced.

9 Transport decentralisation in the Baltic states: the case of Estonia

Anu Kull

9.1 Introduction

This chapter discusses some of the problems connected with the decentralisation of Estonia's public transport. Its aim is to examine the most important features of this still evolving process.

Estonia is a small country with 1.5 million inhabitants, an overall population density of thirty-five persons per sq. km, with a rural density only ten per sq. km, and a dense road network. One reason for the latter is the nature of the settlement pattern. Estonia has been characterised by a dispersed population, which provided the basis for an extensive communication network. In addition to that, almost a third of the population is today concentrated in the capital, Tallinn, which is situated in the north-west of the country. Thus, the transportation links with neighbours to the east and south need to cross the whole territory. The main transport routes are Tallinn – Narva – St. Petersburg; Tallinn – Tartu – Moscow; and Tallinn – Pärnu – Riga, all having both road and rail connections (Figure 9.1).

During forty-five years of occupation, Estonia's economy was gradually integrated into that of the Soviet Union. Today political independence is being restored and the transition from a centrally planned economy to a market economy is going on. Crucial points of this development are: (a) the release of the Estonian economy and state apparatus from the Soviet state and economy; (b) a decentralisation of the economy as a whole. This process started simultaneously with 'perestroika' in the Soviet Union, but took on a more concrete form only after the attempted coup in Moscow in August 1991. The subsequent period has been spent on discussions over different ways to reach an independent economy.

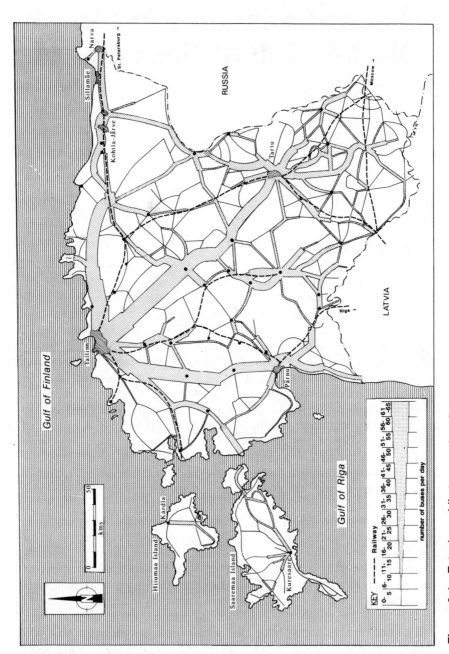

Figure 9.1 Estonia: public transport routes

Within this process of detachment from the immediate past, the country's public transport system is being decentralised and privatised. This is having to take place within the context of a deep economic crisis, although in June 1992 Estonia left the rouble-zone to establish its own currency, the Kroon (Crown). An energy crisis has also developed in relation to a decline of energy production and the transition to world-market prices in raw materials.

It is therefore difficult to provide a longer-term assessment of the processes of decentralisation and privatisation of public transport in Estonia in a context where, for example, routes are being closed in the short term due to a lack of fuel. Under these circumstances this chapter attempts to describe the general background to, and recent trends of, the decentralisation of Estonian public transport. But in so far as Estonia can be used as a general example of the transition from a centrally planned public transport system to a deregulated one, it is hoped that this overview will provide some understanding of the problems connected with the processes which face the peoples of the Baltic countries as well as the rest of Central and Eastern Europe today.

9.2 Special features of privatisation in Estonia

To begin with, the essence of the term 'privatisation' in the Estonian case should be specified because of its close connections with decentralisation. If we consider that the main difference between socialism and capitalism is in their attitudes towards private ownership, then privatisation is central in restructuring the economy. But at the same time the question of the method of privatising state property is unclear. There are three theoretical questions which need to be answered before the transport system is privatised. First, what is the value of the property which is going to be privatised? In the economy we have lived in, the term 'market value' was unknown; instead, the term 'balance value' was used. This denoted the value something had according to the rules of communist book-keeping. The balance value was not connected with supply and demand, and as it was calculated as an initial value minus amortisation, it was usually very low. The opening of the closed economic system gave the people who were inside it, and had access to information, an opportunity to buy (or rather to remove) state property extremely cheaply – for instance, for about 10 per cent of the market value. The consequences which arose from that situation are reflected in the way the former leading communists became leaders of the market economy. These problems are familiar not only in Estonia.

The second question which needs to be answered before privatising public transport concerns finance. With the current high rate of inflation, the monetary system does not function, although the country has now established its own monetary system. Further, during the conditions of socialist economy the accumulation of capital was at an extremely low level, so ways must also be found of privatising other than selling the property because there is no capital with which to buy it (except for the former 'nomenklatura', black marketeers and foreigners).

The third problem is related to the basis of statehood. In the case of Estonia the problem is a dilemma concerning the kind of state Estonia actually is: is it, (a) a state which became independent in the 1920s, was occupied by the Soviet Union in the 1940s and which remains occupied until Soviet troops have left the territory of Estonia? or is it, (b) a state created after the Second World War, which was called the Estonian Soviet Socialist Republic and which became independent in August 1991? The ideology of privatisation is principally different in those two cases. If we accept the latter viewpoint then we accept that the Supreme Soviet and today's government are legal state authorities. But if we accept the first point of view, then we have grounds to demand the dissolution of the parliament and can accuse the government of being illegal because they are nothing more than the tools of the occupying power. That is the essence of the question of Estonian statehood, in a slightly exaggerated form. When we discuss the ways of privatisation it becomes a dilemma: if we accept that Estonia today is a successor of the Estonian Soviet Socialist Republic, the state property will belong either to those who have the closest relationship to it or have money to buy it. But in the second case one must accept that forty-seven post-war years represented a period of occupation, and that accordingly the rights of prior owners must have priority.

9.3 Decentralisation of public transport

As no solution has yet been found to those central problems, the whole process of privatisation has barely started. In the case of public transport, only small private bus firms have so far been established. The actual privatisation of the bus companies and railways has yet to be discussed in Estonia.

Decentralisation of public transport has, however, begun and the strategy for its implementation has been more widely discussed. If we compare the discussion and the whole process in the Estonian case with that in developed market economies, we can find both common and contrasting features. The most important common feature is the need to introduce more commercial reasoning and a higher degree of competitiveness into the heavily subsidised public transport system. The contrasts mainly arise from the different roles of public transport and the different attitudes held towards it.

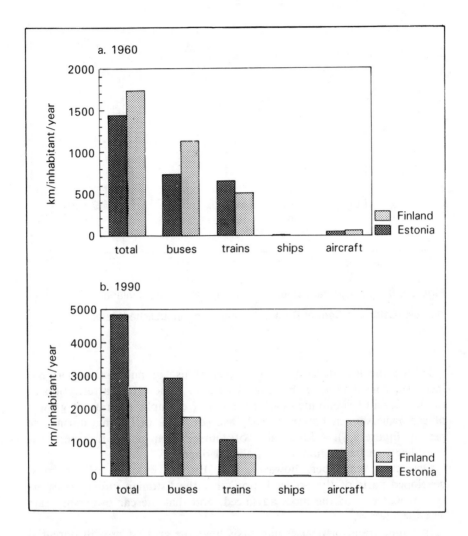

Figure 9.2   Estonia: comparison of use of public transport with Finland
Source: (Estonian) Central Bureau of Statistics, unpublished data.

Estonia has continued to experience a high level of public transport use. This can be clearly illustrated in comparison with Finland, for example (Figure 9.2). Finland today is, of course, much more developed economically than Estonia but Estonian economists are still accustomed to making comparisons with Finland because the two countries were at the same level of development before the Second World War. Looking at the differences now we can get a better understanding of the problems.

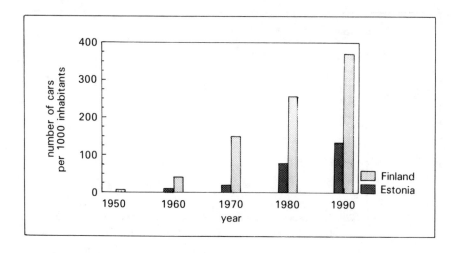

Figure 9.3   Estonia: car ownership – comparisons with Finland

Source: (Estonian) Central Bureau of Statistics, unpublished data.

During the last thirty years the level of use of public transport has increased considerably in Estonia. This is to some extent a reflection of the low level of economic development. For example, the rate of growth of car ownership in Finland clearly exceeded that of Estonia during the period (Figure 9.3). Additionally, of course, cheap public transport was considered to be an important political dogma.

One must remember, however, that Estonia was one of the most developed parts of the Soviet Union, that the Estonian public transport system was one of the most advanced, and that the car ownership rate was the highest.

In public transport, buses and taxis have the greatest growth potential because of the country's small territory and agglomerated population. The dominance of bus transport can be seen from the figures of total number of passenger and passenger-kilometres (Figure 9.4). The most remarkable change in the historical development of the structure of public transport has been the decline in importance of railways, most obviously seen when comparing network configurations of different periods of time (Figure 9.5). It can be seen that before the Second World War a dense network, consisting of narrow- and broad-gauge systems, was established. The most active building phase was between 1923 and 1939, in Estonia's period of independence. After 1950 a programme of rationalising the railway network took place. Through this process all narrow-gauge routes were closed and services were taken over by buses.

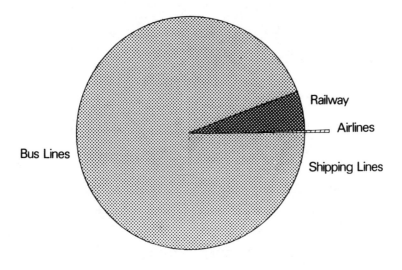

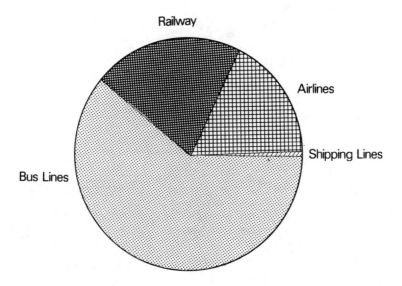

Figure 9.4 Estonia: share of public transport passengers by mode, 1989

Source: (Estonian) Central Bureau of Statistics, unpublished data.

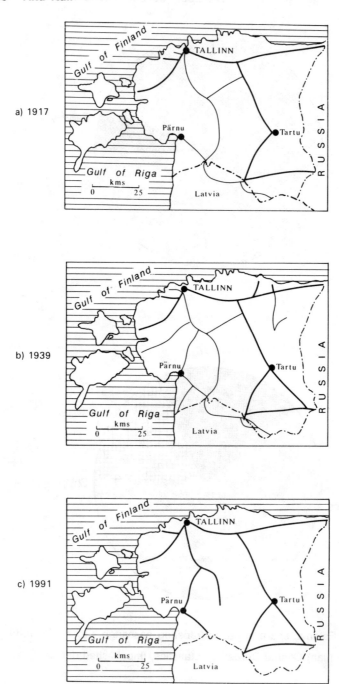

Figure 9.5 Estonia: evolving railway network

The first consideration for any decentralisation of the Estonian public transport system is its relatively developed network and large volume of users, with buses having the greatest load. The second consideration is the previous administrative character of the centralised transport system, which was seen merely as a part of that of the Soviet Union. It was most clearly expressed in the merchant navy and air transport systems, which belonged to two huge Soviet monopolies. The railway network was seen as a part of that of the three Baltic states, which was in turn a component of the Soviet all-union railway system. Only buses, trams and taxis were administered by Estonian authorities.

All public transport was managed according to the principles of a planned economy. It was accompanied by low fares and a lack of economic incentive for the operators. Further, bus purchase and repairs were very narrowly specialised. Most buses purchased in recent years have been produced in Hungary, which was also the only source of spare parts. This has rendered the transport system very vulnerable and has created several problems in maintaining service levels under current changing conditions.

Today, two approaches to the decentralisation of public transport are necessary. For the railway, merchant navy and air transport this requires establishing control over Estonian public transport and separating its administration from the all-union structure. As a general process this actually started some years ago, but only in 1991 was it possible to proceed more resolutely. The situation has advanced most in sea transport, where four competing companies now provide passenger services to Finland and Sweden.

In airline and railway administration the situation is somewhat more complicated. So far, only some international air routes have opened. Before 1989, when a service linking Tallinn with Helsinki was inaugurated, Estonian airports served only domestic routes, and the only legal way to cross the state border by air was either via Moscow or St. Petersburg. Within two years, three more air routes were opened, such that in addition to those to Helsinki, it is now possible to reach Stockholm, Budapest and Frankfurt-am-Main directly. These routes were initially served by Aeroflot, with Soviet equipment, but negotiations concerning renting or buying Western aircraft have been undertaken subsequently. At the same time, Aeroflot began closing down a great share of its domestic flights. It has been superseded by Estonian Air (see also Chapter 4). Similar problems faced the state railway system, where negotiations concerning the separation of the administration from the all-union were undertaken.

In the field of taxi transport, privatisation has already taken place. Private 'taxis' have operated since 1988, when individuals were permitted to use their own cars as taxis; some joined small firms. Later, the country's largest taxi-company was privatised by competitive tender.

Table 9.1 Estonia: income and expenditure of bus operators (in million roubles)

Year	Income	Expenditure
1970	28.8	22.1
1975	31.9	27.1
1980	35.4	38.1
1985	37.0	45.7
1990	39.0	51.3

Source: Central Bureau of Statistics, Tallinn, unpublished data.

9.4 Case study: bus transport

The problems connected with the decentralisation of public transport can be most clearly seen in the case of bus transport. Currently, there are fourteen bus companies, all owned by the state. In 1990 there were about 2,200 buses in total, 74 per cent of which were actually in use. The financial situation of the bus companies revealed an increasing deficit during the previous ten years (Table 9.1). At the same time service provision was constantly increasing (Table 9.2). This was possible only with a relatively high level of subsidies. Today on average 58 per cent of costs are covered from sources other than fare income.

Table 9.2 Estonia: public bus use (in million passenger–kilometres)

Year	Inter-urban	Urban, suburban	Total
1950	49	73	122
1955	166	222	388
1960	437	449	886
1965	682	835	1,517
1970	1,130	1,480	2,610
1975	1,329	1,820	3,149
1980	1,543	2,115	3,658
1985	1,737	2,542	4,279
1990	1,829	2,687	4,516

Source: Central Bureau of Statistics, Tallinn, unpublished data.

There have been two types of subsidy – for passengers and for operators. The subsidising of passengers meant that certain social groups, such as veterans of the Second World War and students, were given fare discounts. But the price difference was paid by the transport operators, not by the authorities responsible for the social policy. At the same time operators also cross-subsidised. Bus companies have been concerned not only with scheduled passenger services, but with other types of passenger services and with the transport of goods. Usually, the latter have been profitable and able to subsidise loss-making scheduled passenger services.

Such manipulations have never been reflected in statistics, and it is thus almost impossible to provide a detailed picture of the level and allocation of subsidies. Service availability was negotiated between local authorities and bus companies. In addition to scheduled routes there were also those organised by enterprises to transport their employees and their children. Mostly operated in rural areas, these were not registered in official statistics and it is difficult to estimate their share of all bus services. Nonetheless, in providing transport for a significant proportion of rural work and school journeys, they acted as a very effective addition to the scheduled services.

In summary, there has been little commercial interest in operating bus services hitherto, due not only to the general character of public bus transport but also to the system of financing it. But in spite of that, or perhaps because of it, a dense network of bus routes with a relatively high level of services was created. Although the comfort of travel has not always been the best, considering the low level of fares, it has been adequate.

9.5 Conclusions

With the transition to a market economy the former principles of passenger transport regulation will inevitably change. A restructuring of the financing system is well advanced. New principles of managing the public bus transport system have been established, according to which the main responsibility for organising bus services has been given to local authorities (at the county level). A new system of licensing has also been established. The authorities who can grant licenses for operating a route at county level are municipalities, and at the state or international level the Ministry of Communications and Transport is vested with appropriate authority. Licences are, in principle, obtainable just by registering the planned service. Operators are free to choose routes and the questions of fares and schedules are negotiated with the authorities. However, because of the national economic difficulties there have been few applicants.

What is going to happen in the longer term is almost impossible to foresee. First the high rate of inflation and the energy crisis are over-shadowing and foreclosing longer-term thinking. The extent to which an independent and capitalist Estonia will be able to maintain the previous level of services and density of transport network is a question left virtually undiscussed. The policy of future subsidisation is now also open to question, and calculations on the profitability of different routes have only just begun. While decentralisation and privatisation of most commercial services are at the top of the restructuring agenda, public transport, as an essentially 'non-commercial' activity, has a low priority, as it is seen as unlikely to return quick or large profits.

10 The role of transport in the development of rural Romania

David Turnock

10.1 Introduction

Any survey of this kind must be tentative, because the new rural land-scape is still in embryonic form and the privatisation of transport is also in its early stages. Some changes have occurred in the provision of services, notably through the increase in rail and bus links between eastern Transylvania and Hungary (laid on to facilitate travel for Romania's largest ethnic minority). But broad assessments of future trends must be based very heavily on the legacy of the old regime. These are the foundations on which any modified transport geography must inevitably rest. Two themes will be explored in this chapter. First the aberrations of socialist investment policy are highlighted, with particular reference to the neglect of road transport during the later years of the 'Ceauşescu Epoch' in favour of developments on the railways and rivers. Railway investment has highlighted electrification (which amounted to only 166 km in 1970 but increased to 2,377 km in 1980 and 3,654 in 1989) but there has also been some enlargement of the rail system, especially in areas where construction in the pre-socialist period was relatively restrained. Nevertheless the ratio between the route-length of railways and roads (also between electrified railways and modernised roads) varies substantially between regions and counties: this could be significant in terms of comparative advantage if modal differences in the cost and efficiency of transport are heightened under privatisation. The second theme emphasises the comprehensive nature of lines of communication even in the sparsely-settled mountain areas. The tradi-tional seasonal rhythm of pastoral activity, followed by the commercial activity of the foresters, has opened up the Carpathian region and provided a substantial potential for tourism which could be exploited under privatisation. Although large investments will obviously depend on a fully-modernised transport infrastructure, there are many opportunities for small-scale labour-intensive developments making use of the existing facilities. This point will be explored with forest transport especially in mind.

10.2 Investment in transport under socialism

Developments under socialism were quite conventional during the early post-war period (Mellor, 1975). At a conference in 1945 the communists gave rail transport prime importance for the development of the national economy, and this priority was reasserted after the party came to power in 1948. A study carried out in 1953 in connection with the 'New Course', following Stalin's death, decided against further expansion of the network but anticipated increases in capacity through widening, dieselisation and electrification (Lupşe, 1954). However, Romania took an independent course through selecting western designs for main-line diesel and electric locomotives. Domestic air services connected Bucharest with the main provincial cities and bus services increased in the rural areas, although they complemented the rail services and were relatively sparse in areas like Banat, where a particularly well-developed rail network existed (a legacy of the pre-1918 Hungarian administration in this area) (Botez *et al.*, 1977: Popescu, 1987). The planners applied the concept of a unitary transport system to avoid unnecessary duplication between different transport modes (Pop, 1984: Turbut, 1981). Industrial development was tied very heavily to the large towns which were regional administrative centres (county centres after 1968), and although this permitted the growth of large cities in backward regions it did little for the rural areas (Moldovan, 1964: Rausser, 1977). Until the 1968 reforms there were nearly 200 districts forming a second tier of local government. But although many of the administrative centres were villages or small towns lacking road access, their industrial growth was restrained and some small projects initiated in the early 1950s were later relocated (Turnock, 1991a) (Figure 10.1). Road transport assumed an important feeder role, but major industrial developments remained tied to the railway network.

Road transport was given greater attention in the 1970s. Many main roads (and some district roads) were fully modernised (or given a light tarmac surface) and this proved useful not only for domestic traffic but for international tourism. Motorways on the German model were proposed as early as 1938, in the shape of an 'Aorta României' running from Bucharest to Braşov, Tîrgu Mureş, Dej and Satu Mare (convenient for journeys to Berlin and Vienna), complemented by several transverse routes (Manoilescu, 1938). A further plan was described in 1972 (Herbst-Rădoi, 1972). But there has been no construction since the 113-km

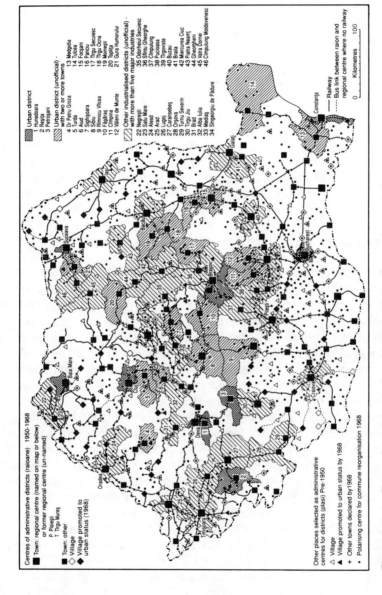

Figure 10.1 Romania: aspects of regional development under socialism

Bucharest–Piteşti autostrada built between 1969 and 1972. There is virtually no dual carriageway and the only other major extensions to the national road network have been the opening of the Danube road bridge near Hîrşova (Giurgeni–Vadu Oii) in 1970, and 'Transfăgărașanul' in 1974: a 95-km highway crossing the Făgăraş Mountains with a summit tunnel at 2,025 m. It should also be noted that the Iron Gates hydropower and navigation project (inaugurated in 1972) included an international frontier crossing for vehicles between Romania and Yugoslavia; while the duplication of the Danube railway bridge between Cernavodă and Feteşti in 1987 included a deck for motor vehicles, so providing a road link between the two towns.

Production of motor vehicles developed from tractor and lorry plants in Braşov (1946 and 1954 respectively) and the production of cross-country vehicles at Cîmpulung in 1957, to car production in the 1970s. There was cooperation with Renault to build the UAP (Uzina de Autoturisme) at Piteşti-Colibaşi in 1967–8, and the production of the Dacia 1300 model began in 1970. This was followed in 1976 by collaboration with Citroën in 1976 in respect of the Oltcit factory at Craiova which was built between 1977 and 1982 with the first cars produced in the latter year. The 1970s was thus a time of reappraisal for road transport, with some modest increase in the level of car ownership. But the momentum was not maintained.

The neglect of road transport in favour of the railways was very evident during the last years of the Ceauşescu period. Tables 10.1 and 10.2 show the trends during the 1970s and 1980s for passenger and freight traffic, considering both the numbers of passengers (or tonnes of freight) and passenger-kilometres (or tonne-kilometres). Plainly rail and road transport together dominate on the domestic front: although overseas shipping makes a significant impression on the total picture for freight, aircraft, river boats and pipelines are of very limited importance. However, the relative importance of rail and road has been changing. Numbers of rail passengers increased by 52.8 per cent during the 1970s and by 38.5 per cent during the 1980s (passenger-kilometres by 30.5 and 52.7 per cent respectively). Yet after the number of road passengers increased much more rapidly – by 187.6 per cent – during the 1970s (205.6 per cent for passenger-kilometres), there was a decline of 15.0 per cent during the 1980s (3.1 in the case of passenger-kilometres). This reflects a switch from buses to metro services in Bucharest, but it also points to a general decline in bus services because of fuel shortages. Freight road transport did experience growth in the 1980s: 28.7 per cent for tonnage and 8.3 per cent for tonne-kilometres; though it was way below the level of 123.5 per cent (114.7 for tonne-kilometres) for the 1970s. However, both sets are higher than for rail transport: 60.2 per cent (57.3) during the 1970s and 11.7 per cent (7.4) during the 1980s.

This situation should be considered alongside data showing the extent

Table 10.1 Romania: passenger transport, 1970–89

	1970				1980				1989			
	A	B	C	D	A	B	C	D	A	B	C	D
Total	0.69	100.0	26.7	100.0	1.39	100.0	50.1	100.0	1.36	100.0	62.4	100.0
Rail	0.33	47.6	17.8	66.5	0.35	25.1	23.2	46.3	0.48	35.2	35.5	56.8
Road	0.36	52.0	7.9	29.4	1.03	74.6	24.0	47.9	0.88	64.4	23.1	37.0
River	–	0.3	–	0.4	–	0.1	–	0.2	–	0.1	–	0.1
Air	–	0.1	1.0	3.7	–	0.1	2.8	5.6	–	0.3	3.8	6.1

A Passengers (billion)
B Percentage share
C Passenger-kms (billion)
D Percentage share

Sources: Comisia Nationala de Statistica, 1971, 1981, 1990.

LIVERPOOL HOPE UNIVERSITY COLLEGE

Table 10.2 Romania: freight transport, 1970–89

	1970				1980				1989			
	A	B	C	D	A	B	C	D	A	B	C	D
Total	1,030	100.0	101.6	100.0	2,203	100.0	191.1	100.0	2,826	100.0	270.9	100.0
I	171	16.6	48.0	47.3	274	12.5	75.5	39.5	306	10.8	81.1	29.9
II	840	81.6	12.9	12.7	1,877	85.2	27.7	14.6	2,416	85.5	30.0	11.1
III	3	0.3	1.3	1.3	12	0.6	2.3	1.2	37	1.3	3.7	1.4
IV	4	0.4	37.5	36.9	16	0.7	80.3	42.0	36	1.3	149.4	55.1
V	11	1.1	1.8	1.8	22	1.0	5.1	2.7	30	1.1	6.7	2.5

A Goods transported (billion tonnes)
B Percentage share
C Goods transported (billion tonnes/km)
D Percentage share
I Rail; II Road; III River; IV Sea; V Air

Source: Comisia Nationala de Statistica, 1990.

of the rail and road systems. Table 10.3 deals with networks at the national, regional and county levels. Electrified railways and surfaced roads are highlighted in addition to the length of all railways and roads; changes during the 1980s are also shown. It reveals that the railway network has grown by 2.1 per cent while the road network has declined by 0.7 per cent (an anomaly which arises from changes in responsibility for maintenance rather than because of outright abandonment). While the modernised roads have increased by 12.5 per cent, the electrified railways have grown much faster: by 54.4 per cent. Some disparity also occurred in the 1970s: the railway system grew by 0.9 per cent while road length declined by 3.3 per cent; and electrified railways increased 14.3 times compared with an increase of 31.8 per cent in the length of modernised roads. Although the data are limited there is enough evidence to suggest that road transport has been restrained because of the state's preference for rail transport. It has also been revealed that 58 per cent of the total length of modernised roads has passed the time stipulated for overhaul and is in a worn-out state. This deficiency also applies to 68 per cent of the 20,500 kilometres of roads with a light tarmac cover (which are additional to the 16,400 km of fully modernised roads) (National Commission for Statistics, 1991, p. 43).

Like other aspects of Ceauşescu's modernisation strategy the discrimination was never acknowledged or justified. But road improvements (and rising levels of car ownership) may well have been associated with individualism, whereas rail transport may have appeared more appropriate at a time when Ceauşescu evidently favoured greater equality and homogeneity. With the economic crisis deepened by the self-imposed burden of foreign debt repayments, the limited investments in traffic were geared to increasing capacities on the railways and extending the scope of the network through branches to towns which had no service (Ianoş, 1982; Turnock, 1987). In addition to the lignite-carrying lines of Oltenia, railways were built to Siret and Tîrgu Neamt in Moldavia; and a branch from Dîngeni to Săveni and Darabani was under construction when the 1989 revolution occurred (Creţu, 1985; Opris, 1987). The Moldavian railways were heavily used by commuters travelling to work in the larger towns like Bacău, Galaţi and Iaşi (Apăvăloaei and Lupu-Bratiloveanu, 1981). Such projects can be justified only by a primitive notion of a national economy with all major components (urban settlements and large enterprises) served directly by the rail network; and with road transport restricted to a local feeder role. This scenario may be extended to include river navigation, which Ceauşescu also supported through the completion of the Danube–Black Sea Canal, the commencement of operations for the Bucharest–Danube Canal, and the initiation of a water transfer scheme between the Siret and the Bărăgan Plain which was expected to mark the first stage in the canalisation of the Siret (Turnock, 1986). Few of Romania's 260 towns

Table 10.3 Romania: rail and road systems by counties, 1980–89

County/Region	Railways					Roads					Ratios	
	A	B	C	D	E	A	B	C	D	E	F	G
ROMANIA	11,343	233	3,654	1,277	47.8	72,816	−548	16,435	1,821	30.7	6.4	4.5
CENTRE	1,405	26	637	377	51.7	7,551	−23	1,867	168	27.2	5.4	2.9
Alba	315	10	148	148	50.6	1,972	20	391	51	31.6	6.2	2.6
Brașov	333		166	72	62.2	1,348	−16	395	7	25.2	4.0	2.4
Covasna	115		46		31.0	810	1	207	48	21.9	7.0	4.5
Hunedora	333	15	229	109	47.5	1,936	−31	554	56	27.6	5.8	2.4
Sibiu	309	1	48	48	57.0	1,485	3	320	5	27.4	4.8	6.7
NORTH	1,722	10	468	168	48.7	9,944	4	2,318	349	28.1	5.8	5.0
Bistrița	365		88	1	68.8	1,304	13	295	104	24.6	3.6	3.4
Cluj	259		129	119	38.9	2,447	5	498	47	36.8	9.4	3.9
Harghita	213	11	165	2	32.2	1,448	34	387	26	21.9	6.8	2.3
Maramureș	232				37.3	1,494	−17	481	69	24.0	6.4	*
Mureș	477	−1	86	40	71.2	1,846	−22	406	24	27.6	3.9	4.7
Sălaj	176				45.7	1,405	−9	251	69	36.5	8.0	*
NORTH-EAST	1,481	55	532	332	40.3	12,696	18	2,568	360	34.5	8.6	4.8
Bacău	226		191	5	34.2	2,301	2	510	55	34.8	10.2	2.7
Botoșani	142				28.6	1,824	54	338	27	36.7	12.8	*
Iași	284	8	127	127	51.9	2,334	−36	384	88	42.7	8.2	3.0
Neamț	134	22	46	34	22.8	1,810	−62	431	46	30.7	13.5	9.4
Suceava	445	21	168	168	52.0	2,329	33	593	52	27.2	5.2	3.5
Vaslui	250	4			47.2	2,098	24	312	92	39.6	8.4	*

Table 10.3 contd.

County/Region	Railways					Roads					Ratios	
	A	B	C	D	E	A	B	C	D	E	F	G
SOUTH-EAST	3,313	90	223	1,056	46.2	21,838	−461	4,865	352	30.5	6.6	4.6
Argeş	225	7			33.1	2,660	−98	555	80	39.1	11.8	*
Brăila	168		119	126	35.6	1,150	−2	202	−15	24.3	6.8	1.6
Bucharest	322	12	9	152	176.9	779	133	365	43	42.8	2.4	2.4
Buzău	232	4	25	108	38.2	2,056	123	307	13	33.9	8.9	2.8
Călăraşi	243	43	47	151	47.9	1,102	28	366	43	21.7	4.5	2.4
Constanţa	392	22	12	77	55.6	2,272	−4	507	3	32.2	5.8	6.6
Dîmboviţa	172	−7		7	42.6	1,736	−38	397	33	43.0	10.1	56.7
Galaţi	291	1	22	22	65.8	1,412	−52	238	12	31.9	4.9	10.8
Giurgiu	113	−19	−2	32	32.2	1,042	−85	327	15	29.7	9.2	10.2
Ialomiţa	276	17	20	50	62.0	1,102	−67	336	3	24.8	4.0	6.7
Prahova	348	2	−9	163	74.1	2,024	−93	477	3	43.1	5.8	2.9
Teleorman	294	9	3	73	51.0	1,431	−71	301	26	24.8	4.9	4.1
Tulcea	68				8.1	1,183	16	186	15	14.0	17.4	*
Vrancea	169	−1	6	102	34.8	1,889	−153	301	78	38.8	11.2	3.0
SOUTH-WEST	1,011	79	70	487	34.7	9,951	−40	2,270	192	34.1	9.8	4.7
Dolj	221	−2	−5	74	29.8	2,116	−65	470	47	28.5	9.6	6.4
Gorj	264	37	80	225	46.8	1,886	26	582	63	33.4	7.1	2.6
Mehedinţi	129		−5	124	26.3	1,878	45	370	89	38.3	14.6	3.0
Olt	233			64	42.3	2,043	−32	343	59	37.1	8.8	5.4
Vîlcea	164	42			28.7	2,028	66	505	134	35.5	12.4	*

Table 10.3 contd.

County/Region	Railways					Roads					Ratios	
	A	B	C	D	E	A	B	C	D	E	F	G
WEST	2,311	−125	110	467	63.8	10,836	−123	2,547	200	29.5	4.7	5.5
Arad	485	−35	93	196	63.4	2,087	−51	478	22	27.3	4.3	2.4
Bihor	474	7			62.9	2,491	−58	573	21	33.1	5.3	*
Caras-Sev.	267	−103	12	160	43.2	1,889	−18	695	30	22.2	7.1	4.3
Satu Mare	298				67.7	1,511	7	280	31	34.3	5.1	*
Timiş	787	6	5	111	90.5	2,858	−2	521	95	32.9	3.6	4.7

A Length in km
B Change 1980–89
C Length of electrified railways/surfaced roads
D Change 1980–89
E Kilometres of railway per thousand square kilometres of territory/road per hundred square kilometres of territory
F Kilometres of road per kilometre of railway
G Kilometres of modernised road per kilometre of electrified railway
* Unofficial micro-regions as used in the author's previous researches (Turnock, 1991a, p. 321)

Sources: Comisia Nationala de Statistica, 1981, 1990.

lie more than five kilometres from a railway line or from navigable water, and further rail construction was contemplated to deal with some of these cases (Banister, 1981; Iacob, 1987). Almost all of the twenty-three new towns promoted in 1989 under the 'sistematizare' programme enjoyed good rail access and the entire rural development programme may well have been geared to a radical consolidation of settlements (reducing the villages from some 13,100 to between 5,000 and 6,000, including some 550 additional towns) linked as closely as possible with an ideologically-appropriate transport system.

While this scenario must be to some extent speculative, it is well known that Ceauşescu was committed to the building of socialism in the most literal sense, and eccentric schemes of social engineering were widely feared by the Romanian people as a sequel to the paying-off of foreign debts. The new Romania, which is energetically re-establishing its links with the rest of Europe, therefore faces the problem of road improvements to a greater extent than other Central and East European countries. Further motorways will have to be considered as a matter of urgency and it is likely that the Bucharest–Piteşti autostrada will be extended eastwards to Constanţa and north-westwards along the Olt valley and into Transylvania. But it will be a long time before the quality of the road system and the level of ownership of motor vehicles approaches Western levels. Foreign investment may become limited to places with motorway access and all forms of investment in rural areas may be conditioned by the quality of the rail tracks and road surfaces. At present there are great variations in the balance between the two systems. Over the whole country there are 6.4 km of roads for every kilometre of railway; but lower figures of 4.7 km in the West, 5.4 km in the Centre and 5.8 km in the North (compared with 6.6 km in the South-east, 8.6 km in the North-east and 9.8 km in the South-west) highlight the historic contrast between the 'Old Kingdom' (pre-1918 Romania) and the former Habsburg provinces. When individual countries are considered, the contrasts are widened further. Apart from the figure of 2.4 km for Bucharest all the lowest values fall to the post-1918 provinces: 2.4 km for Arad (West), 3.6 km for Bistriţa (North) and Timiş (West), 3.9 km for Mureş (North) and 4.0 km for Braşov (Centre). Meanwhile the highest figures concern parts of the Old Kingdom: 12.4 km for Vîlcea (South-west), 12.8 km for Botoşani (North-east), 13.5 km for Neamţ (North-east), 14.6 km for Mehedinţi (South-west) and 17.4 km for Tulcea (South-east). However, the historical legacy is not so clear when the ratio of surfaced roads to electrified railways is considered: across the country there are 4.5 kilometres of surfaced road for each kilometre of electrified railway. But the lowest figures fall to the Centre (2.9 km) followed by the South-east (4.6 km), the South-west (4.7 km) and the North-east (4.8 km): the highest values fall to the North (5.0 km) and West (5.5 km). This is confirmed by reference to individual counties with 1.6 km for Brăila (South-east), 2.3 km for Harghita (North); and 2.4 km for Braşov (Centre), Bucharest (South-east), Călăraşi (South-east) and Hunedoara (Centre) – compared with nine countries with no electrified railway whatsoever: Argeş (South-east), Bihor (West), Botoşani (North-east), Maramureş (North), Sălaj (North), Satu Mare (West), Tulcea (South-east), Vaslui (North-east) and Vîlcea (South-west). These variations may be academic for the moment, but if variations in cost and efficiency emerge they could affect local economic potentials across the countryside, a possibility which will be examined through further rural research (Turnock, 1992).

10.3 Rural accessibility: the Carpathian forests

Although the quality of Romanian transport may be generally indifferent by European standards, the availability of access routes to all parts of the country is an asset which should favour small-scale labour-intensive rural development concerned with the intensification of agriculture and the growth of tourism. The density of population is just below the European average (97 persons per sq. km compared with 101), yet unsurfaced roads and tracks are available throughout the arable lands and adjacent meadows and pastures; and they also extend to the mountain grazings far removed from permanent settlements. The Carpathians have been fully occupied by the peasantry for centuries and are readily accessible through a remarkably comprehensive system of paths and trackways. The development of modern communications was relatively slow because the main Carpathian watershed comprised one of the most durable of international frontiers, undermined only by Romania's annexation of the Habsburg territories already referred to. At that time there was only a limited number of railways and roads crossing the mountains. Most local roads went no further than the limits of permanent settlement. However, the commercial exploitation of the forests required transport facilities and over the years modern communications have been provided along all the major valleys (Giurescu, 1980). Far more investment in essentially rural transport has gone to the Carpathian area during this century than other sections of the Romanian countryside. Furthermore, the need for better inter-regional linkages between Transylvania and the provinces of the pre-1918 Romanian state (Moldavia and Wallachia) has meant that further connections across the watersheds have been made. Hence the scope for rapid penetration of the mountains has been greatly increased. This reduces the isolation of mountain communities and increases the potential for private investment (Turnock, 1990; 1991b).

10.3.1 Forest transport before the Second World War

The commercial exploitation of Carpathian forests was very limited until the development of a main-line railway network. The navigable rivers were used for floating timber (sometimes in the form of rafts) and the traffic was particularly significant along the (Moldavian) Bistriţa and Siret to Galaţi on the Danube; and by the Mureş of Tisa to the Pannonian Plain (in the latter case cargoes of salt were carried from Transylvania) (Anania, 1900; Engli, 1940). The railways opened the prospect of large-scale transfers of timber to Central Europe, and foreign capital was therefore invested to establish sawmills at railheads convenient for the exploitation of each Carpathian basin. The relatively short hauls from the forests to the sawmills were accomplished in a variety of ways, including the traditional method of floating (assisted by dams on the rivers or by artificial canals) and the use of animal haulage in conjunction with plankways, railways or lubricated chutes (Opletal, 1913). However, narrow-gauge railways using steam locomotives were found to be most satisfactory. They catered for all types of timber (beechwood was too heavy to float) and could handle large quantities of material at all times of year. Over the years many forest railway systems were built, although not all were operating simultaneously (Turnock, 1991c).

Most operations were concerned with a single drainage basin, and timber transport involved a simple downstream journey. However, where very steep gradients were involved it was sometimes impossible to extend a railway to the highest part of a valley and so tap the fir and spruce trees lying beyond the beech forests. Under these circumstances it was less expensive to extend lines of communication across the watersheds and exploit timber in adjacent basins by means of funiculars or inclined planes (Burghelea, 1941). Timber from the highest part of the Lotru Valley (above the gorges) was taken by funicular to the Sadu Valley (with rail access to the sawmill of Tălmaciu) while wood below the Lotru gorges was carried downstream to the sawmill at Brezoi. The most remarkable arrangements, however, applied to Vrancea: the very long hauls from the main railway line (serving Rîmnicu Sărat, Focşani and Mărăşeşti) to the rich spruce forests of the Giurgiu, Goru and Lăcăuţ mountains meant that railways in Transylvania (serving Covasna and Comandău) were extended over the watershed to the Năruja and Zăbala valleys of Vrancea (Lacriteanu *et al.*, 1987–8) (Figure 10.2). These arrangements date back to the years before 1914, and demonstrate that close coordination of woodcutting was possible on both sides of what was then an international frontier. Further connections were made across watersheds with the closure of the forest railway from Mărăşeşti to Lepşa around 1930: funiculars extended into the upper reaches of the Putna basin from Caşin in Moldavia and Tîrgu Secuiesc in Transylvania.

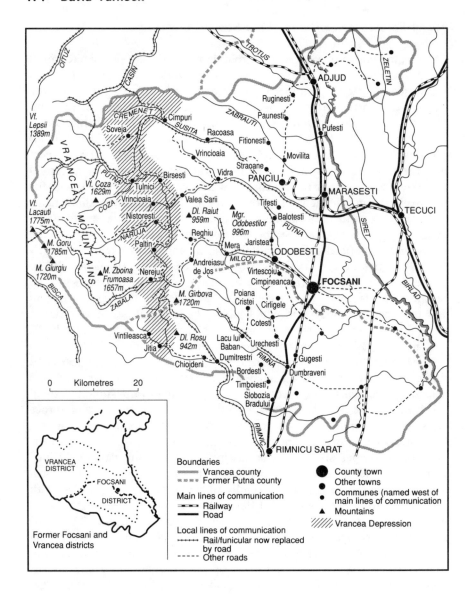

Figure 10.2   Romania: the Vrancea Depression – changing transport arrangements

Plate 10.1   A typical forest railway scene: Riusor on the Stilpeni system north of Pitești. The woodyard is situated at a point of contact between rail and road transport. Timber is sorted and there is some processing, including charcoal burning (note the conical heap at the top right). (David Turnock)

10.3.2 The transition to road transport

The introduction of motor vehicles in considerable numbers during the 1930s suggested that forest roads would ultimately be the best way of solving the problem of inaccessibility and enabling the working of the entire Carpathian forest on a sustained yield basis (Sburlan, 1938; Timiş, 1962). New technology to utilise the beechwood (much of which had previously been used only for firewood) helped to rationalise transport within each basin (Bereziuc *et al.*, 1958). There were already 1,150 kms of forest roads in Romania in 1948 but the earmarking of Romanian oil for the Soviet Union (as war reparations) meant a renewed rail programme in the 1950s when nationalisation of the forests brought large-scale commercial exploitation to all the Carpathian valleys (Manoiliu, 1959; Bălănescu and Tatomir, 1959). By the late 1950s, however, radical change was on the way (Marin, 1966). There was now more oil for the domestic economy and a new generation of timber lorries was available; moreover, the decision to undertake more sophisticated processing at large wood industrialisation complexes meant longer hauls from the forests which could only be accomplished by rail with a break of bulk between narrow-gauge and standard-gauge. Road building, related to the needs of each district woodcutting enterprise, has been persistent over the last three decades and most railways disappeared by 1970. Particularly radical change occurred in Vrancea where the 'export' of timber from what was then the Galaţi region to the neighbouring regions of Bacău, Braşov and Ploieşti was curtailed under a road-building programme to feed the timber down-valley to a new processing combine based in Focşani. This plan was then activated by the county administration in Focşani after 1968 and the reorientation was completed during the 1970s (Ielenicz, 1971; Stan and Pasoi-Barco, 1964). However, the subsequent rise in world oil prices prompted a decision to retain those railways still available and they continue to operate (Hofmeister, 1986).

10.3.3 The significance of forest transport

Although intended primarily to expedite the handling of timber, the forest transport is of considerable importance in 'humanising' the Carpathians (Giurcăneanu, 1988). It simplifies the deployment of forest workers, both the silviculturists who live permanently in the forests, within each 'canton', and the woodcutters who usually stay in dormitories in the forest during the week and return to their villages at the weekend. It has led to all-year occupation of some formerly temporary settlements. And, within zones of permanent settlement, forest transport often provided an official public service (for example between Tîrgu Jiu, Tismana and Apa Neagră) before the introduction of a bus service (Peto, 1937). Forests close to the frontier railways and roads have a strategic significance, enabling the military to reach barracks established to provide accommodation for frontier patrols. And the network of forest roads has also been important in connection with prospecting for minerals and surveying for hydro-electric schemes. Miscellaneous items of freight can be handled: thus mica from the Lotru valley could be taken by pack ponies to Voineasa and transferred to the forest railway, ultimately reaching the main-line railway at Brezoi. In some cases, railways no longer required by the district woodcutting organisations have been taken over for other industrial purposes. The Topliţa–Borsec line is now used to transport mineral water, and the line from Băbeni along the valley of the (Oltenian) Bistriţa is now used to take limestone from the Arnota quarry to the chemical plants of Govora and Rîmnicu Vîlcea.

A major ancillary role lies in tourism (Paladian, 1967). Forest railways were useful to some extent, although limited capacity and uncertainty over scheduling meant that only a small number of intrepid travellers

Plate 10.2 Voineasa in the Lotru Valley in the heart of the Southern Carpathians. This is an old centre of woodcutting transformed into a substantial resort through the development of the forest road network (replacing the original railway) and a major hydro-electric project. (David Turnock)

used the trains to reach hunting chalets in the mountains. Silviculture has been traditionally associated with wildlife conservation, and hunting is regulated through a network of lodges accessible by forest roads and railway. Hunting has been an important foreign-currency earner in recent years. The harshest measures were taken to eliminate casual hunting in order to maintain stocks for the tourist industry and also for the late president (for whose benefit selected animals were retained by regular feeding and chalets maintained in readiness). However, the extensive road network (which is generally open without formality) is now an excellent means of access for all who wish to enjoy remote mountain country (with opportunities for camping or chalet accommodation) (Mocanu, 1970). Vehicles built for unsurfaced roads can operate on the principal forest roads without difficulty during the summer months, although cars built for western roads would admittedly face problems. Forest road building has also created new possibilities for the extension of the public highway system. The Vrancea funiculars which once crossed the Caşin-Cremenet and Putna-Covasna watersheds have been replaced

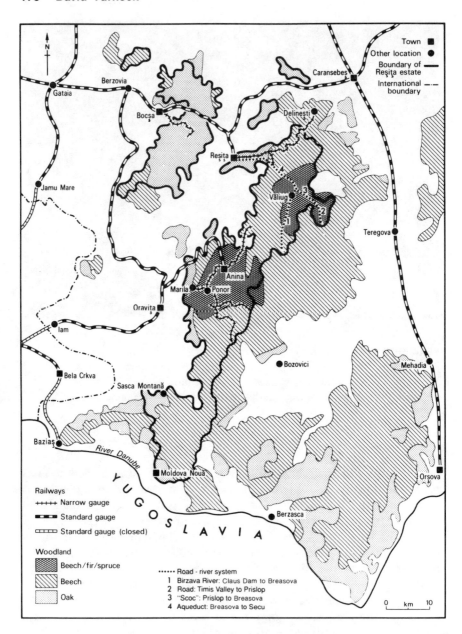

Figure 10.3 Romania: the STEG/UDR estates in the Reşiţa and Anina area.

by roads which now afford direct access between Braşov, Covasna, the Vrancea Depression and the Trotuş Valley. One of the more prominent conservational controversies before the revolution of 1989 was the proposal to link the Jiu, Motru and Cerna valleys: this would also have given a direct connection between Petroşani, Băile Herculane and the Iron Gates. The idea was opposed (successfully) by naturalists wishing to restrict access to the Retezat National Park and it is likely that proposals for new forest roads will be even more carefully scrutinised in future.

10.3.4 A case study: Reşiţa

From the eighteenth century the Habsburg Empire took great interest in the timber and mineral resources of the Banat. An iron furnace was lit at Reşiţa in 1771 and this metallurgical enterprise (owned until the First World War by the Austro-Hungarian company STEG: Staatseisen-bahngesellschaft) managed extensive woodlands around Văliug in the Anina and Semenic Mountains (Păsărica, 1935) (Figure 10.3). Some minor works were put in hand to regularise the Bîrzava, for there were 'greble' (dams) installed at Reşiţa, Cîlnic and Bocşa when timber was first taken from the Semenic Mountains to the Danube in 1785 (though the system was not successful and had to be given up in favour of horse traction in 1803). At the local level, however, timber was floated downstream to Reşiţa with the aid of the Claus barrage (above Văliug), built in 1865 and repaired in 1894. Soon after this the complete canalisation of the river between Văliug and Reşiţa was undertaken in association with the generation of hydro-electricity (to supplement the first thermal stations built at Anina and Reşiţa from the 1880s). The Grebla station was opened on the eastern edge of Reşiţa in 1904, but proximity to the plant (avoiding long-distance transmission of power) combined with an adequate head of water was only achieved by means of a ten-kilometre aqueduct. This was a major piece of engineering, since the crossing of tributary valleys required six tunnels (with a combined length of five kilometres) and five metal bridges with a total length of 700 m. In 1916 a second hydro-power station was built above the origin of the aqueduct at Breasova, where a 12.6-ha storage lake was impounded. These waterworks were also useful for the transport of timber from the Upper Bîrzava to Reşiţa.

Where timber had to be taken down a steep mountainside it was useful to instal a dry canal in the form of a wooden tube but more usually a chute or trough (known in the area as a 'scoc'), so that trunks would slide down in a controlled manner (with the assistance of grease or water) to a stockpile at the riverside (Malaesescu, 1938). These installations were temporary or permanent depending on the level of production. The 'scoc' from Prislop in the Semenic Mountains to the Bîrzava at Crainicel formed part of the supply system for Reşiţa. The Semenic funicular (1909–1932) was also installed to bring timber from the Timiş Valley to the top end of the Prislop 'scoc'. Extraction of timber was also expedited by narrow-gauge railways from Reşiţa to Secu (1873) and Delineşti (1911), which were used for coal and manganese respectively, as well as timber. The railhead of Anina, with its coal mines, iron furnace and power station, was connected with the Paulasca and the Caras Valley between 1908 and 1911, with an extension to Mindrisaga in 1915.

During the inter-war years the integration of forestry with mining and metallurgy continued through the ownership of large estates in the area by the Romanian company UDR (Uzine de Fier şi Domeniilor din Reşiţa) and some further narrow-gauge railways were reported in the 1920s (notably the Plesiva and Racasdiana extensions to the Anina system in 1925). Although the significance of timber in the metallurgical industry was much reduced by the switch to coke smelting, considerable quantities were required in the mines and for construction purposes. But since nationalisation the traditional integration of lumbering and metallurgy has been eroded still further. Cutting is now carried out by the district IFET based at Caransebeş, using the greatly-extended road network (Tomoioaga, 1968). Other means of transport (rail at Anina and river/canal at Văliug) have been abandoned because road transport is the cheapest way of delivering wood to the large industrialisation plants which have superseded a number of the local sawmills. It also avoids the material losses involved with the use of canals and associated funiculars and chutes. The canal system on the Bîrzava is retained for hydro-electricity, but the funiculars have been dismantled. The 'scoc' from Prislop to Crainicel can still be used, but it is present policy to take all timber out by road.

The Prislop 'scoc' operates in conjunction with the Semenic Canal which augments the Bîrzava water supply by bringing water from the Trei Ape storage in the adjacent Timiş Valley (using off-peak power from pumping). This canal (and the Zanoaga Canal further south, which diverts water from the Nera basin) is part of a large post-war development of water management. It has involved primarily a new 66.2-ha storage at Gozna above Văliug (finished in 1953) serving a third power station at Crainicel. There is also a lake at Secu, just above Reşiţa, for water supply only. All this has contributed to the development of tourism which began in the Semenic Mountains in the 1930s when the Club Turistic Banatean built cabins and marked out paths in the forests. The original huts (supplied with chairlift access in 1942) have been joined by a hotel complex which is accessible by surfaced road. The potential for winter sports will justify a major expansion from the present level of 300 beds to an eventual 1,500. Other developments are directly related to the water storages for the complex at Crivaia, developed in the 1970s out of the camp provided for construction workers on the Gozna reservoir.

There is a hotel and a cluster of hostels (some of them owned by enterprises in Reşiţa). Similar facilities are available at Trei Ape, while day recreation close to the city is provided for at Secu.

The Reşiţa case study is quite unusual as regards the scale of development which has followed from the exploitation of the forests in the Upper Bîrzava basin. But it does illustrate some of the linkages which can be found on a smaller scale in other areas. Forest transport systems have become extensive throughout the forested zones of the Carpathians to overcome the old problem of inaccessibility. Various other developments have been assisted by the infrastructure already in place, and hamlets associated entirely with silviculture and woodcutting have sometimes grown into larger communities concerned with agriculture (Cerna Sat in the Cerna Valley), border patrols (Faina in the Vaser Valley) or tourism (Cumpana in the Argeş Valley). Tourism is likely to be more important in future, since privatisation should provide a stimulus for growth in areas remote from the principal resorts which benefited so much from the regime of central planning. Tourist facilities may be provided on outlying farms which could only have been contemplated under the old regime if they could have been brought under the umbrella of a cooperative organisation (Rey, 1979).

10.4 Conclusions

Transport in Romania is certainly far below European standards of comfort and efficiency, except in the case of a small number of linkages involving the major cities. The mixture of modes available in the various counties is also variable. Yet given the relatively low density of population the means of access are quite comprehensive, even in areas beyond the limits of permanent settlement. There is therefore an effective infrastructure to support a large number of small rural development projects where modest capital reserves can exploit reserves of cheap labour, perhaps through family businesses which can depend on kinship relations. This may lead to the intensification of agriculture and the expansion of processing of local raw materials, including the exploitation of resources for tourism. But the fairly widespread distribution of projects of this kind may be complemented by a high level of locational concentration of large businesses attracting foreign investment. Selective improvement in transport, perhaps through the construction of more motorways, may only reinforce this trend in the short and medium term and thereby separate the rural areas and the small towns from the large cities. Such a centre–periphery dichotomy (suggested by the local election results of 1992 which expressed a swing against the government in the larger towns, especially in Transylvania) would plainly increase the significance of traditional peasant resourcefulness which must now be stimulated in every possible way after the appalling frustrations suffered by small-scale rural enterprise under the former regime.

11 Geopolitics, transport and regional development in the south Slav lands

Colin Thomas

11.1 Introduction

Following the removal of communist governments in Central and Eastern Europe in 1989–90 (Hawkes, 1990), one of the least expected consequences was the appearance of a series of independent states to replace the Socialist Federal Republic of Yugoslavia. These entities had undergone a wide range of social and economic development experiences, the understanding of which may best be achieved by an appreciation of their diverse environmental, cultural and political characteristics.

Central to any such understanding is an awareness of the constant historical interplay between the rival super-powers of the day and indigenous nationalities, giving rise to tensions which often extended far beyond regional politics to encompass the whole continent, as during the First and Second World Wars. The military and ideological triumph of Tito's partisan forces in 1944–45 culminated in the creation of a federation of six republics and two autonomous provinces (Clissold, 1966). This was committed to a socialist programme of radical transformation, yet operating outside the strait-jacket of Soviet domination after the rift with Stalin in 1948. It was organised on a distinctive system of polycentric development and workers' self-management in industrial and commercial enterprises. Non-alignment in foreign policy and maintenance of open borders with Italy and Austria produced their own economic benefits. The inter-war monarchy, initially founded as the Kingdom of Serbs, Croats and Slovenes, and riven by nationalist antagonisms, had, like the other new East European states, suffered a period of economic depression within a decade of its formation, although historical ties had attracted speculative foreign capital and a perpetuation of external entrepreneurial involvement in primary and secondary industries. Those,

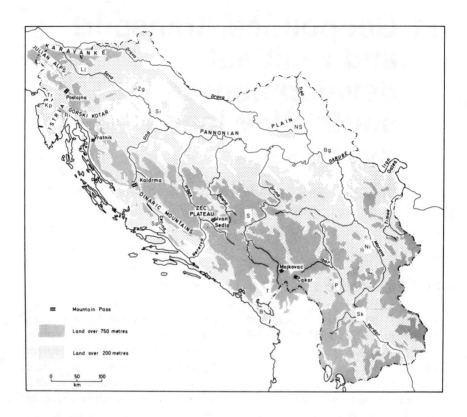

B	Bar
Bg	Belgrade
Kp	Koper
Lj	Ljubljana
Ni	Niš
NS	Novi Sad
P	Priština
Ri	Rijeka
S	Sarajevo
Si	Sisak
Sk	Skopje
Sp	Split
T	Podgorica (former Titograd)
Tr	Trieste (Italy)
Zg	Zagreb

Figure 11.1 (Former) Yugoslavia: topography and main towns

in turn, could be traced back to the pre-1914 centralist political structures out of which Serbia and Montenegro, as the first pair of independent states, emerged like a chrysalis from the decaying folds of the Austro-Hungarian and Turkish empires, which, to the north and south respectively, had together dominated the peninsula since the fourteenth century.

Underlying the successive administrative frameworks, more durable environmental elements acted as resource bases for, and constraints on, settlement distribution and lines of communication between communities (Figure 11.1). Broadly identified as Alpine, Dalmatian, Dinaric, Danubian (Pannonian) and Aegean, each distinct region possesses unique development opportunities and problems, the integration and resolution of which presented a formidable challenge to the post-1945 government. The discrete nuclear areas of the medieval quasi-states which were the forerunners of the present units were all essentially land-locked, but collectively were bounded on three sides by water – the Adriatic Sea, the river Danube and its tributaries, and the Aegean Sea – which were just as significant as the northern land frontier in shaping their subsequent economic development and colonial histories.

A crucial consequence of periodic ebb and flow of imperial power and its internal administration was that when the South Slav state was constituted in 1918 its 2,989 km of international borders extended 2,173 km across land and 711 km along rivers, bringing direct contact with seven other countries (Rogić, 1982, pp. 15–19). The new state also had over 2,000 km of coastline; within the then kingdom and subsequent federation, each constituent territory became framed by historic provincial boundaries that acquired inherent long-term significance. Serbia remained land-locked, its only international land borders being with postwar communist Hungary, Romania and Bulgaria, together with a stretch of the Danube at the Djerdap Gorge. Macedonia maintained only two frontier posts along its 262-km border with Greece. Croatia's horse-shoe formation meant that its land border with Hungary was complemented by a virtual monopoly of Yugoslavia's coastline (Pavić, 1980). Compact Slovenia's nineteen crossing points acted as the only direct land connections with western Europe via Austria and Italy. This series of open doors gave Slovenia incalculable economic and political advantages that could not be matched by any other federal component (Grčić 1984).

The disposition of quasi-state territories in the western Balkans further guaranteed that the environmental characteristics of each differed appreciably from those of its neighbours. Earlier geographers undoubtedly exaggerated the role of the great river valleys in south Slav life, yet the Drava–Sava–Danube plains in Croatia and Vojvodina, the Morava–Vardar basin in Serbia and Macedonia, and the Una, Vrbas, Bosna and Drina leading from the barren uplands of Bosnia-Hercegovina have perpetually channelled migrations and trade between contrasting societies. Only the Neretva opened south to the sea from its precipitous head-streams, and between the Pannonian plains and sub-Mediterranean Dalmatia no easily traversable routes crossed the High Karst from Rijeka to the Gulf of Kotor. For Croatia, this meant a strong trend towards littoralisation, expressed in Grčić's (1984, p. 83) assertion that 'Yugoslavia is an Adriatic country'.

Commercially and strategically, the juxtaposition of land and sea ensured that, from the later nineteenth century in particular, the south Slav lands functioned as a bridge between transalpine and Mediterranean Europe, the latter acting as a maritime spring-board to the Atlantic and Indian Oceans after the opening of the Suez Canal in 1869. Culturally, for two millennia the Balkans became synonymous not only with internal fragmentation and relative under-development, but also with bewildering complexities of ethnic mixtures, between Roman Catholic, Orthodox, Jewish and Islamic creeds, and Germanic, Romance, Slavonic and Turkic language groups (Thomas, 1987, 1990; Petrović, 1992).

11.2 Transport networks

The profound general disparity between areas to the north and south of the Sava–Danube line is nowhere better illustrated than in land communications networks (Figure 11.2), whose scales and functions within the respective republics further highlight peculiarities of regional development (Nicod, 1982).

11.2.1 Rail transport

The South Slav lands were peripheral to the Austro-Hungarian state core during the major period of communications expansion in the second half of the nineteenth century. This is exemplified by the points of origin of the future Yugoslav railway system (Figure 11.2a) and directions of growth, as well as by the actual growth phases and functions of the regional components.

From the viewpoint of a land empire, the paramount need was for access to the sea. Barred from an Atlantic outlet by distance and a series of other states, Austria sought alternatives within its own territory, devoting huge investments to the creation of artificial ports at Trieste and Rijeka (Fiume) at the head of the Adriatic. Consequently, the first railway outside the imperial heartland was directed from Vienna and Graz through the easiest pass in the Eastern Alps to Maribor and on via Ljubljana to Trieste (1857). This took the line through the Postojna Gap, at 609 m the lowest breach in the northern Alpine rim of the Mediterranean between the Rhone valley

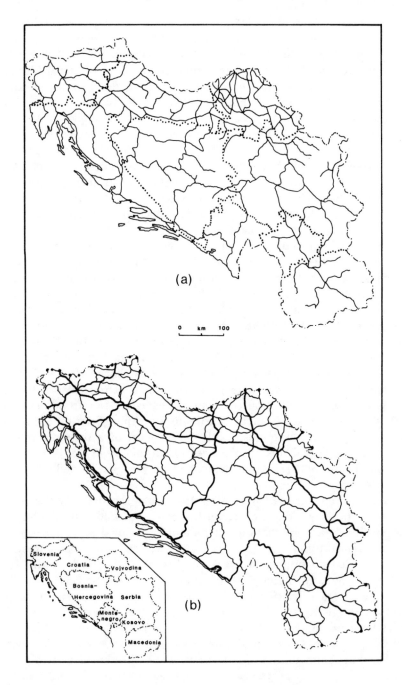

Figure 11.2 (Former) Yugoslavia: transport networks
(a) Railways
(b) Main roads

and the Aegean (Moodie, 1945). Following the development of branch lines along the Sava valley from Zidani Most to Zagreb, Sisak and Karlovac by 1865, a direct link from Budapest through Zagreb to Rijeka was completed in 1873 to serve the Hungarian half of the Dual Monarchy (Zuljić, 1978). All routes stopped short of the Bosnian border, beyond which the Turkish authorities only belatedly became convinced of the potential value of railways, having constructed a single track from Salonika to Skopje and Kosovska Mitrovica and an isolated line from Bosanski Novi to Banja Luka (1872). Until 1878 the whole area south of the Kupa–Sava–Danube was effectively a railway desert, graphically symbolising the polar contrast in economic and strategic values and transport technologies of opposing empires, one reluctantly accepting retreat from a neglected frontier, the other eager to penetrate its difficult terrain in search of new mineral and forest resources.

In 1878, having acquired Bosnia as a protectorate, Austria immediately began constructing a dendritic rail system southwards from Croatia-Slavonia, for example from Bosanski Brod to Sarajevo, while innumerable private companies built narrow-gauge tracks to extract specific raw materials. Even after Austria's annexation of Bosnia-Hercegovina in 1908, with the exception of strategic lines to the naval base at Pula in Istria, only two links existed across the High Karst linking Pannonia to Dalmatia: from Bosanski Novi via Knin to Split, and Sarajevo via Mostar down the Neretva valley to Ploče. Meanwhile, the northern plains themselves were provided with a dense network to tap their grain and timber resources, and a single line ran from Belgrade south through Niş to Istanbul, partly to underpin German economic expansionism in the Near East, with the prospect of a tortuous and as yet incomplete lateral link through central Bosnia from Banja Luka to Višegrad. Prior to 1918, Montenegro had only 43 km of railway from Bar to Vir Pazar.

Few extensions occurred until after 1945 when the first five-year plan adopted a positive policy of reconstruction and modernisation of all transport media as a mechanism for promoting regional economic growth (Table 11.1). Priority was given to electrification (after diesel traction had superseded steam), double-tracking of trunk routes, and the standardisation of gauge to harmonise with European networks. Eradication of narrow-gauge track by 1976 enabled axle-loads and average speeds to be increased on up-graded lines, yet in the early 1980s speeds averaged only 36 km/hour on commercial passenger trips and 18 km/hour for freight, both being well below technical limits. While the total network decreased to 9,567 km from a peak of 11,882 in 1959 (Sirotković and Stipetić, 1982), two important projects were completed. The first of these was to greatly expand port facilities at Koper (1967), while the other was the extremely costly and technically difficult Belgrade–Bar line (1976) (Wilson 1971; Singleton and Wilson 1977; Kolarić 1977), the completion

Table 11.1 (Former) Yugoslavia: transport development, 1946–89

	1946	1951	1961	1971	1981	1989
Rail						
Network length*	9,900	11,581	11,867	10,332	9,393	9,567
% Double track	3.8	5.9	6.1	7.2	9.5	9.9
% Electrified	–	0.9	2.1	17.5	35.3	39.5
Freight†	19.5	41.9	64.2	75.4	85.6	84.8
Passengers°	78.4	169.5	195.0	145.6	104.9	117.0
Average journey*	51	45	51	72	100	100
Road						
Motorcycles‡	99.5	92.5	72.2	372.3	162.0	89.9
Buses‡	0.6	1.1	1.5	16.4	26.4	29.4
Cars‡	6.2	6.9	75.6	875.3	2,568.1	3,323.9
Freight†	1.4	7.7	25.6	122.8	188.5	124.5
Inland waterways						
Freight†	1.7	3.3	5.9	17.0	22.7	19.2
Oil/gas pipeline†	–	–	–	0.4	6.2	9.4

Key * kilometres
     † million tonnes
     ‡ in thousands
     ° in millions

Source: Statisticki Godisnjak, 1990.

of which realised a century-old Serbian dream of an outlet to the Adriatic through Montenegro.

It is significant that even the new lines emphasised the inherited port-orientation of the network, which itself became reflected in the rail system's basic freight-carrying function and a source of the system's relative decline in recent decades. Whereas the average length of rail freight haul increased by one third to over three hundred kilometres between 1961 and 1989, the volume carried had declined in absolute terms since 1984 (to 85 million tonnes), and its share of total freight had fallen from 65 to 32 per cent in the 1961–89 period. Similarly, the number of passengers travelling by train was halved between 1965 and 1989, the rail share of total passenger journeys collapsing from 52 to 12.5 per cent.

Partly responsible for this dramatic reversal of fortunes in the closing years of the unified Yugoslav Railways was the growing volume of petroleum carried by pipeline. This represented both domestic requirements, the Rijeka-Pancevo pipeline being completed in 1979, and also transit functions from the Omišalj terminal to Central Europe. Technological innovations within the rail system itself were a contributory

LIVERPOOL HOPE UNIVERSITY COLLEGE

factor too, as demand for coal, lignite and timber for its own fuel was reduced. Moreover, the early post-war government operated a multiplicity of tariffs with wide differentials (twenty-five rates with a ratio of 14:1 between highest and lowest in 1960). These tended to favour wasteful long hauls of low-value commodities, drawn predominantly from the southern republics and processed nearer the market, thereby superficially promoting internal trade. Both the number of tariff grades and their range were radically cut by 1978 to five rates with a ratio of 1.6:1. The railways relinquished their obligation to carry large quantities of low-tariff goods while simultaneously reducing their profitability (Sirotković and Stipetić, 1982, p. 397). Only in international and transit traffic have the railways retained their former importance.

11.2.2 Road transport

As expected, the Yugoslav road network displays a more comprehensive spatial cover and a more even density than that of railways, although its greater tolerance of steep gradients does not entirely remove negative areas from the overall distribution pattern, notably in the Alpine and Dinaric regions (Figure 11.2b). Yet it, too, had its arterial origins, in this case in both Roman and early modern Habsburg times, deriving from the imperial strategic and commercial requirements to link interior plains and valley nodes to the Adriatic on one side and the Danubian *limes* on the other. Nevertheless, in both density and quality the north–south disparity has long existed. In the later nineteenth century in central Bosnia, for example, while the Austrians were extending their railways, the Turks were only beginning to construct motor roads. The spatial dichotomy between animal- and mechanical-based transport systems could not be better illustrated than in the recollections of Jovan Cvijić (1918) who, not long before the First World War, met camel caravans in southern Serbia. Surviving Turkish stone bridges, such as those at Mostar and Višegrad, bear further witness to a different technology, capable of powerful and elegant structures, but not adapted to bulk movement of freight.

The application of steam power to transport, in first providing the capacity to transfer goods over long distances at greater speed than by pack-horse or bullock-cart, ensured that railway supremacy would be prolonged in a part of Europe that was marginal to large-scale concentrated industrial activity. Here internal markets were relatively small, and certainly localised, by reason of production techniques, limited rural commodity needs, population distribution and low purchasing power. When the advent of motorisation did eventually occur, much later than in western Europe, the transformation was rapid and far-reaching in its effects.

An ideological and pragmatic predisposition towards public transport

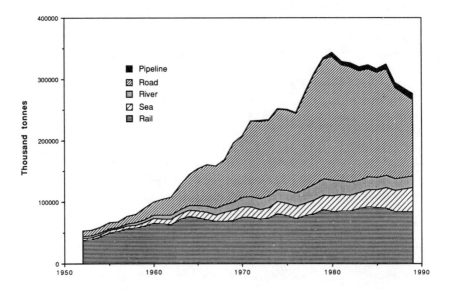

Figure 11.3 (Former) Yugoslavia: freight traffic by mode of transport, 1952–1989

Source: Statisticki Godisnjak, 1990

saw the number of buses increase ten-fold between 1946 and 1962, and a further five-fold by 1989, creating webs of routes that spread from virtually every urban settlement. In remoter areas, and for individuals requiring local access to bus routes, numbers of mopeds and motorcycles increased dramatically, especially between 1956 and 1961. With gradually augmented disposable incomes, the demand for family transport changed the primary journey-to-work purpose of motorised mobility. The production of private cars began in 1954 (Antanasković and Djekić, 1986), at first under licence from Fiat. Having started at Kragujevac, paradoxically in one of the less advanced republics, car assembly was later initiated in Slovenia (Novo Mesto, Koper), Bosnia (Sarajevo), Vojvodina (Kikinda) and Kosovo (Priština). In time, dependence on imported engines and components from France and Germany in joint ventures diminished and a wider range of private and commercial vehicles was introduced as production diversified and sub-contracting spread. In 1979 annual production peaked at over 200,000 cars, 80 per cent from Zastava factories, and more than 2.25 million private cars were registered in Yugoslavia.

Meanwhile, road freight experienced a phenomenal boom, with its volume growing from 36 to 201 million tonnes in 1965–80 as industrial production dispersed into the countryside, and its share of total internal commodity movement overturned the railways' former dominance (Stanković, 1975; Sirotković and Stipetić, 1982, p. 385) (Figure 11.3). Despite the early 1970s fuel crisis, partly offset by exploitation of oilfields in Vojvodina and eastern Croatia, the superior adaptability of road transport to Yugoslav industrial and settlement conditions had become irreversible. Road transport can move small loads to and from specific dispersed points, minimising delays by its greater spatial freedom and technical modernity. It represents unchallenged efficiency in breaking bulk cargoes, carried longer distances by sea, river and rail, for localised delivery. Road transport also has an ability to operate over difficult terrain as well as along valleys and plains. All of these factors contributed to the pronounced transformation of the modal composition of freight movement.

Simultaneously, changes may be discerned in the types of goods handled and in road transport organisation which reflect the underlying metamorphosis of the economy and society in general. Formative phases of industrial and urban growth saw heavy traffic of construction materials (steel, cement, sand, gravel, timber), ores and fuels on road and rail alike, with lesser quantities of foodstuffs such as grains, fruit, vegetables, milk and meat, travelling over short distances to widespread processing installations. By the later 1980s the non-metallic material cargo share of total road freight had been reduced to half of its 1970 volume, and in absolute terms, at 23.8 million tonnes, reverting to its earlier level after an intervening rise to twice or three times that amount. Solid and liquid fuel freight had grown absolutely, but stabilised relatively, as industrial and domestic consumption became more efficient, and rail and pipelines took on the extra burden. Contemporaneously, changes in manufacturing promoted the movement by road of household goods and processed foods to retail distributors in even the most remote villages, while use of public sector freight transport diminished as more producer enterprises branched out into their own transport services. For example, *Emona*, based in Ljubljana, began as a retail outlet for food production on its own farms, then expanded into hotels and catering, and finally tourism, all cemented by its own goods and passenger fleet with full technical support.

Fundamental improvements in the route network were a pre-requisite for this scale of reorganisation. In addition to these internal demands, one stimulus for trunk-road modernisation in width, surface and alignment quality was the pressure imposed by the heavy volume of transit traffic through Yugoslavia from Turkey, Greece, Bulgaria and Romania to Austria, Italy and central Europe. Accordingly, investment was directed towards upgrading sections of the E75 (Budapest–Belgrade–Niš–Istanbul/Sofia), E65 (Koper–Split–Dubrovnik–Titograd–Priština–Skopje), E70 (Ljubljana–Zagreb–Belgrade), and E59 (Maribor–Zagreb–

Plate 11.1 The Adriatic Highway, southern Croatia. The original coastal road may be seen several hundred metres above the present route. (Colin Thomas)

Karlovac–Rijeka) routes, helping to integrate the whole country with the wider European road system, a feature made all the more desirable by the steady increase in lorry capacity and internationally permissible axle-loads. Although road improvements were disjointed, two rationales may be distinguished in their pattern. Firstly, the symbolic and practical unifying significance of two NW-SE arterial routes, the Ljubljana–Belgrade (*Bratstvo i jedinstvo*) *autoput* and the Adriatic Highway (Plate 11.1), cannot be underestimated, especially since the latter encouraged massive foreign currency earnings from tourism during the summer. Secondly, embryonic toll motorways took shape from 1976 with the construction of the Vrhnika (later Ljubljana)–Postojna–Razdrto and Zagreb–Karlovac sections (Sić, 1980–1). Both reinforced traditional orientation towards the ports, Koper and Rijeka, aimed at joining the two southward trunk routes and, most importantly, were contained within their respective republics, Slovenia and Croatia. Interpretations of such network developments as demonstrating separatist tendencies is justified when one remembers that 85 per cent of all investment in roads came from republican, not federal, funds, primarily from fuel revenues (Depolo, 1974; Vasilijević, 1989).

Synchronised with headline projects of this nature, and of far more immediate concern to the majority of Yugoslav motorists, was the systematic improvement of district and local roads. Most significant were extensions to inter-community linkages and increases in the proportion of all-weather (asphalt, cobble, concrete) surfaces at the expense of macadam and dirt, often ravaged in severe winters. In that sphere, too, inter-republican and indeed local variations may be identified, and the enduring difficulties of contact between the coast and interior, particularly over the notorious Čakor, Lovćen and Ivan Sedlo passes, continue to impede broader social and economic progress in those localities.

11.2.3 Coastal and inland waterways

Water-borne transport vividly depicts the contrasting opportunities afforded to different republics endowed with distinctive environmental resources. Most notable are Croatia's almost complete dominance of the Adriatic coast and offshore islands, and northern Serbia's position astride the Danube, with less traffic diverting along the lower Sava, separating Croatia and Bosnia, as far as Sisak. Both systems appear to be linear transverse/diagonal arteries of freight and passenger movement, but are now of only minor importance because of reluctance both to invest in recent technological innovations in cargo handling and to overcome restrictions imposed by nature on the size of the transport unit (Plate 11.2). For example, only the Danube is navigable for vessels of

Plate 11.2   King Alexander I (Franz Josef) Canal, Savino Selo, Vojvodina. Constructed between 1855 and 1872, it was primarily intended for irrigation in southern Bačka and was largely superseded by improved navigation along the Danube after the Second World War. Note the shelter-belts along its unprotected earthen banks. (Colin Thomas)

3,000 tonnes, and most Dalmatian harbours are unable to handle larger ocean-going ships, having developed historically only to cope with small regional trade and local fishing craft (Naval Intelligence Division 1945; Thomas 1978). Introduction of mechanised bulk-cargo handling equipment has lagged behind at coastal and river ports alike. Consequently, in 1989 on the Danube only Pančevo, Smederevo, Belgrade and Prahovo processed more than a million tonnes of freight each. Prahovo and Smederevo being preoccupied with international transit traffic, itself considerably augmented by canalisation of the Iron Gates section, completed in 1970 (Hall, 1972; Thomas, 1973).

The seaports of Slovenia, Croatia and Montenegro, like many of their counterparts would-wide, have surrendered their purely coast-wise traffic to the roads (the Adriatic Highway having no rail competitor) and therefore function primarily as discrete points of injection or extraction of international freight in relation to the overall system, supplemented by the heavily seasonal passenger traffic in transit, to the islands. In 1989,

Plate 11.3   Bakar Bay, Croatia. Arguably the best natural harbour on the Adriatic coast, it lies in a belt of flysch between two limestone/dolomite ridges, a breach in one of which provides its only narrow sea entrance to the south-west. The modern oil terminals are situated around the headland to the right (west). Rail access from Zagreb to the port facilities is by means of a serpentine single track to the left (north-east). (Colin Thomas)

32.6 million tonnes of foreign trade entered or left Yugoslav maritime ports – 88 per cent of their total cargo.

Regarding rank, 77.6 per cent of port traffic fell to Croatia and within that republic activity was dominated by the Kvarner Bay complex, focused on Rijeka. This port's prosperity had recovered only after the Second World War as the Yugoslav rival to Trieste, having previously been cut off from its natural hinterland by the Italian occupation since 1920, and the false border imposed by the Rapallo Line. In 1989 the Rijeka cluster handled half of Croatia's sea trade (12.25 million tonnes), five times more than Split and three times more than Ploče (Kardeljevo), its cargoes heavily distorted by large imports to the terminals at Omišalj and Bakar (Plate 11.3). That situation had arisen mainly since the mid-1960s, with the realisation that Rijeka's port congestion could only be alleviated by dispersal of its comprehensive services to more specialised smaller neighbouring harbours. As a result, shipbuilding and repairs were transferred to Martinscica, new oil storage facilities and jetties were constructed at Omišalj, on the island of Krk, and near the entrance to the magnificent natural harbour of Bakar Bay, where an iron-ore terminal was also located. All were provided with improved transit access to the interior, by pipeline to Sisak's oil refinery and through electrification of the railway to Zagreb (Stražičić, 1989).

Two further port developments of that period assume considerable geopolitical relevance in the light of the dissolution of the Yugoslav federation. First, Slovene acquisition of 46 km of coastline from the Treaty of London's (1954) adjustment of the Italo-Yugoslav border soon stimulated the decision to create a modern port at Koper, partly to perform a transit function for Central Europe via a rail link though the Postojna Gap and Ljubljana. Beside the picturesque medieval peninsular town there spread out separate facilities for bulk raw materials, grain, tropical fruit, timber, vehicles, oil and containers, and in the thirty years to 1990 Koper's port traffic increased from 0.1 to 5.5 million tonnes, 90 per cent of which originated in, or was destined for, Austria, Hungary and Czechoslovakia (Jeršič, 1992). Second, at the southern end of Dalmatia, construction of the Belgrade–Bar railway promoted similar developments on a lesser scale, Bar in 1990 handling 2.5 million tonnes, a hundred-fold increase on its 1960 traffic, but in this case directed towards the needs of Serbia and Montenegro.

11.3 Regional development policies

Although possessing divergent living standards, partly attributable to environmental and historical peculiarities, all the successor states to the Yugoslav federation possess the resource substructure for adequate food supply, energy production and raw materials for construction and manufacturing (Table 11.2). Where they differ most acutely is in their capital accumulation (Vinski, 1963), infrastructural quality and demographic characteristics, which result in disparities in consumption levels and in the future prospects for rates and scales of improvement.

Bićanić (1973) considered that at the outset of the first five-year plan in 1952 the whole country could have been regarded as underdeveloped, not least because of war-time devastation. More specifically, on any criteria, the people of Bosnia-Hercegovina, Macedonia, Montenegro and Kosovo-Metohija (together representing one-third of the total population) experienced the worst economic and social privations. Political, economic and ethical imperatives demanded efforts to reduce the ratio of 3:1 between the gross social product per capita of the 'richest' and poorest territories. This was to be undertaken according to socialist principles and by institutional means via the public sector, while upholding administrative cohesion under the constitution.

Table 11.2 (Former) Yugoslavia: selected regional indicators, 1989

	Yu	Slovenia	Croatia	Vojvodina	Serbia	B-H	Mont.	Maced.	Kosovo
Rail km/100 km^2	3.8	5.3	4.7	8.0	3.7	1.9	1.6	2.6	3.1
Road km/100 km^2	43.9	72.0	46.2	33.6	51.7	36.5	26.4	36.2	37.1
Modern road %	60.2	66.5	68.3	81.1	54.1	49.7	65.9	46.1	38.2
Dirt road %	12.2	0.0	0.9	16.9	21.8	9.5	6.3	40.0	28.7
Cars/thous. popn.	142	280	176	152	149	95	97	107	43
Workers/thous. popn.	–	436	333	299	282	234	255	248	122
Ind. workers/thous. empl.	–	299	178	169	164	150	122	155	79
Social product per cap.	*	201	125	121	98	68	78	65	26
Net investment per cap.	*	174	114	117	93	83	134	59	61

* Yugoslav average = 100

Source: Statisticki Godisnjak, 1990

The socialist development programme, like its counterparts elsewhere in Central and Eastern Europe, was predicated on a belief in the virtues of industrialisation, initially in the production of basic goods and only later shifting towards consumer durables. Both reconstruction of plant devastated by war and new industrial locations (Hamilton, 1963, 1968) emphasised historic centres and raw material nuclei. The depleted unskilled labour force for construction and heavy industry was largely drawn from the countryside, a process that itself required personal mobility and simultaneously alleviated severe problems of rural over-population, while permitting equally essential agrarian reform.

Pragmatic and humanitarian considerations dictated that priorities be established, so that initially whole republics were designated as development areas, Slovenia and Croatia being excluded from special status because of their comparatively satisfactory conditions. During the second five-year plan (1957–61), the Croat-favoured refinement of identifying sub-republican special areas was adopted, with the result that extra investment continued to be directed to Kosovo, Macedonia, Montenegro and all of Bosnia-Hercegovina except the north-east, but southern Croatia and parts of south-east Serbia also now qualified (Singleton and Carter, 1982). This gradual sharpening of spatial focus channelled central funds more realistically to genuinely deprived communities, especially after the creation in 1965 of the Federal Fund for Crediting Faster Development in Economically Underdeveloped Republics and Provinces (Mladenović, 1982; Mihailović, 1975, pp. 120–46), and the emergence of regional planning mechanisms (Fisher, 1971; Gregory, 1973).

Following the new Constitution (1963) and economic reform (1965), which never fully implemented market criteria in investment allocation, there occurred a distinct shift away from centralism towards autarkic concepts of development, allowing republican financial institutions to reach independent decisions regarding funding priorities (Milanović, 1987). Consequent ideological contradictions merely accentuated regional tensions in a multinational state, colouring the intellectual debate among economists as to the most effective means of combating spatial inequalities. Among alternatives discussed were those of 'Danubian' versus 'Adriatic' strategies: the former emphasising interior resources, essentially in the primary and secondary sectors, eastward-looking yet vulnerable in the Cold War; the latter hoping for benefits from trade and tourism with the West. Both prospects contained clear broad political implications, as well as reflecting conflicting national outlooks, for instance between Serbs and Croats respectively.

Apart from theoretical debates over bi-polar (Belgrade–Zagreb), oligocentric or polycentric concepts of development, uncertainty persisted over criteria for defining 'underdeveloped' areas (Briški, 1978; Miljovski, 1980). Analysis of national income per capita for the 498 communes (Figure 11.4a) at the end of the Tito era (1980–81) has shown that the

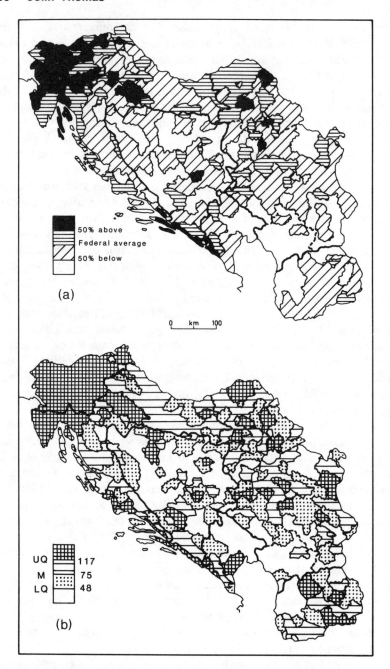

Figure 11.4   (Former) Yugoslavia: socio-economic indicators
(a) social product per capita
(b) cars per thousand population

Source: Statisticki Godisnjak, 1990.

mean value for the upper octile was over thirteen times greater than that for the lowest octile. Despite thirty-five years of varied policies, achieving remarkable absolute progress and dramatic structural changes in the economy, numerous indicators still revealed inter-republic disparities of great magnitude, and the gulf between the richest and poorest communities actually widened. Moreover, at the extremes, twenty-six of the thirty-nine most prosperous communes were in Slovenia and fourteen of the least prosperous twenty-three in Kosovo, which, together with Montenegro, Macedonia and Bosnia-Hercegovina had no representation in the former category. Conversely, no Slovene, Croatian or Vojvodina districts featured in the poorest group.

11.3.1 Personal mobility

Of considerable significance in relieving these regional disparities in living standards is the capacity of people to move within the country. Migration is clearly one strategy adopted in the search for improved employment, housing or social status (Thomas, 1982), but the extent of travel-to-work journeys has long been recognised as crucial in enabling wider processes of socio-economic transformation to proceed (Friganović, 1970; Gosar, 1975). Mobility of individual family members not only reveals a level of public transport service, but private car ownership (Figure 11.4b), as one indicator of disposable incomes, also provides opportunities for employment choice, the exercise of consumer preferences, access to educational and cultural amenities, and social interaction.

In 1957, when the age of motorisation was still in its infancy in Yugoslavia, the Statistical Bureau had the foresight to survey the extent of journeys to work in seventy-five of the largest urban centres. Daily commuters then accounted for seventeen per cent of employees, a figure that has since increased rapidly. Spatial spheres of movement were then very restricted: for 72.5 per cent of those sampled, the distance between residence and place of work was no more than twenty kilometres, and only 3.3 per cent travelled over fifty kilometres. When analysed by republic and province, distinct variations in mean distances emerged. Allowing for regional contrasts in basic settlement pattern, spatial mobility for employment purposes was least extensive in the poorest territories (Macedonia, Montenegro and Kosovo), indicating few opportunities and poverty of infrastructure services. However, a similarly high value for short-distance commuting was also recorded in Slovenia, where its explanation lay in terms of an already advanced stage of dispersed industrial employment in the countryside (Vrišer, 1988).

Under quite different circumstances, Vrišer (1990) for Slovenia and Bjelovitić (1978) and Grčić and Marić (1986) for Bosnia-Hercegovina have traced the development of secondary and tertiary employment from the colonial period to the 1980s. Both areas show common trends that may be attributed to successive industrial location policies, the pace of job creation accelerating steadily from nineteenth-century origins in primary production to diversified and spatially diffuse manufacturing by the 1960s. From 1965 a related feature of deliberate post-war policy was a gradual relative shift away from historical industrial regions, such as the Ljubljana basin and central Bosnia, the beneficiaries of new investment being the less developed peripheral regions of the respective republics. While the success of that strategy should not be accepted uncritically (Zečević, 1991), it did serve to spread higher incomes and skills to areas formerly dependent on peasant agriculture, and could not have been accomplished without increased spatial mobility of labour on a daily or weekly, as opposed to a permanent, basis.

11.4 Post-independence issues

The most obvious consequence of the political disintegration of federal Yugoslavia in 1991 was that former internal borders became international ones, and the military conflict demonstrated that in some cases even these borders were disputed between rival ethnic groups. Creation of separate jurisdictions, with divergent social and economic priorities, endows territorial limits with functions of defining levels of customs duties, freight tariffs and restrictions on personal movement. Of immediate interest, therefore, is the medium- or long-term impact that these boundaries will have in the sphere of transport and regional economic development. In the short term, the war in Croatia and Bosnia-Hercegovina, provoking UN sanctions against Serbia-Montenegro, has drastically reduced west–east movements of goods by rail and road along former axial lines of communication. Even in Slovenia, not directly involved in the conflict, road freight transport along the E70 has dwindled to a trickle as international carriers have sought to avoid the war zone of eastern Croatia and the Croatia–Bosnia border along the middle Sava. Traffic intended for the Balkans and Near East has been diverted northwards through Hungary and Romania. That temporary response to increased risk may settle into a new, permanent, orientation of freight movement along the as yet incomplete motorway network from Iberia through southern France and the Po valley, using the Slovene 'bridge' between Trieste and Vienna/Budapest, thereby pumping new life into the nineteenth-century artery (Černe, 1992).

Between those new independent states maintaining relatively amicable relations, it is also probable that common interest will eventually reduce present customs barriers and reinstate previous cross-border traffic flows, such as between Slovenia and Croatia, or Croatia and Bosnia, towards Istria and Dalmatia. Conceivably, if capital becomes available, existing local road links may even be improved. A demand already exists for reciprocal journey-to-work flows, access to farmland, and normal consumer and recreational mobility by people living in border communities. In the absence of open hostility, it is wholly illogical and mutually damaging to attempt to funnel freight and passenger movements through a few official crossings and to try to discourage them everywhere else. The outcome of bilateral negotiations will influence the precise scale and nature of future commodity flows on those routes, but most parties are conscious of the need for maximum participation in increasing physical and economic integration with Central and Western Europe. The same considerations of sustained or expanded markets for manufactured goods, and continuation of transit trade, will surely safeguard the operation of pipeline, rail and road linkages through Slovenia and Croatia north from Koper, Rijeka, Bakar and Omišalj, together with planned improvements in their facilities. Among the projects most fervently advocated are completion of motorways across the Karst to the northern Adriatic, and a low-level rail route between Karlovac and Rijeka, via two very long and immensely costly tunnels, approximating more closely in alignment to the motorway and eliminating long gradient-reducing deviations at low speed on the existing line through Delnice (Šimičić, 1981).

At present, only Slovenia and Croatia seem suitably placed to attract the necessary external investment to underpin those developments, and irrespective of their achievement, the continued widening of the gulf between those republics and the rest of the former federation remains likely, with all that implies for the volume and type of trade and modernisation of transport networks between them. An alternative scenario, of conscious introspective separatism in political and economic life, for example, in Serbia-Montenegro, would create its own distinctive, but quite different, patterns within those territories. At present, the future status and prospects of the poorest areas, Macedonia and Kosovo, is quite unforeseeable, yet it is certain that, with their land-locked position, lack of capital, weak infrastructure, and severe population pressure on meagre resources, the outlook cannot be very hopeful, unless a radical reappraisal is made of their economic-political alignment. In that context, sympathetic attitudes on the part of neighbouring countries and substantial positive action by third parties are absolutely fundamental.

With regard to implementation of novel policies derived from ideological reorientation, again it is too soon even to discern precisely what forms of administration will eventually crystallise out in the successor states. Public lip-service has been paid to notions of so-called 'free-market' economics, ignoring or overlooking the fact that favoured models in Western Europe, with which convergence is envisaged, embody considerable elements of state intervention in various economic sectors and by various means, together with other procedures operated by large corporations and institutions that may not be appropriate or entirely beneficial in the Balkans. For example, political fragmentation has resulted in the partitioning of the unified Yugoslav Railways between the separate states, yet it would be totally irrational for those parts now to go entirely their own ways in technology, standards, and operating methods. Road-building norms also imply high levels of liaison, if not coordination, if regional systems are to be integrated cost-effectively into a continental network.

De-nationalisation of the dominant state-owned or municipally-directed firms has proceeded very little and in some spheres of provision it is debatable that it should. Not least among the advantages of the former Yugoslav self-management system and territorially devolved administrative structure was a potential for diversity and flexibility in organisation that is particularly relevant for transport. Some complex enterprises began as local bus operators in centres such as Koper, Kranj, Nova Gorica, and Novo Mesto, subsequently branching out into private vehicle sales, repairs and servicing, freight transport, and domestic or foreign coach tourism. Others specialised in international freight, such as *Špedtrans* (Maribor) and *Interevropa* (Koper), while oil companies like *Istrabenz* (Koper) operate their own delivery vehicles. Although large numbers of private sector enterprises already existed under the former dispensation, legal constraints obliged them to be small in scale. Numerous private hauliers and taxi firms perform vital local services, as did their forebears, the peasant farmers seasonally active in the carting trade.

Whereas indicators of deprivation usually relate to population areas, actual problems tend to be alleviated by activities promoted at specific points, in the expectation of spread effects. Realistically, such nodes cannot survive in isolation, but depend on diverse linkages, giving rise to notions of development 'corridors', for example along motorways or railways. In the Balkans the concept requires refinement into that of strings of varied-sized beads of only moderate industrial urbanism laid over an irregular fabric of rural backwardness. Regional socio-economic disparities may have environmental and cultural roots, but their diminution clearly depends on structural transformations, in which improved transport and communications networks for freight and passengers are crucial. Over-arching all these objectives are motives rooted in national and international policies, themselves deeply embedded in the past.

11.5 Conclusions

From 1845 to 1945 transport developments in the south Slav lands were moulded primarily by external politico-economic forces of continental scale, and etched in detail by constraints imposed by the local environment. In contrast, the following forty-five years in a federal Yugoslavia were characterised by indigenous centralist and, later, devolved economic and social policies to alleviate regional disparities which simultaneously reflected and were partly created by inherited physical and cultural networks. Technological transformations, structural shifts in employment, spatial transfers of population between countryside and town, improved living standards and increased personal mobility all contributed to a fundamental reappraisal of available modes of transport. Dramatic changes ensued in the absolute and relative shares held by rail, road and waterborne traffic of freight and passengers alike, as interaction between communities was intensified and extended. The struggles for independence in Slovenia, Croatia and Bosnia-Hercegovina in 1991–92 disrupted both the unitary and loosely-articulated pre-existing communications systems at a time when the socio-economic gulf between the more and less developed republics continued to widen. Prospects for limiting further ethnic and geographical divergence in the Balkans undoubtedly rest in the first instance on international political negotiations and specific internal policies, but central to all material and social progress is the extent to which all these communities are physically linked to each other and functionally integrated with broader European transport systems.

12 Transport implications of tourism development

Derek Hall

12.1 Introduction

This chapter aims to explore some of the implications of recent and likely future trends in the tourism industry for the region's transport development. Transport would appear to have three basic roles in relation to tourism development: (a) enabling tourists to travel between their home area and tourist destination; (b) providing a service for tourists at their destination; and (c) as a variant on the latter, supporting the ocean cruise industry, whereby the tourist 'destination' may cover a very wide area.

Transport functions at tourism destinations which are specifically aimed at the tourist normally involve equipment which is of a higher standard than local public transport (such as luxury coaches), is often highly specialised (for air, sea or river excursions), and often involves direct organisational linkages with accommodation, airline and holiday tour operation companies (car rental, coach excursions). More recently, as expressed in 'heritage' and innovatory guises, transport has become an object, as well as a facilitator, of the tourism experience. In Central and Eastern Europe, Budapest would appear to be leading the field in this respect, with its horse carriages, 'vintage' open-top double-decker buses, single-deck open-top buses (Plate 12.1), and a regular minibus service operating within the Castle district, the focus of tourism in Old Buda. The city also boasts a narrow-gauge cog railway climbing the Buda hills (Plate 12.2) which links with the former 'young pioneer' rail line.

This chapter will concentrate largely on the first of transport's three functions, that of enabling tourists to travel between their home area and the tourist destination. This assessment is set within the perspective that transport and communications, together with other regional shortcomings, exerted major infrastructural constraints on tourism development during the communist period. The evaluation is also placed within a context whereby such countries as Hungary, Czechoslovakia and even Albania are looking to tourism as a major source of income and

Plate 12.1 Budapest tourist transport 1: open single-deck Ikarus vehicle embellished with silhouettes of the major features of Old Buda's Castle area, facilitating the tourist gaze to fall upon St Stephen's cathedral. (Derek Hall)

employment-generation during the difficult times of transition and restructuring. Conclusions are drawn concerning the changing relationship between tourism development and transport provision.

12.2 Tourism and economic development

12.2.1 Key elements

A number of key elements condition the relationship between tourism, transport and economic development:

(a) The national economic context: notably the availability of capital investment to develop the necessary infrastructure, not least transport and communications.
(b) Scale: small economies are more likely to depend upon imports.
(c) Level of development: lower levels of development, including that

Plate 12.2   Budapest tourist transport 2: this narrow-gauge cog railway in the Buda hills also acts as an important element in the local public transport system. (Derek Hall).

of domestic tourism, produce poor economies of scale for suppliers.

(d)   The organisation of capital: the extent of the penetration of international capital may be critical in assisting development and/or leading to leakages of income abroad through payment of royalties, profits and dividends which the economy may ill afford. The roles of foreign tour companies, carriers (notably airlines) and transport manufacturers (of, for example, luxury tourist coaches), are significant here.

(e)   Nature of tourism and background of tourists: tourists' contribution to economic development may vary considerably in terms of per capita spending power, infrastructural demands and the forms of tourism in which they participate.

12.2.2 Tourism as an invisible export

The importance of tourism in processes of national economic development can be measured in a number of ways, the most important of which relate to its direct contribution to the balance of payments, to income and GDP, and to employment generation, as well as indirectly to a wide range of other sectors of the economy, such as transport and communications infrastructure. As an activity with very explicit economic impacts, the tourism industry differs from international trade in a number of ways (Foster, 1985, pp. 104–9; Mill and Morrison, 1985, p. 223):

(a) Most of the supply components are *in situ* in the 'exporting' country: 'distribution' is concerned with taking the 'consumer' to the 'product' rather than the reverse. In advance of this, however, there is a need to disseminate information required by potential tourists, who also subsequently need to receive confirmation of reservations and tickets. 'Distribution' in the tourism industry therefore also involves the movement of substantial paperwork, although this has been simplified and speeded up considerably by computerisation.

(b) The demand for tourism is subject to instability, posing problems for planning and increasing business risk. Reasons for this include:

   (i) pronounced seasonal variations in, and high elasticity of, demand, arising from habit, climate, tradition or institutional factors such as school holidays, factory or office annual vacation periods. It may also be oriented to specific events such as Christmas/New Year;

   (ii) sudden, often unpredictable impacts on the host country of external or domestic factors, such as economic recession or boom. Destinations may also lose favour due to the appearance of health hazards. Sudden political and economic changes in host countries, as experienced in the region recently, can close or open frontiers, to both tourists and international capital, impeding or encouraging potential tourism development. When both the Chernobyl nuclear reactor accident and the US bombing of Libya took place just prior to the main 1986 tourist season, North Americans' desire to spend a vacation across the Atlantic that year was considerably inhibited (Table 12.1);

   (iii) international tourism being usually both price and income elastic: external impacts may easily bring about changes in 'product' price, and thus in the demand for the product, while changes in the disposable income levels of potential customers (such as the impact of high interest and mortgage rates or salary increases) may also bring changes in the volume of demand. Changes in either of these two variables normally result in a more-than-proportional change in pleasure travel;

   (iv) quantitative and qualitative changes in the demand structure reflecting general changes in consumer tastes and preferences,

Table 12.1   North Americans' repulsion from Europe in 1986

Country	Arrivals of US citizens			Arrivals of Canadian citizens		
	% of total tourist arrivals		% change	% of total tourist arrivals		% change
	1985	*1986*		*1985*	*1986*	
Albania	nd			nd		
Bulgaria	0.24	0.13	− 45.0	nd		
Czechoslovakia*	1.72	1.32	− 11.8	nd		
GDR	nd			nd		
Hungary	1.08	0.65	− 34.3	0.23	0.18	− 13.6
Poland	nd			nd		
Romania	0.51	0.29	− 45.1	0.08	0.05	− 38.9
Soviet Union	nd			nd		
Yugoslavia	2.83	1.74	− 38.3	0.47	0.41	− 12.8
Austria	6.51	3.38	− 48.4	0.62	0.51	− 19.2
FR Germany	20.74	15.16	− 29.6	1.62	1.44	− 14.3
Switzerland	20.73	12.99	− 41.2	1.94	1.65	− 20.1
United Kingdom	21.91	16.53	− 27.7	4.37	4.01	− 12.1

Notes: nd: no data
*   figures for all non-European arrivals

Source: WTO *Yearbook*, 1987.

with changes in the fashionability of resorts/countries often created by media coverage. Because of an often wide choice of resorts and strong competition between Western tour companies, with a considerable degree of potential substitution to be made, there may be little customer loyalty either to destinations or to modes of transport, type of accommodation and trade intermediaries.

(c)   In the case of transport, incoming Western tourists to Central and Eastern Europe can choose from a range of travel modes, and between their own national airline or another Western company. In terms of comfort and service these have been preferable to the region's airlines which have hitherto mostly used Soviet-built aircraft (Chapter 4) and have been stigmatised for surly or inefficient on-board service (although they have often been able to undercut Western fares, particularly for group rates). Central and Eastern Europeans, by contrast, until 1991 had usually been restricted to their own national airline as the only carrier willing to accept their inconvertible currency for fare payment. This is now generally no longer the case, with most transactions being conducted in convertible currencies, thereby acting further to constrain travellers from the region in the short to medium term (Hall, 1991c, pp. 56–8, 104–12).

(d) The tourism industry's supply components – accommodation, airports, railways and roads – exhibit a rigidity and inelasticity due to:

    (i) the need for such capital-intensive items to have long lead times for completion and opening following initial approval and planning;

    (ii) the difficulty of conversion once facilities are created;

    (iii) the need for skilled and semi-skilled staff who may not be readily available, such that considerable advance training may be necessary.

(e) By using specific fiscal measures, the 'exporting' country can manipulate exchange rates so that those for tourists are higher or lower than those for other foreign trade markets. Also, tourists are permitted to buy in domestic markets at the prices prevailing for the local residents, and at an advantage in the hard currency shops.

(f) Tourism is a multifaceted industry that directly affects a wide range of economic sectors – transport, accommodation, retailing, catering, entertainment and handicraft production – and indirectly affects many others, such as equipment manufacturers and utilities. Complementarity and equilibrium are therefore necessary between the different tourism components.

(g) Tourism brings a wider range of social and cultural benefits and costs than other export industries.

12.3 Tourism patterns of the post-communist transition

In interpreting post-war tourism trends in Europe three distinctive elements have been recognised: long-term growth, cyclical movements, and short-term erratics (Williams and Shaw, 1988). In the case of the new Central and Eastern Europe we may be viewing a convergence of all three elements: (a) an overall increase in growth, reflecting absolute lower levels of tourism activity in the region, and in part the response to a perceived 'saturation' of tourism in Western Europe; (b) a shorter-term growth cycle related to creeping liberalisation from the mid-1980s; and (c) the major 'erratic' of the 1989 revolutions, generating substantial short-term curiosity value and a longer-term actual and perceived improvement in accessibility and attitudes (Hall, 1991b, p. 112).

The few years since 1989 have seen enormous changes and uncertainty in the tourism industry of Central and Eastern Europe (Figure 12.1), and these are likely to continue for some time. Four major factors have contributed to increased tourism activity: (a) the easing of entry, exit and currency restrictions; (b) the changed 'image' of, and more substantial

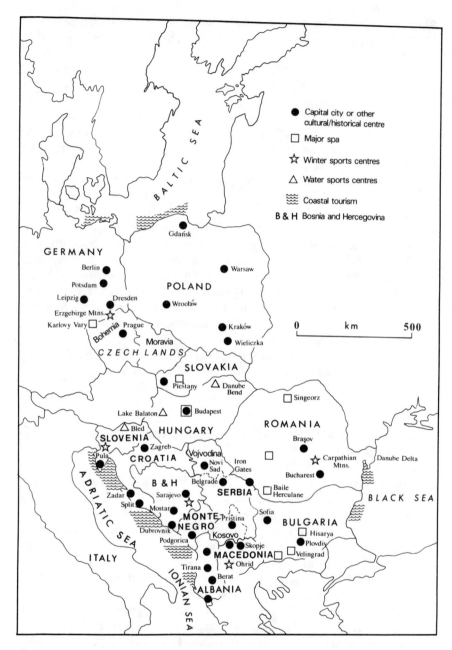

Figure 12.1   Central and Eastern Europe: major areas for tourism

Table 12.2 Central and Eastern Europe: international tourist arrivals, 1970–90 (millions)

	1970	1980	1985	1986	1987	1988	1989	1990	% change 1985–88	% change 1988–89	% change 1989–90
Albania	nd	nd	nd	nd	nd	nd	nd	nd		nd	
Bulgaria	2.5	5.5	3.4	3.5	3.6	4.0	4.3	4.5	15.8	8.8	4.3
Czechoslovakia	3.5	5.1	4.9	5.3	6.1	6.9	8.0	8.1	41.4	16.7	0.8
GDR	nd	1.5	1.6	2.0	2.1	2.2	3.1	–	43.5	39.0	–
Hungary	4.0	9.4	9.7	10.6	11.8	10.6	14.5	20.5	8.6	37.2	41.5
Poland	1.9	5.7	2.7	2.5	2.5	2.5	3.3	3.4	–9.2	32.0	3.2
Romania	2.3	6.7	4.8	4.5	5.1	5.5	4.9	6.5	15.5	34.6	–12.0
USSR	nd	nd	4.3	4.3	5.2	6.0	7.8	7.2	38.4	29.0	–7.1
Yugoslavia	4.7	6.4	8.4	8.5	8.9	9.0	8.6	7.9	6.9	–4.1	–8.8

Notes: nd: no data

Sources: WTO *Yearbook*, 1991, vol. 1, p. 104, 1992, vol. 1, p. 103; author's calculations.

Western media attention paid to, the region; (c) increasing Western involvement in aspects of tourism development; and (d) the newly-found mobility of Central and East Europeans themselves.

12.3.1 Patterns of tourist numbers

In terms of numbers of tourists (as opposed to all types of visitors), Table 12.2 records that during the second half of the 1980s considerable growth in arrivals was experienced, particularly for the non-beach holiday states of Central Europe: Czechoslovakia (41.4 per cent increase 1985–88, 16.7 per cent rise 1988–89), the then German Democratic Republic (43.5 and 39.0 per cent), and Hungary (8.6 and 37.2 per cent), together with the then Soviet Union (38.4 and 29.0 per cent). Poland fared less well (– 9.2 per cent 1985–88), but recovered in 1989 (32.0 per cent up). The traditional beach holiday destinations – Yugoslavia, Bulgaria and Romania – showed modest growth up to 1988, but both Yugoslavia and Romania saw downturns in 1989, a trend to be continued subsequently in the former, but arrivals in Romania in 1990 showed a 34.6 per cent increase, albeit in large part because of a cross-border influx of low-spending Soviet citizens. Hungary has revealed by far the most spectacular growth in tourist arrival numbers in the early transition period, with increases of 37.2 per cent for 1988–89 and 41.5 per cent for 1989–90.

12.3.2 Patterns of tourist receipts

The second half of the 1980s up to 1988 witnessed increases in tourism receipts for all countries of the region except Romania, reflecting that country's increasingly desperate economic and political situation (Table 12.3). Considerable increases over the 1985–88 period in certain countries – 90.8 per cent for Yugoslavia and 98.0 per cent for Czechoslovakia – reflected the significant role of high-spending tourists from the West. Romania, by contrast, experienced a 6.0 per cent decrease and for the 1980–88 period a 47.2 per cent downturn. In terms of receipt growth per tourist, Poland recorded the best performance for 1985–88 with an increase of 92.5 per cent, while Romania, along with Bulgaria and the USSR, saw decreases.

During the early stages of transition, as tourist numbers were gradually increasing, particularly day trippers responding to the easing of cross-border movement, receipts generally did not increase proportionately, such that for 1989, all except Romania and the USSR saw a decrease in receipts per tourist, and for 1990 only Bulgaria, Yugoslavia and again the Soviet Union recorded per capita increases, in the latter two cases reflecting declining rather than increasing tourist numbers.

Table 12.3 Central and Eastern Europe: international tourist receipts, 1980–90 (US $ millions)

	1980		1985		1988		1989		1990	
	a	b	a	b	a	b	a	b	a	b
Albania	nd	nd	nd	nd	nd	nd	nd	nd	nd	nd
Bulgaria	260	47.3	343	100.1	359	90.5	362	83.9	394	87.6
Czechoslovakia	338	66.3	307	63.1	608	88.3	581	72.3	470	58.0
GDR	nd	nd	nd	nd	nd	nd	nd	nd	nd	nd
Hungary	504	53.6	512	52.7	758	71.8	798	55.1	1,000	48.8
Poland	282	49.5	118	42.9	206	82.6	202	61.3	266	78.2
Romania	324	57.9	182	38.1	171	31.0	167	34.4	106	16.2
USSR	nd	nd	163	37.6	216	36.0	250	32.2	270	37.5
Yugoslavia	1,115	174.2	1,061	125.8	2,024	224.9	2,230	258.0	2,774	352.0

	% change							
	1980–88		1985–88		1988–89		1989–90	
	a	b	a	b	a	b	a	b
Albania	nd	nd	nd	nd	nd	nd	nd	nd
Bulgaria	38.1	− 8.5	4.7	− 9.6	0.8	− 7.3	8.8	4.4
Czechoslovakia	29.0	− 53.1	98.0	39.9	− 4.4	− 18.1	− 19.1	− 19.8
GDR	nd	nd	nd	nd	nd	nd	nd	nd
Hungary	50.6	33.6	48.0	36.2	5.3	− 23.3	25.3	− 11.5
Poland	− 31.6	56.0	74.6	92.5	− 1.9	− 25.8	31.7	− 27.5
Romania	− 45.7	− 44.7	− 6.0	− 18.6	− 2.3	11.0	− 36.5	16.2
USSR	nd	nd	32.5	− 4.3	15.7	− 10.6	8.0	16.3
Yugoslavia	81.5	29.1	90.8	78.8	10.2	11.2	24.4	36.5

Notes: nd: no data
     a   receipts (US $ millions)
     b   average income per tourist arrival (US dollars)

Sources: WTO *Yearbook*, 1991, vol. 1, p. 104, 1992, vol. 1, p. 103; author's calculations.

A sample of more recent unconfirmed figures for Hungary can exemplify that country's position as the region's leading tourist destination in terms of numbers, and, since the Yugoslav upheavals, also in terms of tourist receipts.

Hungary derived an income surplus from tourism of $170 million for the first seven months of 1991, a 30 per cent increase on the previous year's figure: the industry is now the country's largest balance of payments contributor. For the first six months of 1992, despite a 6 per cent decrease in tourism income, Hungarians travelling abroad spent 21 per cent less than in the same period for the previous year, thereby providing a surplus of $202.1 million: an increase of $30 million.

By contrast, the Balkan countries, despite possessing the most favourable climate and coastal conditions for mass tourism, have experienced stagnation or even decline in tourist numbers, reflecting an initial lack of clarity of political change, continuing instability, and a

LIVERPOOL HOPE UNIVERSITY COLLEGE

lower degree of transport accessibility from major West European markets. Additionally, tourists from the northern part of the region, no longer tied to Soviet-bloc vacation destinations, have been forsaking their post-war Black Sea coast holiday playgrounds for more enticing Western venues. However, in Bulgaria at least, preliminary figures for 1992 showed an increase of 23–25 per cent in foreign visitors compared to the previous disastrous year.

Beset by internal conflict and long-term uncertainty, (the former) Yugoslavia, previously unique in the region with its predominance of Western tourists (Hall, 1991c), has encapsulated the worst consequences of the 'new world order': fragmentation, intense nationalism suppressed for almost half a century and now exacting revenge for Second World War experiences, and the destruction of geographical frameworks established for Europe in the ruins of the First World War (Chapter 11). In terms of tourism, discussion of which appears almost obscene in the face of the mass cruelty and destruction being perpetuated there, the lands of the former Yugoslavia experienced a decrease in tourism earnings of 69 per cent during the first seven months of 1991, with 62 per cent fewer foreign visitors and 68 per cent fewer overnight stays. A decline in numbers had begun in 1989, and a 40 per cent reduction in 'domestic' tourists on the Adriatic riviera was recorded during the first six months of 1990, reflecting the Serbs' abandoning of Croatian resorts. Pegging the dinar rate to the Deutschmark also rendered Yugoslavia's once inexpensive resorts relatively costly for foreigners, and although a $2 million publicity campaign was initiated in Austria and Germany to ameliorate the imbalance, it was soon overtaken by events. In neighbouring Albania, international tourism activity, never excessive, had come to a virtual halt by 1992 (Hall, 1991a, 1992c).

12.4 Modal split of international visitor arrivals

Although the data are far from complete, Table 12.4 indicates that in the late 1980s, road transport was the predominant mode for visitor arrivals in the region, ranging from 56 per cent of all arrivals in Romania (1988) to 88 per cent in Yugoslavia (1988). The figures for several countries, but notably Yugoslavia and Bulgaria, are distorted by high levels of transit traffic, predominantly road-borne. Romania had a high proportion of arrivals by rail (36 per cent), reflecting its dependence on the regional market in 1988. Western 'packages' accounted for most of the air arrivals in Yugoslavia and Romania and Bulgaria, although the overall proportion of arrivals by air (between one and 12 per cent), was far lower than for West European 'package' holiday destination countries (Hall, 1991c).

Table 12.4 Central and Eastern Europe: visitor arrivals by mode of transport, 1988–90

Visitor arrivals by mode of transport, 1988–90 (per cent)

Countries	Air			Rail			Road			Sea/river		
	a	b	c	a	b	c	a	b	c	a	b	c
Albania	nd	nd	nd	nd	nd	nd	nd	nd	nd	nd	nd	nd
Bulgaria	12.2	12.1	7.0	7.8	10.0	8.9	79.1	76.8	83.4	0.9	1.1	0.8
Czechoslovakia	1.7	1.4	nd	24.0	25.1	nd	74.1	73.3	nd	0.2	0.2	nd
GDR	3.0	nd	nd	28.8	nd	nd	67.4	nd	nd	0.8	nd	nd
Hungary	3.6	2.7	1.6	20.5	20.2	16.6	75.4	76.6	81.6	0.6	0.5	0.3
Poland	nd	nd	nd	nd	nd	nd	nd	nd	nd	nd	nd	nd
Romania	5.5	nd	nd	36.2	nd	nd	55.9	nd	nd	2.3	nd	nd
Yugoslavia	5.3	nd	nd	4.2	nd	nd	88.3	nd	nd	2.2	nd	nd

Visitors arrivals by mode of transport, 1989–90, in millions

Countries	Air			Rail			Road			Sea/river		
	b	c	d	b	c	d	b	c	d	b	c	d
Bulgaria	0.99	0.72	−27.7	0.82	0.92	12.5	6.32	8.61	36.3	0.09	0.08	−14.4
Hungary	0.68	0.60	−12.1	5.03	6.24	24.0	19.10	30.70	60.7	0.11	0.10	−9.5

Totals

Countries	b	c	d
Bulgaria	8.22	10.33	25.65
Hungary	24.92	37.63	51.02

Notes: a 1988
b 1989
c 1990
d 1989–90 % change
nd no data

The data in this table refer to all 'visitor arrivals', the only statistics broken down by transport mode in WTO *Yearbooks*. By contrast, data in Tables 12.2 and 12.3 refer specifically to the more narrowly defined 'tourist arrivals'.

Source: WTO *Yearbooks*, Vol. 2, 1990, 1991, 1992.

Table 12.5 Bulgaria and Hungary: major changes in visitor arrivals by mode of transport, 1989–90 (per cent)

a. Major changes in arrivals by air, 1989–90		
Source	*Bulgaria*	*Hungary*
'Eastern Europe'	– 38.3	– 65.8
Czechoslovakia	– 27.3	– 53.7
Poland	– 40.6	– 55.0
Austria		– 34.9
Finland	– 31.8	
Hungary	– 30.6	–
All Europe	– 29.9	
Soviet Union		– 29.7
Netherlands		+ 18.2
Turkey	+ 33.0	
USA	(– 5.6)	+ 35.0
UK		+ 36.0
France		+ 42.1
Romania	+ 147.5	+ 400.0

b. Major changes in arrivals by road, 1989–90		
Source	*Bulgaria*	*Hungary*
'Eastern Europe'	+ 73.5	+ 75.5
Romania	+ 758.5	+ 936.0
Netherlands		+ 329.4
Soviet Union	+ 235.2	(– 1.3)
France		+ 200.0
Yugoslavia	+ 13.1	+ 90.4
UK		+ 56.7
Turkey	+ 32.7	
Czechoslovakia	– 28.9	
Austria	– 39.4	
Hungary	– 44.6	–

Source: WTO *Yearbook*, Vol. 2, 1992.

Although subsequent data available from the WTO (1991, 1992) are more limited, for Bulgaria and Hungary at least, the political and economic changes of 1989–90 appear to have had at least a three-fold effect on patterns of visitor arrivals: (a) substantially increasing overall numbers of arrivals (to Bulgaria by over 25 per cent between 1989 and 1990, and to Hungary by over 51 per cent); (b) raising the proportion as well as absolute numbers of arrivals by road (to Bulgaria by over 36 per cent, to Hungary by over 60 per cent); and (c) stimulating a decrease in arrivals by air both proportionately, and perhaps a little surprisingly, in absolute terms (with Bulgarian air arrivals down nearly 28 per cent and those to Hungary by 12 per cent). Of the other two recorded modes of arrival, rail-borne travellers increased in number to both Bulgaria and Hungary, although they decreased in relative terms. The small water-borne sector recorded both absolute and relative declines at the turn of the decade.

The relationship between road and air arrivals in Bulgaria and Hungary for 1990 is interesting (Table 12.5). While both countries experienced significant proportional decreases of air arrivals from Eastern Europe (with the notable exception of newly-freed Romanians, although the 147.5 per cent increase for Bulgaria represented only an additional two thousand arrivals), the response of West Europeans was far less uniform, with Bulgaria recording mostly losses but Hungary making some notable gains. For arrivals by road, much greater numbers of Romanians, and, for Bulgaria, also Soviet citizens, distort the picture for incoming East Europeans. The number of Romanians entering neighbouring Bulgaria by road increased from a 1989 figure of 181,921 to a hefty 1.562 million for the following year, raising their share of all road arrivals to Bulgaria from 2.88 to 18.13 per cent; for Hungary the change was even more dramatic, the country being seen by many Romanians as a gateway for escape to the West: numbers increased from 100,000 to 7.036 million, raising the Romanian share of road arrivals to Hungary from 0.52 to 22.92 per cent. In respect of this latter consideration, Romanians arriving in Hungary by rail in 1990 increased by 403.1 per cent compared to the previous year, again by far the largest increase of any source country.

Clearly for Bulgaria there is a Balkan emphasis in these figures, while for Hungary, aside from the Romanian skewing, and the increase in Yugoslavs – presumably Serbs turning away from the Croatian coast – the strengthening of a number of West European markets for overland travel boosted significantly that country's arrival figures.

12.5 Transport implications of international tourism development

As a support and facilitator of international tourism development, the role and nature of transport can be viewed alongside the region's other structural and infrastructural shortcomings. These arise both from an inheritance of the priorities and prejudices of the communist period and from the current uncertainty of post-communist transition (Hall, 1992d). The consequent implications of greater Western-oriented international tourism for transport development are several:

1. The quality of the region's tourist services has been low and very variable by accepted Western standards and requires comprehensive improvement. Transport and communications, as well as accommodation, catering and utilities have suffered from decades of neglect in which the economic and ideological cost of upgrading infrastructure to meet the needs of foreigners was considered too high. Even in a country such as Hungary, by 1992 only 60 per cent of hotel staff possessed training qualifications and just a third could speak a foreign language, emphasising the considerable requirement for appropriate staff training. This was recognised by American Express in 1991, when the company launched a $500,000 fund to develop personnel skills for the tourism industries of Czechoslovakia, Hungary and Poland: those countries of the region most advanced in the improvement of service provision (Hamilton, 1991). In the following year the EC Phare programme allocated 4.5 million Ecus to Poland for the development of a national tourism plan with an emphasis on training and promotion.

2. In parts of Central and Eastern Europe uncertainty, instability and conflict are creating an organisational vacuum within which the priorities for developing a tourism industry and for investing in an appropriate transport infrastructure cannot be firmly established. The former Yugoslavia is the obvious example where such infrastructure is being destroyed. Yugotours, then Yugoslavia's largest tour operator, abandoned its 1991 programme in August of that year, and for the 1992 season forsook its home 'country' to promote Mediterranean sailing holidays and packages to Malta, Greece and Turkey. Knock-on effects of the conflict, and the impact of UN sanctions against Serbia, saw the Bulgarian Committee for Tourism anticipating a loss of $20 million in 1992 from the absence of five million Middle Eastern transit passengers. MALÉV expected to lose four million forints a month due to the suspension of its weekly flights to Belgrade. In Albania, social unrest, fuel and food shortages coupled with uncertainties over future privatisation prevented the state tourist organisation Albturist from promoting tourism plans for 1992.

3. While exit visa requirements for Central and East Europeans have been abolished, freedom of movement to the West has been constrained both by administrative and economic impediments: a 'dollar curtain' has replaced the former 'ferrous' drape across the continent. For example, while Britain has visa-free agreements with Czechoslovakia, Hungary and Poland, citizens of other Central and East European countries still require visas to travel to Britain, at a substantial financial disadvantage. At the time of writing, the cost of a UK visa for a Romanian citizen was equivalent to about half a month's income.

Plate 12.3 Tourist coaches from France, Austria, Portugal, Russia and Germany congest Heroes Square in Budapest behind less conventional four-wheel mobility. (Derek Hall)

4. The social, cultural and physical environmental impacts of tourism activities in the region may be severe as the industry expands with a new generation of indigenous entrepreneurs looking for quick profits. Tourist traffic congestion is but one element of this (Plate 12.3). Such problems may generate a strong negative reaction from host populations: involving local communities more closely in the tourism development process can be a means of ameliorating such situations. Yet experience of bottom-up development is limited in the region. Questions of defining and recognising 'carrying capacities' and 'saturation levels' are particularly pressing for the region's more sensitive environments. This has been apparent, for example, in Romania's Danube Delta, where the use of inappropriate leisure craft has endangered fragile ecosystems (Hall, 1988, 1991a). On the other hand, the poor environmental image which has been projected of certain parts of Central and Eastern Europe has acted as a sub-regional force of tourism repulsion (Table 12.1). Atmospheric and water pollution and toxic waste problems, reinforced by the after-math of the Chernobyl accident in 1986 will take some time and a

great deal of Western finance to diminish (Carter and Turnock, 1992; Hall, 1992e).

5. With absolute numbers of Western tourists in Central and Eastern Europe being far greater than before, the proportion going to a few specific locations may well increase as more package holidays are organised, as accommodation and transport economies of scale for host countries are realised, and as disparities in service levels and tourist investment in the region increase. In the longer term, however, the need to diffuse tourism pressures will be paramount, with considerable implications for transport and communications infrastructure. But with growing differentiation of perceived tourism attractiveness between countries, particularly with continuing Balkan instability, an international polarisation may increasingly take place, perhaps replicating and reinforcing the differing levels of Western support for the region's economic restructuring (Chapter 2). This will be exacerbated by the fact that the region is very vulnerable to tourism fashion changes, which are themselves sensitive to instability and the short-term problems with which the region is currently beset.

6. Nonetheless, the region's diversity of physical and cultural environments and attractions provides a wide range of tourism 'products' for marketing purposes. The need to target niche markets, preferably high spending groups with minimal adverse impact and season-extending activities, points to the need for an emphasis upon conference/business tourism, and the availability of commensurate transport facilities. With market segmentation, specialist emphasis is likely to be placed upon the region's health resorts and wildlife wealth, and such attractions clearly require sensitive and effective management, including appropriate transport planning and management.

12.6 Transport for tourism development: East–West partnerships

In attempting to respond to some of the above problems, the creation of joint ventures with Western capital, and of other forms of partnership, is being sought in the region. Improving both the supply and quality of services and facilities are the major reasons for such ventures, reinforced by the need to compensate for the inability of the region's partners to finance development themselves due to lack of capital. The ability of transnational corporations to guarantee product quality is important in items subject to major competition, while at the same time helping to upgrade local facilities through the pressure of competition and demonstration effects (Buckley and Witt, 1990).

Both quality and capacity problems within the region's transport and communications systems have constrained all forms of tourism, as they have done in other economic sectors. Eliminating such obstacles will continue to embroil the region for some considerable time. Other chapters in this volume have focused on the wider economic, social and environmental implications of transport upgrading. In relation to the specific needs of the international tourism industry, a number of areas of East–West partnership clearly require attention:

1. With the monopolistic position of the old state-sponsored travel agencies breaking down, East–West partnerships in travel and tour organisation have been required to facilitate outbound tourism to locations formerly denied to citizens of the region. An early notable development was the partnership between the then East German state airline Interflug and the West German Touristik Union International, which opened a travel agency in the GDR early in 1990 to offer travel packages to holiday destinations in the Mediterranean and to far-eastern destinations such as Singapore. The Hungarian agency Ibusz, in partnership with the Italian Aviatour company, set up a travel agency for holidays to Asia. Such partnerships need to bring the expertise of outbound tourism operations to destinations previously outside the experience of the region's travel companies and to open new tourism horizons at least for the region's citizens with access to sufficient hard-currency funds.

2. Substantial road transit traffic has been experienced in the region for at least the past quarter century, associated with migrant labour movement between South-Eastern and Western Europe, increasing freight trucking between Western Europe and the Middle East, and growing tourism flows. Although problems vary locally, the region's road infrastructure and service provision is desperately in need of upgrading to meet the new demands of tourism generation. The IBRD arm of the World Bank has been funding development of the Baltic to Adriatic Trans-European Highway. Such a north–south spine motorway system would encourage greater tourism movement from the north to the south of the region. However, although about 800 km of the 1,183 km trans-Yugoslav highway had been completed by 1991, conflict and subsequent Western sanctions against Serbia rendered the 1994 completion date untenable, and the likelihood of longer-term tension in the Balkans must bring into question the tourism value of such a project.

3. New coach services have been opened within the region and from Western Europe. An early development was the inauguration in May 1990 of an operation between Vienna, Prague and Karlovy Vary, running six times a week. With a scheduled journey time of five hours, this provides a faster connection between the two capitals

than the existing rail service. Several UK travel operators have extended regular continental routes into eastern Germany, Hungary, Czechoslovakia and Poland. The speeding up of border formalities is a crucial element in the competitive development of such services.

4. Plans to connect Central and Eastern Europe to the expanding Western European high-speed rail network (Figure 1.1) would appear to be aimed at business passenger traffic rather than the leisure market or indeed necessarily improving freight movement. The enormous costs of upgrading infrastructure will require substantial dependence upon the major international funding institutions, but the current Balkan crisis, as in the case of planned trans-European highway development, has at least postponed the construction of significant elements of the network. For example, a 507-km double-track upgrading for 200-kph speeds through 'Greater Serbia' from the Hungarian border at Subotica to the Bulgarian frontier at Dimitrovgrad had been planned for completion by 1998. Costing some $3.5 billion, this development was dependent upon European Investment Bank support, currently suspended.

5. In many respects air transport is the key link for future tourism development: the region's revenue passenger miles are expected to rise from fifteen billion in 1990 to forty billion by 2005 (Kateraas, 1991). Motivated by new business opportunities, as well as by tourism development potential, a number of new joint venture airlines have been established to fill gaps in the existing structure. New Western technology is being taken up for improved economy and passenger comfort, joint ventures, if not full privatisation, are being entered into (Table 13.1), and most of the region's airlines are adopting new 'images', including designer fleet liveries and logos (eg. Plate 4.3). Improved customer services and staff training programmes are required, and new routes are essential to better open up the region for both tourism and business opportunities.

The expansion and improvement of facilities at major airports is also being undertaken (Figure 1.1), usually with Western assistance, to cope with new and likely future demands. The bringing into civil air use of secondary- and tertiary-level airports and landing strips, previously operated by the (often Soviet) military, reflects the need to make provincial centres accessible to tourists and business travellers. For example, four Hungarian provincial airfields were reopened in 1989, in response to growing demands for charter tourist flights, domestic air services, air taxis and recreational air services, including sports flying.

12.7 Conclusions

As with most elements of the region's infrastructure and service sector, transport for tourism development is in urgent need of substantial and comprehensive upgrading. Transport and communications are pivotal in connecting the region with the world's leisure and business markets, yet it is just these areas which were grossly underfunded and neglected under the communists. Growth in business and conference tourism will be particularly stimulated by coordinated upgradings in air transport, high-quality accommodation, conference facilities and telecommunications systems, which, it would appear, only Western involvement can currently provide. Far from being altruistic, this will depend upon: (a) a recognition of profitable returns on investment; (b) a virtual elimination of CoCom restrictions; (c) the availability of Western aid, being provided with the explicit aim of hastening the restructuring of economies to market orientation, such as the one million Ecus provided by the EC for the privatisation of the Bulgarian tourism industry; and (d) a continuing fashionability and long-term market value.

Likely future trends include:

(a) the growth of a highly segmented market: this has only taken place to a limited extent, although new 'niches' are opening up;
(b) complex and dynamic tourist flows reflecting technological and political influences on transport. Increasing levels of car ownership and mobility across the region will be matched by improved air technology. Further technological changes and governmental attitudes towards transport deregulation and privatisation will continue to have a substantial impact, given the poorer technology and rigidity of governmental restrictions hitherto experienced; and
(c) the region's participation in, and contribution to, a growing concentration and internationalisation of capital. Transnational fleet ownership will act as the most obvious outward symbol of increasing vertical and horizontal structural linkages within the industry, entailing air and surface transport operation, travel agencies and tour operation.

13 Key themes and agendas

Derek Hall

13.1 Transport and economic restructuring: sustainable?

The major components of economic restructuring in Central and Eastern Europe can be summarised as:

(a) elimination of the predominant state ownership of the means of production, transport and trade through privatisation;
(b) elimination of the planning apparatus and institutions administering a centralised economic system;
(c) introduction of currency convertibility and market-led price reform;
(d) reform of inward investment and foreign trade regulations;
(e) establishment of a private banking system;
(f) introduction of a tax system commensurate with a market economy;
(g) formulation of bankruptcy laws;
(h) establishment of stock exchange activities.

Privatisation is central to such comprehensive systemic change, and has been proceeding at differing rates in different countries, not least in the transport sector. In most cases, new private operators have entered the market while old state enterprises continue alongside, often in a dominant role. For example, in the Hungarian road freight haulage business, by 1991 only 30 per cent of the lorry fleet was privately owned (Chapter 6).

The unprecedented privatisation of substantial elements of national economies is proceeding far from smoothly. As part of the philosophy's baggage, restructuring has been predicated on the assumption that privatisation generates greater enterprise efficiency. But the evidence is at best inconclusive. Disputed property and land rights and the rise of private monopolies – a not unfamiliar theme in the privatised UK bus operating industry, for example (Knowles and Hall, 1992) – are but two immediate structural problems. One estimate now suggests that at current rates it will take Czechoslovakia, Hungary and Poland an average of twenty-eight years to privatise just one half of the state companies still on their hands (Reynolds and Young, 1992).

Notably varying approaches to restructuring are being taken; for example, in the case of the region's air transport industry, where most national flag carriers (Table 13.1) are preparing for privatisation. On the one hand, LOT has been divesting itself of uneconomic aircraft and a wide range of service activities. At Warsaw's Okęcie international airport, an Australian group has taken over the franchise for twelve duty-free shops, Scandinavian Airlines System (SAS) is now managing the airport's in-flight catering arrangements under a seven-year agreement, and AMR Services (US) has responsibility for ticketing, luggage handling, aircraft maintenance and defrosting, and freight management. MALÉV, on the other hand, plans to keep its fleet of Tupolevs after privatisation for use on charter flights and other secondary activities. Air Budapest Ltd was set up for this purpose in the spring of 1991, leasing two TU-154s for excursions to the Canary Islands and Malta. An important consideration in MALÉV's potential market capitalisation is the extent to which it will continue to have monopoly rights on aviation fuel supply and duty-free shop operation in the country's airports. The demonopolisation of such activities and their opening to international tendering is thus rapidly changing the character of the region's airports.

While perhaps most explicit in the air industry, joint ventures with Western capital are also being created for the improvement of both supply and quality of transport technology, infrastructure and services across the region's transport sectors. They also help overcome the lack of capital held in the region to finance development, and to upgrade facilities and guarantee product and service quality through the pressure of competition and demonstration effects. But as noted in earlier chapters, the spatial and structural distribution of such ventures is notably, and increasingly, skewed. By the end of 1991, Hungary had attracted 11,000 joint ventures, representing $2 billion foreign capital investment. During the first half of 1992 a further 3,000 were added constituting one half of all such ventures in the region during that period. By contrast, joint venture growth in the Balkans was minimal. In sectoral terms, some 60 per cent of all the region's JVs are in manufacturing, 30 per cent in trade, and, surprisingly, only 10 per cent are in services (Warr, 1992).

Large proportions of transport and other sectors of Central and Eastern Europe's economies are still far removed from a thoroughgoing restructuring, while the living standards of the region's citizens continue to fall. In Hungary and Poland the state-owned sector was still responsible, at mid-1992, for two-thirds of the national economy, and in other countries of the region the figure rose to up to 90 per cent. A recent analysis argued that up to two-thirds of state enterprises in each economy were on the brink of collapse (Reynolds and Young, 1992).

Table 13.1   Central and Eastern Europe: restructuring the flag carriers

Country	Airline	No. of aircraft	Fleet upgrading*	Restructuring position
Albania	Albanian Airlines	2	Canadian 36- and 50-seaters	JV with Tyrolean Airways inaugurated 1992
Bulgaria	Balkan	38	4 Airbus A320s 3 Boeing 737s 2 Boeing 767s	Converted to a joint-stock company 1992. Privatised 1993 with up to 49% foreign airline share ownership
CIS†	Aeroflot	1,900	5 Airbus A310s	From 31.3.92 replaced by 92 independent units both within and outside of the CIS. The Airbuses, delivered in 1992, are operated by Russian International Airlines
Croatia	Croatian Airlines	3	3 Boeing 737s (ex-Lufthansa) (initially 2 MD-82s leased from Adria)	50% state owned: established 1991
Czechoslovakia	ČSA	27	2 Airbus 310s 5 Boeing 737s 4 ATR-72s	Legally a Czech company 1992 controversial 'sale': 60% state, 40% Air France/EBRD
Estonia	Estonia Air	16	(ex-Aeroflot TU-134s and Yak-40s)	Established 1992
Hungary	MALÉV	25	6 Boeing 737s 2 Boeing 767s 1 BAe 146	Privatised 1992/3: state 51%, foreign airlines 30%, employees 8%
Latvia	Baltic International Airlines	37	(ex-Aeroflot TU-134s, 154s and An-24s)	Established 1992
Lithuania	Lithuanian Airlines	104	1 Boeing 737 sub-leased from MALÉV (ex-Aeroflot Tu-134s, Yak-40s, 42s, An-24s and 26s)	Established 1992
Poland	LOT	24	9 Boeing 737s 3 Boeing 767s 4 ATR-72s	Privatised 1993: state 51% foreign airlines and guaranteed employers' stake 49%

Table 13.1 contd.

Country	Airline	No. of aircraft	Fleet upgrading*	Restructuring position
Romania	Tarom	35	3 Airbus A310s	To be 30% 'privatised'
Slovenia	Adria	10	(Ageing DC9s)	Previously existed alongside JAT
Yugoslavia	JAT	32	9 Boeing 737s (Ageing DC9s, DC10s, B-727s)	Converted to a joint-stock company February 1992 with Republic of Serbia holding 51%.

* In fleet or on order, owned or leased
† see also Chapter 4
CIS: Commonwealth of Independent States
EBRD: European Bank for Reconstruction and Development
JV: Joint venture

Sources: Various issues of: *BBC Summaries of World Broadcasts: Eastern Europe*; *Business Eastern Europe*; *Business Europa*; *East European Markets*; *EuroBusiness*; *The Economist*; *Flight International*; Hall, 1991.

13.2 Realisable road and rail plans?

Aspirations to extend the growing West European high speed rail network eastwards (Figure 1.1) will be constrained by the enormous costs of upgrading infrastructure and by political instability and upheaval in the Balkans. A high-speed rail system linking Paris and Warsaw via Berlin, for example, would cost Poland alone $4 billion. More realistic and potentially important sub-regional developments include the planned linking up of Albanian, Macedonian and Bulgarian rail systems to establish a through route from the Adriatic at Durrës to the Black Sea at Varna, for onward ferry connections with the Ukraine and overland routes to Turkey and the Middle East. Such a line would considerably shorten the distance for shipping goods from Italy to Eastern Europe, and could substantially enhance Albania's role within the region. Albania once sat astride the major routeway from Rome to Byzantium – the Via Egnatia – and the site of its present major port, Durrës (Bërxholi, 1986), was the landfall for the movement of goods and people eastwards across the Adriatic. That port could gain considerable advantage from such a development, particularly if coupled to free port status. Discussions have also taken place on the possible construction of a road from Macedonia to the Adriatic: certainly overland links are poor at present.

International financing for the construction of key sections of the long-projected Trans-European Highway connecting the Baltic with the Adriatic and the Middle East continues. In the short- to medium-term, however, the diversion of South-East–West European transit traffic away from Balkan instability is exposing major infrastructural shortcomings and is focusing minds and investment on the need for upgrading Central Europe's road links.

Although both Hungarian and Czechoslovak governments have embarked on placing the construction of new motorways in the hands of outside contractors on a concessionary basis, the effort to upgrade infrastructures in the absence of immediately available finance will be a very long-term process. In Czechoslovakia, for example, where the transport ministry estimates the cost of upgrading the country's transport infrastructure to be over $8 billion, the need to extend the existing 540-km network of motorways to 1,800 km by the end of the century has seen the first foreign tenders invited for a link between Plzen and the German border. In Hungary, bidding for concessions for the first motor-way toll section – the 48-km M1 completion from Györ to Hegyeshalom (Austrian border) and Rajka (Czech border) – began in 1992. In the case of both of these land-locked Central European states, governments argue that motorway links with Western neighbours provide the best means to boost economic growth. The role of Western institutions such as the EBRD in this process is notable. Poland, for example, has sought EBRD and World Bank financial assistance for plans to set up a motorway construction agency to oversee the building of 2,000 km (Chapter 7).

Environmental opposition to new highway construction has been limited largely to eastern Germany, where the planned 290-km motorway between Lübeck and Szczecin has been the subject of much rancour. Greenpeace has led a consortium of groups threatening to take the Bonn government to the European Court of Justice, claiming that the official justification for the development was based upon false traffic statistics. The Poles have shown a disinclination to extend such a link from Szczecin to Kaliningrad, as the Germans would wish, for fear of exacerbating the already potentially precarious status of Poland's sea ports. Progress of the Via Baltica will be watched with interest (Chapter 7).

13.3 New equipment and technology: who pays? who benefits?

The region's motor vehicle industry, noted for its high debt and low technology, has been the recipient of substantial inward investment since 1989. Central and Eastern Europe is viewed by Western and Asian manufacturers as a promising market in the medium to longer term, with a current level of car ownership at 117 per thousand population compared to an EC average of 360. Poland, for example, has undertaken a series of joint ventures which could generate significant employment and establish the country as an important bridgehead for Western car manufacturers seeking to exploit a highly-skilled but low-paid ($200 per month) labour force (Wellisz, 1992; Hall, 1993).

Hungary, noted for the export performance of its Ikarus buses, did not have a motor car industry under the communists, but since 1989 Suzuki has established an assembly plant, Ford has a components production unit and General Motors has set up an engine factory. The knock-on impact on infrastructural development of such inward investment can be substantial. The General Motors plant at Szentgotthard, for example, opened in July 1992 to produce 200,000 petrol engines a year, has required the construction of a 30-km high-pressure gas pipeline, and has encouraged the opening of six extra crossing points along the Austrian border.

Former modal inflexibility is changing, with the take-up in the region of bi-modal transport systems such as road-railers, in anticipation of considerable container traffic development. Overburdened with transit freight traffic diverted from 'Yugoslavia', in 1992 the Hungarian government reduced by 90 per cent the road tax on foreign lorries which reached their destination on Hungarian territory by rail or ship instead of by road. Hungary's leading transporters have set up a partnership with Austrian and German interests to employ truck-carrying trains and ships between Budapest/Sopron and Hamburg/Bremen. Promotion of truck transport by ship on the Danube has also been pursued.

All the region's airlines, with the exception of Yugoslavia's JAT, operated only Soviet-designed aircraft up to 1989. Subsequent political aspirations and the demands of world market competition have seen the adoption of new marketing approaches – including designer liveries and logos – and Western aircraft technologies (Chapter 4; Table 13.1). Improved performance, passenger comfort, fuel efficiency and the ability to reduce ground staff requirements have resulted from the latter. Lease or purchase of such massive capital investment has been a question related to each airline's particular financial circumstances and long-term requirements. When MALÉV leased the region's first modern Boeings (737s) from the Irish company Guinness Peat Aviation (GPA), the airline was in no financial position to undertake outright purchase, but did seek a relatively rapid, symbolically important service inauguration of Western equipment. More recently, the Hungarian flag carrier has been negotiating the purchase of Boeing 767s with Japanese creditors. Balkan Bulgarian, on the other hand, is leasing its first 737s (Table 13.1) from an Australian company.

LIVERPOOL HOPE UNIVERSITY COLLEGE

13.4 Competition for hegemony?

With German and Italian ports and trade centres competing to extend their hinterlands deep into the region, a diversion of maritime traffic away from Central and Eastern Europe appears to be a medium-term consequence of change, with Rostock, the former GDR's only major port, becoming a prime victim (Hall, 1992b), due to: (a) its disadvantageous geographical location – up to four days' sailing time can be saved by calling at Hamburg or Bremen/Bremerhaven and trucking overland; and (b) the port's inferior infrastructure, particularly its inability to handle larger container ships.

German unification, bringing to an end the independence of the East German deep sea merchant fleet (Cranfield, 1991), has seen Hamburg, in the vanguard of other western German ports, intent on supplanting Rostock as the natural entry and exit port for eastern Germany, a region which could be generating 840,000 container units annually by the end of the decade, as part of the process of regaining the 'natural' hinterland of Czechoslovakia and Hungary which Hamburg dominated before the Second World War (Morgan, 1948, 1949; Weigand, 1956). Long-term plans to upgrade the river Elbe, an artery for Czechoslovakia, will further assist Hamburg's aims. Bremen/Bremerhaven are also competing for Eastern trade, with regular flows to and from eastern Germany and Poland, and agreements with Czechoslovakia and Hungary for containers to be trucked overland to and from the ports. Rostock's long-term future is likely to be as a ro-ro/feeder port for the eastern Baltic (Eller, 1990b).

The north-east Italian port of Trieste (Moodie, 1945; Mihelič, 1969; Navak, 1970) has been countering competition from north European ports by negotiating reductions in freight tariffs on goods transiting from Czechoslovakia, Hungary, Austria and the former Yugoslavia (Eller, 1990a), and expanding its main container terminal by 50 per cent (Haberman, 1990). In addition to an international offshore financial centre developed to stimulate links with Central and Eastern Europe, scientific collaboration with the region has been strengthened with the establishment of a business innovation centre and science park (BIC-Trieste). This has promoted similar innovation centres at Koper in Slovenia, Pécs in Hungary, and St. Petersburg.

The rivalry between Italy and Germany/Austria for regional economic influence has been most apparent on the very edges of the Balkan theatre of conflict. Slovenia has debated the relative merits of giving priority to an east–west or north–south motorway axis. The first route would connect northern Italy, Hungary and the Ukraine, and has been supported by the Trieste-based regional government of northern Italy, claiming that construction costs could be met by a consortium in return for thirty-five years' toll collection. A north–south alignment would link Germany and Austria with Slovenia and Croatia, and a feasibility study was presented to the Slovenian government by a German company early in 1992. It has the advantage of employing the Karawanken tunnel through the Alps between Austria and Slovenia. An Austrian–German construction company claimed to have already secured the Croatian government's approval for a 116km DM8,400 million highway from Spielfeld in Austria to Zagreb.

The Italians have also been seeking an expansion of pipeline links in the region, and Rome has emphasised its desire to consolidate its former areas of influence in the Danube–Alpine–Adriatic region rather than allow German–Austrian interests to dominate.

13.5 Competition for hub status

The expansion and improvement of facilities at potential major hub airports is being undertaken on a considerable scale with Western assistance, to cope with new and likely future demands. Berlin, Prague, Budapest and Warsaw will all be competing for major hub status in the region in the coming decade, and Western financiers, construction firms and service suppliers will be similarly competing to gain the development contracts.

For Prague, a Canadian–US company and British Aerospace have concluded an agreement to finance, build and operate a new terminal at the existing Ruzyne airport with an annual capacity of 4.8 million passengers per year. Yet both here and in Warsaw, other Western interests have put forward plans to develop new international hub airports on former Soviet-controlled military airfields based on private-sector financing. For the Prague site, 30 km north-east of the city, support for an economic development zone, construction of a magnetic levitation transport link to the capital and promotion of the scheme for creating the 'European air travel crossroads for the next century' have been robustly advanced by the potential developers. Similarly, for Warsaw, with a new terminal building recently completed at Okęcie international airport, a military airfield at Modlin has been proposed as the site for Central and Eastern Europe's biggest airport and transit centre by a German–Italian–UK–US consortium with support from the EBRD.

Disharmony has surrounded the debate concerning the site for a new Berlin international hub, with the Bonn government, City of Berlin and the state of Brandenburg each having different priorities and preferred locations. With the best chance of being Europe's third most important airport with 40 million passengers by 2010, the development is seen as vitally important for generating up to 100,000 new jobs at a time of depression for the eastern German economy.

Both of the region's land-locked countries also acknowledge the need to establish hub roles in relation to the new international waterway links secured by the 1992 completion of the Main–Danube Canal (Korompai, 1977; Turnock, 1979; Wulf, 1983; Mellor, 1984; Seidenfus, 1987; Bryson, 1992), which closed the final gap in the 3,488-km link between the North and Black Seas. Recognising the enhanced potential for the transport of lower-value bulk goods between Western and Eastern Europe, Czechoslovakia has been further pursuing a canal scheme to link the Oder with the Danube, for completion early in the twenty-first century. To further enhance Slovakia's Danubian role a new container terminal has been established at Bratislava with Austrian cooperation, adding to the pre-existing oil terminal facilities there. Downstream, at the Csepel free port to the south of Budapest, Hungary has opened a new international cargo terminal in a joint venture with a German forwarding company. Hungary realises little more than 10 per cent of the carrying capacity of her 450-km section of the Danube, and there exists the particular need to further expand container storage and ro-ro facilities. While these developments represent competing aims of neighbouring land-locked states, for a number of observers, not least the Italians, they also express a further dimension of the German–Austrian re-assertion of influence in the region.

As part of their competitive armoury, governments of the region have designated free ports/free trade zones (Clough, 1991; Kuźma, 1990) as an inducement to inward investment for employment generation, technology diffusion and skill enhancement, offering a variety of tax concessions, relaxed import procedures and lower customs duties, land availability, low rents, qualified staff and cheap skilled labour.

Yet lack of legal clarity, particularly in such areas as insurance and repatriation of funds, has inhibited some potential investors. Further, as foreign investment liberalisation takes hold across the region it is likely that free trade zones will become progressively less attractive to Western companies. They are likely to be most successful in conjunction with the movement of bulk goods both westwards and further eastwards. Notable in this respect are Romania's free trade zones on the Black Sea, notably at Constanţa Sud, in conjunction with the 64-km Danube–Black Sea Canal, completed in 1984 (Spulber, 1954; Sharman, 1983; Turnock, 1987), and on the Danube, with the completion of the Black Sea–North Sea canal system in mind (EIU, 1991, pp. 22–3).

13.6 Conclusions

It requires little foresight to suggest that political and economic instability is likely to continue for some time, particularly in the Balkans. If one assumes, optimistically, that the division of Czechoslovakia will provide only a temporary setback to Central Europe's relative stability, it is likely that disparities in levels of development and inward investment between that part of the region and the high-risk Balkans will intensify. Initial advantage, EC association and cultural factors will reinforce such a gulf. This will be further reflected in the geographical bias of developing transport systems.

Second, the two dimensions of regional competition are likely to be intensified. On the one hand, the states of Central Europe will be competing increasingly with each other to gain ascendancy in regional transport hub status. With the likelihood of continued rising unemployment, the prize of an inter-continental airport and its employment generation potential will appear increasingly seductive. On the other hand, there will be heightened competition for trade and political influence between Germany–Austria and Italy as they vie with each other to re-assert their pre-war transport roles in the region. This will also be reflected in transport orientations and the extent to which northern or southern patrons assist technology transfer and service upgrading.

Transport and communications are pivotal in connecting the region with the world's leisure and business markets. Growth in business and conference tourism, for example, particularly from within Europe and from North America, can be particularly stimulated by coordinated improvements in air transport, high-quality accommodation, conference facilities and telecommunications systems. Although the region has attracted limited investment from outside of Europe and North America, the very process of developing a modern transport and telecommunications infrastructure in a region with continuing low labour costs is likely to tempt Middle Eastern and Far Eastern investors wishing to enter the EC market by the back door.

However, the imposition of 1980s free-market policies cannot continue unabated, and increasingly governments at all levels within the region will be taking more time to consider the long-term social and political implications of producing large pools of unemployment, and of the environmental and cultural consequences of implementing motorway, airport and high-speed rail policies based on other people's money and expertise. There is an underlying danger that Central and Eastern Europe could slip into a dependency relationship with the West, becoming dominated by Western multinational companies and consortia, and increasingly burdened with levels of debt repayment. On the other hand, the growing participation of the self-employed and small businesses in road transport activities is widening the indigenous base of entrepreneurial expertise.

But there exists a serious mis-match between need and supply of advice from the West. Indeed, it is highly questionable whether the West European/North American context is the most appropriate model for application in Central and Eastern Europe. The example of East Asian enterprise should also be examined for ways of competing successfully in international markets and of more realistically relating to the indigenous level of economic development and appropriate government intervention. If current post-communist policies have not turned around the region's economies and living standards within five years, there is a strong likelihood that the reform process will become politically and socially unsustainable, and other solutions will be sought, perhaps from the grass roots (Reynolds and Young, 1992; Simmons, 1992).

Research agendas therefore need to encompass assessments of:

(a) the social, cultural and environmental implications of current transport policies;
(b) the extent to which new transport and communications technology liberates the region or merely renders it more vulnerable to international monopolist penetration;
(c) individual transport sectors' development – including inter-modal and bi-modal change – and national policy-making processes;
(d) the long-term impact of the funding policies of such bodies as the EBRD, to help clarify any hidden agendas the West may have for Central and Eastern Europe in the new world order.

The emerging transport geography of the region is an important element in a developmental jigsaw which may take some time to put together. Transport and communications are fundamental for assisting the interlocking of disparate pieces. The fear is, however, that the pieces are being fitted into the wrong-shaped frame.

References

Abbati, C., 1986, *Transport and European integration*, Commission of the European Communities, Brussels.

ABSEES (*Abstracts: Soviet and East European Studies*), London, quarterly.

Adam, J., 1984, 'The regulation of labour supply in Poland, Czechoslovakia, and Hungary', *Soviet Studies*, **36** (1): 69–86.

Ambler, J., Shaw, D.J.B. and Symons, L., 1985, *Soviet and East European transport problems*, Croom Helm, Beckenham.

Anania, M., 1900, *Descrierea pădurei Tarcău și plutaria pe Bistrița*, Tiparul Gutenberg, Bucharest.

Andrews, M., 1991, *The birth of Europe*, BBC Books, London.

Anon., 1990a, 'East Europe: sharp rise in energy demand forecast', *Petroleum Economist*, **57**(7): 4.

Anon., 1990b, 'East Europe after the wall', *Petroleum Economist*, **57**(1): 19–22.

Antanasković, S. and Djekić, Dj., 1986, 'The passenger car industry', *Yugoslav Survey*, **27**(2): 89–104.

Apăvăloaei, M. and Lupu-Bratiloveanu, N., 1981, 'Mobilitatea forţei de muncă pe căile ferate din Moldova', *Analele Stiinţifice ale Universitatea A.I. Cuza din Iaşi IIb*, **27**: 117–20.

Äripäev, Tallinn, daily.

Ash, G.T., 1990, 'Mitteleuropa?', *Daedalus*, **119**: 1–21.

Aslund, A., 1984a, *Private enterprise in Eastern Europe*, Macmillan, London.

Aslund, A., 1984b, 'The functioning of private enterprise in Poland', *Soviet Studies*, **36**(3): 427–44.

Aviation Week, London, weekly.

Bălănescu, E. and Tatomir, E., 1959, 'Importante realizări în transporturile forestier', *Revista Pădurilor*, **74**: 531–5, 594–8.

Banister, C.E., 1981, 'Transport in Romania: a British perspective', *Transport Reviews*, **1**: 251–70.

Baum, V., 1990, 'Marriage of opposites', *Petroleum Economist*, **57**(7): 8–11.

BBC, daily, *Summaries of World Broadcasts: Eastern Europe*, BBC, Caversham.

BBC, daily, *Summaries of World Broadcasts: Soviet Union*, BBC, Caversham.

BEE (*Business Eastern Europe*), fortnightly, Business Eastern Europe, London.

Bereziuc, P. *et al.*, 1958, *Drumuri forestiere*, Editura Agrosilvică, Bucharest.

Berman, Z. and Alvstam, C.G., 1985, *Investment policy in the Polish transport sector*, Occasional Paper, Department of Human and Economic Geography, University of Gothenburg, Gothenburg.

Bërxholi, A., 1985, *Vlora and its environs*, 8 Nëntori, Tirana.

Bërxholi, A., 1986, *Durrës and its environs*, 8 Nëntori, Tirana.

Betts, P., 1992, 'Boeing sells $470m jets to Romania', *Financial Times*, 10 September, p. 7.

Bićanić, R., 1973, *Economic policy in socialist Yugoslavia*, Cambridge University Press, Cambridge.

Bjelović, M., 1978, 'Razvoj privrede Bosne i Hercegovine', *Geografski Preglad*, **22**: 25–47.

Blades, D. (ed.), 1991, *Statistics for a market economy*, OECD, Paris.

Boardman, A. and Vining, A., 1989, 'Ownership and performance in competitive environments', *Journal of Law and Economics*, **32**: 1–33.

Borotvás, E. and Veroszta, J., 1992, 'A magyar közlekedés fejlődése nemzetközi összehasonlításban', *Közlekedéstudományi Szemle*, **42**(1): 1–20.

Borowicz, S., 1988, 'The development of the Polish merchant fleet and its role in the national economy, 1988', in Zurek, J. and Winkelmans, W. (eds), *Maritime transport in Belgium and in Poland*, State University Centre, Antwerp, pp. 78–90.

Botez, C. *et al.*, 1977, *Epopeea feroviara românească*, Editura Sport-Turism, Bucharest.

Boyes, J.R.C., 1990, 'What the USSR needs is a lot of help from its friends', *Containerisation International*, **24**(11): 21–8.

Brišski, A., 1978, 'Pospeševanje skladnejšega regionalnega razvoja v SR Sloveniji', *Geografski Vestnik*, **50**: 127–39.

British Petroleum Company, 1991, *BP statistical review of world energy*, Ashdown Press, London.

Bryson, B., 1992, Main–Danube Canal: linking Europe's waterways, *National Geographic*, **182**(2): 2–31.

Buckley, P.J. and Witt, S.F., 1990, 'Tourism in the centrally-planned economies of Europe', *Annals of Tourism Research*, **17**(1): 7–18.

Burghelea, D., 1941, 'Funicularul ca mijloc de transport', *Revista Pădurilor*, **53**: 579–80.

Burles, D.A. (ed.), 1991, *Energy map of Europe*, The Petroleum Economist, London.

Carter, F.W. and Turnock, D. (eds), 1992, *Environmental problems in Eastern Europe*, Routledge, London.

Černe, A., 1992, 'European aspects of the Slovenian transport system', in Maier, J. (ed.), *Slowenien auf dem Weg in die Marktwirtschaft*, Universität Bayreuth, Bayreuth, pp. 24–38.

Cleef, E. van, 1945, 'East Baltic ports and boundaries', *Geographical Review*, **35**: 256–72.

Clissold, S. (ed.), 1966, *A short history of Yugoslavia*, Cambridge University Press, Cambridge.

Clough P., 1991, 'Russia seeks to create a "Hong Kong" in the Baltic', *The Independent*, 23 September.

Comisia Nationala de Statistica (CNS), annual, *Anuarul statistic al R.S. Romania*, CNS, Bucharest.

Compton, P.A., 1972, 'Internal migration in Hungary between 1960 and 1968', *Tijdschrift voor Economische en Sociale Geografie*, **63**: 25–38.

Coopers and Lybrand, 1991, *Distribution systems in Eastern Europe*, Coopers and Lybrand, London.

Corbo, V., Coricelli, F. and Bossack, J. (eds), 1991, *Reforming Central and Eastern European economies: initial results and challenges*, The World Bank, Washington D.C.

Cranfield, M., 1991, 'East German deep sea shipping 1953–1990', *Ships Monthly*, **26**(7): 20–3.

Crawford, W., 1991a, 'Poland needs more than moral support', *Interavia Aerospace Review*, **46**(11): 32–5.

Crawford, W., 1991b, 'Lot flirts with privatisation', *Interavia Aerospace Review*, **46**(11): 49–50.

Creţu, F., 1985, 'Noua căile ferate Siret-Dorneşti', *Terra*, **17**(1): 50.

Cuny, P. (ed.), 1991, *Lloyd's ports of the world*, Lloyd's of London Press, London.

Cvijić, J., 1918, *La péninsule balkanique*, Librairie Armand Colin, Paris.

Depolo, B., 1974, 'Road transport', *Yugoslav Survey*, **15**(1): 53–66.

De Waele, A., 1991, 'Consequences of closer East–West relations', in ECMT, *Prospects for East–West European transport, international seminar, Paris*, ECMT, Paris, pp. 9–42.

Drozik, L., 1991, 'Development prospects for freight transport in the Eastern European countries', in ECMT, *Prospects for East–West European transport, international seminar, Paris*, ECMT, Paris, pp. 145–88.

Dziewoński, K., 1989, 'Changing goals of spatial policies and planning in Poland', *Geographia Polonica*, **56**: 9–16.

Economist, The, weekly, Economist Publications, London.

ECMT (European Conference of Ministers of Transport), 1991, *Prospects for East–West European transport, international seminar, Paris*, ECMT, Paris.

EIU (Economist Intelligence Unit), 1990, *Yugoslavia country profile 1990–91*, Economist Intelligence Unit, London.

EIU (Economist Intelligence Unit), 1991, *Romania Country Report No. 2, 1991*, Economist Intelligence Unit, London.

Eller, D., 1990a, 'Caution prevails over Eastern Europe', *Containerisation International*, **24**(1): 49–50.

Eller, D., 1990b, 'Emden enters the container age', *Containerisation International*, **24**(9): 77–9.

Eller, D., 1990c, 'Europe's railways signal go', *Containerisation International*, **24**(8): 49–52.

Eller, D., 1990d, ''Twixt plans – the choice for Cuxhaven', *Containerisation International*, **24**(10): 79–81.

Eller, D., 1991, 'New era for main German ports', *Containerisation International*, **25**(1): 51–7.

Elkins, T.H., 1986, 'The island of Rügen and new Baltic ferry links with the USSR', *Geography*, **71**: 358–9.

Endres, G., 1991, 'Baltic independence hatches new airlines', *Interavia Aerospace Review*, **46**(11): 19–21.

Engli, E., 1940, 'Plutaritul pe Mureş', *Revista Geografică Romănă*, **3**: 227–33.

Euromonitor, 1991, *Consumer Europe, 1991*, Euromonitor, London, 8th edn.

Euromonitor, 1992, *European marketing data and statistics, 1992*, Euromonitor, London, 27th edn.

Europa World Yearbook, 1992, Europa Publications, London, 2 vols.

Farrington, J.H., 1985, 'Transport geography and policy: deregulation and privatisation', *Transactions, Institute of British Geographers (New Series)*, **10**(1): 109–19.

Financial Times, London, daily.

Fisher, J.C., 1971, 'The emergence of regional spatial planning in Yugoslavia:

the Slovenian experience', in Hoffman, G.W. (ed.), *Eastern Europe: essays in geographical problems*, Praeger, New York, pp. 301–53.

Flight International, London, weekly.

Foster, D., 1985, *Travel and tourism management*, Macmillan, London.

Friganović, M., 1970, 'Commuting in Croatia as an index of the socio-economic mobility of population', *Geographical Papers* (Zagreb), 1: 95–103.

Frohnmeyer, A., 1992, 'EC transport policy: the consequences of German unification', in Heisenberg, W. (ed.), *German unification in European perspective*, Brassey's, London/Washington/New York, pp. 342–61.

Fuchs, R.J. and Demko, G.J., 1978, 'The postwar mobility transition in Eastern Europe', *Geographical Review*, **68**: 171–82.

Funck, R.H. and Kowalski, J.S., 1987, 'Impact of transportation bottlenecks on production – the Polish case', in Tismer, J.F. *et al.* (eds), *Transport and economic development – Soviet Union and Eastern Europe*, Duncker and Humblot, Berlin, pp. 292–305.

Gál, Z., 1990, 'The new boss is about to slim the airline', *Népzsabadsag*, 1 August.

Gál, Z., 1991a, 'Agreement about Malev', *Népzsabadsag*, 2 July.

Gál, Z., 1991b, 'Charter flights to Japan', *Népzsabadsag*, 10 July.

General Directorate of Public Roads, 1992, *Perspectives for primary road network development and its connections with neighbouring countries*, Paper presented at International Symposium Via Baltica, Helsinki-Tallinn.

(German) Ministry of Transport, 1992, *Bundesverkehrswegeplan*, Ministry of Transport, Bonn.

Giurcăneanu, C., 1988, *Populatia şi aşezările din Carpaţi româneşti*, Editura ştiinţifică şi Enciclopedică, Bucharest.

Giurescu, C.C., 1980, *A history of the Romanian forest*, Editura Academiei RSR, Bucharest.

Gorst, I., 1990, 'It's tough being free', *Petroleum Economist*, **57**(12): 5–6.

Gorst, I., 1991, 'Don't count on gas', *Petroleum Economist*, **58**(7): 18–19.

Gosar, L., 1975, 'Prometna dostopnost v Sloveniji', *Geografski Vestnik*, **47**: 91–106.

Grčić, M., 1984, 'Geopolitichki polozhaj Jugoslavije u proshlosti i danas', *Zbornik Radova PMF Beograd*, **31**: 79–95.

Grčić, M. and Marić, Dj., 1986, 'Strukturne promjene i regionalna diferencijacija industrije u Bosni i Hercegovini 1961–1987', *Geografski Pregled*, **30**: 37–48.

Gregory, M.B., 1973, 'Regional economic development in Yugoslavia', *Soviet Studies*, **25**: 213–25.

Grzybowski, K., 1990, 'Le Conseil D'Aide Économique Mutuelle (CAEM) et la Communauté Europénne (CE)', *Revue d'Études Comparatives Est–Ouest*, **21**: 113–24.

GUS (Polish Central Statistical Office), annual, *Statistical Yearbook*, GUS, Warsaw.

Haberman, C., 1990, 'Long-dormant Trieste sees an opening to the East', *International Herald Tribune*, 27 October.

Hall, D.R., 1972, 'The Iron Gates scheme and its significance', *Geography*, **57**(1): 51–5.

Hall, D.R., 1988a, 'A driving force in Eastern Europe', *Town and Country Planning*, **57**(12): 342–43.

Hall, D.R., 1988b, 'The sickness on the Danube', *Town and Country Planning*, 57(3): 80–1.

Hall, D.R., 1990a, 'Introduction: geographic dimensions of change', *Geography*, 75: 239–44.

Hall, D.R. (ed.), 1990b, 'The changing face of Eastern Europe and the Soviet Union', *Geography*, 75: 239–77.

Hall, D.R., 1990c, '"The communist world" in the 1990s', *Town and Country Planning*, 59(1): 28–30.

Hall, D.R., 1991a, 'Albania', in Hall D.R. (ed.), *Tourism and economic development in Eastern Europe and the Soviet Union*, Belhaven, London, pp. 259–77.

Hall, D.R., 1991b, 'New hope for the Danube Delta', *Town and Country Planning*, 60(9): 251–2.

Hall, D.R. (ed.), 1991c, *Tourism and economic development in Eastern Europe and the Soviet Union*, Belhaven, London.

Hall, D.R., 1992a, 'Czech mates no more?', *Town and Country Planning*, 61(9): 250–1.

Hall, D.R., 1992b, 'East European seaports in a restructured Europe', in Hoyle, B.S. and Pinder, D.A. (eds), *European port cities in transition*, Belhaven, London, pp. 98–115.

Hall, D.R., 1992c, 'Skills transfer for appropriate development', *Town and Country Planning*, 61(3): 87–9.

Hall, D.R., 1992d, 'The challenge of international tourism in Eastern Europe', *Tourism Management*, 13(1): 41–4.

Hall, D.R., 1992e, 'The West's nuclear dumping ground?', *Town and Country Planning*, 61(1): 28–30.

Hall, D.R., 1993, 'Impacts of economic and political transition on the transport geography of Central and Eastern Europe', *Journal of Transport Geography*, 1(1).

Hamilton, D., 1991, 'A more European Germany, a more German Europe', *Journal of International Affairs*, 45: 127–49.

Hamilton, F.E.I., 1963, 'The changing pattern of Yugoslavia's manufacturing industry', *Tijdschrift voor Economische en Social Geografie*, 54(3): 96–105.

Hamilton, F.E.I., 1968, *Yugoslavia: patterns of economic activity*, Bell, London.

Hamilton, F.E.I., 1990, 'COMECON: dinosaur in a dynamic world?', *Geography*, 75: 244–6.

Hamilton, G., 1991, 'Amex sets initiative for EE tourism development', *Business Eastern Europe*, 20(46): 412.

Hawkes, N. (ed.), 1990, *Tearing down the curtain: the people's revolution in Eastern Europe*, Hodder & Stoughton, London.

Herbst-Rădoi, A., 1972, 'Aspecte actuale ale geografiei transporturilor din ţara noastră, *Terra*, 4(2): 29–40.

Hofmeister, F., 1986, *Mit Dampf durch die Karpaten: Waldbahnen in Rumanien*, ECM-Buch/Bayerisches Eisenbahnmuseum, Munich.

Hoyle, B.S. and Knowles, R.D. (eds), 1992, *Modern transport geography*, Belhaven, London.

Hupfer, R., 1992, 'Az évtized végéig terjedő időszak magyar közlekedéspolitikája, kapcsolata a korábbi magyar és a jelenlegi nyugat-európai koncepciókkal', *Közlekedéstudományi Szemle*, 42(5): 161–8.

Iacob, G., 1987, 'Potenţialul forestier al bazinului hidrografic Lăpuş şi valorificarea lui', *Lucrările seminarului geografic "Dimitrie Cantemir" Iaşi*, 8: 277–84.

LIVERPOOL HOPE UNIVERSITY COLLEGE

Ianoş, E., 1982, 'Noi trasee feroviare şi importanţa lor economică, *Terra*, **14**(1): 38–42.

Ielenicz, M., 1971, 'Construirea retelei drumuri forestiere in bazinul Buzaului si dinamica proceselor actuale', *Revista Padurilor*, **86**: 421–5.

Interavia Aerospace Review, London, monthly.

International Energy Agency, 1988, *Energy in non-OECD countries*, OECD, Paris.

International Energy Agency, 1991, *Energy statistics and balances of non-OECD countries: 1988–1989*, OECD, Paris.

Jeršić, M., 1992, 'The port of Koper', in Pak, M. and Adamič, M.O. (eds), *Slovenia: geographic aspects of a new independent European nation*, Association of Geographical Societies of Slovenia, Ljubljana, pp. 87–91.

Journal of Transport Economics and Policy, 1990, 'Bus deregulation' (theme issue), *Journal of Transport Economics and Policy*, **24**(3): 237–350.

Kapitany, Z. *et al.*, 1984, 'Reproduction of shortage on the Hungarian car market', *Soviet Studies*, **36**(2): 236–56.

Kassel, P. and Rothengatter, W., 1990, *Scenario for transport development with the GDR and Eastern Europe*, Study commissioned by the Federal Ministry of Transport, Freiburg.

Kateraas, E., 1991, 'Boeing: keeping pace with competition in Eastern Europe', *Business Eastern Europe*, **20**(41): 352–3.

Kenedi, J., 1981, *Do it yourself*, Pluto Press, London.

Kessel, P. *et al.*, 1990, *Szenario zur Verkehrsentwicklung mit der DDR und Osteuropa*, Untersuchung im Auftrag des Bundesministers für Verkehr (FE-Nr. 98105/90), Bonn.

Kolarić, V., 1977, 'Neue Eisenbahnstrecke Beograd-Bar', *Verkehrsannalen*, **24**: 11–17.

Korboński, A., 1990, 'CMEA, economic integration, and perestroika, 1949–1989', *Studies in Comparative Communism*, **23**: 47–72.

Kornai, J., 1980, *Economics of shortage*, North Holland, Amsterdam.

Kornai, J., 1982, *Growth, shortage and efficiency*, University of Berkeley Press, Berkeley.

Korompai, G., 1977, 'The effects of the Europa Canal Rhine–Main–Danube', *GeoJournal*, **1**: 33–44.

Kostrzewa, W. and Schmieding, H., 1989, 'EFTA option for the reform states of Eastern Europe', *World Economy*, **12**: 501–14.

Kovács, Z., 1992, '1991 évi gazdasági folyamatok alakulása a közlekedés gazdasági ágazatban', *Közlekedéstudományi Szemle*, **42**(13): 199–202.

Kowalski, J., 1983, 'On the relevance of the concept of the centrally planned economies', *Jahrbuch für Socialwissenschaft*, **2**: 255–66.

Kowalski, J., 1986, 'Regional conflicts in Poland: spatial polarization in a centrally planned economy', *Environment and Planning A*, **5**: 599–639.

Kowalski, J., 1987, 'Rational expectations in centrally planned economies', in Pejovich, S. (ed.), *Socialism: institutional, philosophical and economic issues*, Kluwer Academic Publishers, Dordrecht, pp. 175–208.

Kowalski, J., 1990, 'Privatisierungsstrategien in Polen: eine ordnungspolitische Aufgabe', *Zeitschrift für öffentliche und gemeinwirtschaftliche Unternehmen*, **13**(3): 337–43.

Kowalski, J., 1991, 'Privatisierung in osteuropäischen Ländern: die Erfahrungen der ersten zwei Jahre', *Zeitschrift für öffentliche und gemeinwirtschaftliche Unternehmen*, **14**(3).

KPS (Komisioni i Planit të Shtetit), 1989, *Vjetari statistikor i R.P.S. të Shqipërisë*, Komisioni i Planit të Shtetit, Drejtoria e Statistikës, Tirana.

Kuziemkowski, R. (ed.), 1981, *Transportochłonność gospodarki narodowej*, WKŁ, Warsaw.

Kuziemkowski, R., 1984, 'Koncepcje przekształceń struktury transportu', *Przeglad Komunikacyjny*, **12**: 329–33.

Kużma, L. (ed.), 1982, *Ekonomika portow morskich*, Wydawnictwo Morskie, Gdańsk.

Kużma, L., 1988, 'The development of Polish seaports and their role in the national economy', in Zurek, J. and Winkelmans, W. (eds), *Maritime transport in Belgium and in Poland*, State University Centre, Antwerp, pp. 66–77.

Kużma, L., 1990, 'External conditions for the state and development of Polish sea ports', in Mosiewicz, M. (ed.), *Maritime transport in Belgium and in Poland*, Gdańsk University Press, Gdańsk, pp. 23–8.

Lacriteanu, S. *et al.*, 1987–8, 'The Covasna forestry railway and incline', *The Narrow Gauge*, **117**: 15–9.

Lijewski, T., 1980, 'Wpływ współczesnych tendencji lokalizacyjnych na wzrost transportochłonności gospodarki w Polsce', *Miasto*, **9**: 1–5.

Lijewski, T., 1982, 'Transport in Poland', *Transport Reviews*, **2**: 1–21.

Lijewski, T., 1986, *Geografia transportu Polski*, PWE, Warsaw, 2nd edn.

Lipton, D. and Sachs, J., 1991, 'Privatisation in Eastern Europe: the case of Poland', *Brookings Papers on Economic Activity*, **1**: 293–341.

Lupşe, P., 1954, 'Despre dezvoltarea planificată a transportului in RPR', *Probleme Economice*, **7**(1): 55–72.

Lydolph, P.E., 1987, 'Soviet marine transport in an overcrowded market', in Tismer, J.F. *et al.* (ed), *Transport and economic development – Soviet Union and Eastern Europe*, Duncker and Humblot, Berlin, pp. 140–74.

Machon, P. and Dingsdale, A., 1989, 'Public transport in a socialist capital city: Budapest', *Geography*, **74**(2): 159–62.

Malaesescu, A., 1938, 'Din trecutul Reşiţei forestiere', *Viaţa Forestieră*, **6**: 230–2.

Manoilescu, M., 1938, *Ideea de plan economic naţional*, Imprimerie Naţională, Bucharest.

Manoiliu, T., 1959, 'Construcţiile forestiere în perioadă 1944–1959', *Revista Pădurilor*, **74**: 482.

Marin, G., 1966, 'Realizările constructorilor forestieri din regiunea Oltenia în perioadă 1955–1965', *Revista Pădurilor*, **81**: 594–9.

Mellor, R.E.H., 1975, *Eastern Europe: a geography of the Comecon countries*, Macmillan, London.

Mellor, R.E.H., 1984, 'A future for the Rhine–Main–Danube Canal', *Geography*, **69**: 338–41.

Mieczkowski, B (ed.), 1980, *East European transport: regions and modes*, Martinus Nijhoff, London.

Miettinen, M., 1992, *Via Baltica, A road to the future*, Paper presented at International Symposium Via Baltica, Helsinki-Tallinn.

Mihailović, K., 1975, *Regional development: experiences and prospects in Eastern Europe*, Mouton, The Hague.

Mihelić, D., 1969, *The political element in the port geography of Trieste*, University of Chicago, Department of Geography, Research Paper No. 120, Chicago.

Milanović, B., 1987, 'Patterns of regional growth in Yugoslavia, 1952-83', *Journal of Development Economics*, 25(1): 1-19.

Milanović, B., 1991, 'Privatisation in postcommunist societies', *Communist Economies and Economic Transformation*, 3(1): 5-39.

Miljovski, K. (ed.), 1980, *Neravnomerni regionalni razvoj u ekonomskoj teoriji i praksi*, Makedonska Akademija na Naukite i Umetnostite, Skopje, 2 vols.

Mill, R.C. and Morrison, A.M., 1985, *The tourism system*, Prentice-Hall, Englewood Cliffs, NJ.

Ministry of Transport, Telecommunications and Water Management, 1991, *Statistical pocket book of the nationwide vehicle fleet*, Budapest.

Ministry of Transport, Telecommunications and Water Management, 1992, *Hungarian transport policy*, Budapest.

Misztal, K., 1990, 'Internal conditions for the state and development of Polish sea ports', in Mosiewicz, M. (ed.), *Maritime transport in Belgium and in Poland*, Gdańsk University Press, Gdańsk, pp. 29-36.

Mladenović, M., 1982, 'Development of economically underdeveloped republics and the Autonomous Province of Kosovo', *Yugoslav Survey*, 33(2): 3-22.

Mocanu, C.G., 1970, *Drumurile forestiere din România*, Universitatea din Bucureşti Doctorat, Bucharest.

Moldovan, R., 1964, 'Dezvoltarea economică a regiunilor relativ ramase în urma în trecut', in Malinschi, V. *et al.* (eds), *Industriei României 1944-1964*, Editura Academiei RPR, Bucharest, pp. 135-62.

Monigl, J., 1991, 'A Budapesti Közlekedési Vállalat átvilágitása – helyzetjelentés a konzultánsok szemszögéből', *Városi Közlekedés*, 32(3): 146-50.

Moodie, A.E., 1945, *The Italo-Yugoslav boundary, a study in political geography*, George Philip, London.

Morawski, W., 1980, 'Trzy refleksje w sprawie teoretycznych podstaw badań transportochłonności', *Problemy Ekonomiki Transportu*, 3.

Morgan, F.W., 1948, 'The pre-war hinterlands of the German North Sea ports', *Transactions, Institute of British Geographers*, 28.

Morgan, F.W., 1949, 'The pre-war hinterlands of the German Baltic ports', *Geography*, 34: 201-11.

Morgan, F.W. and Bird, J., 1958, *Ports and harbours*, Hutchinson, London, 2nd edn.

Moyes, T., 1992, 'Five years of British bus deregulation', *Geography*, 77(1): 70-2.

Myant, M., 1989, *The Czechoslovak economy 1948-1988: the battle for economic reform*, Cambridge University Press, Cambridge.

Nasiłowski, J., 1986, 'Kilka refleksji z okazji 50-lecia elektryfikacji PKP', *Przeglad Komunikacyjny*, 3: 53-6.

National Commission for Statistics (NCS), 1991, *The social state and the economy of Romania in 1990*, NCS, Bucharest.

Navak, B., 1970, *Trieste 1941-1954: the ethnic, political and ideological struggle*, University of Chicago Press, Chicago.

Naval Intelligence Division, 1945, *Geographical handbook: Jugoslavia, volume III*, Admiralty, London.

Nicod, J., 1982, 'Les transformations et le rôle structurant du réseau de transport intérieur yougoslave', *Méditerranée*, **44**(1): 19–27.

Nicolson, D., 1992, 'Unblocking an inland artery', *Geographical Magazine*, **64**(9): 30–33.

North, R., 1987, 'Current developments in transport and traffic between the Soviet Union and Eastern Europe', in Tismer, J.F., *et al.* (eds), *Transport and economic development – Soviet Union and Eastern Europe*, Duncker and Humblot, Berlin, pp. 270–91.

OECD, 1991, 'The transition to a market economy', *OECD Observer*, **169**: 5–10.

Opletal, J., 1913, *Das forestliche Transportwesen in der Bukowina*, n.p., Vienna.

Opris, V., 1987, 'Calea ferate Pascani-Tirgu Neamt: aspecte geografici', *Terra*, **19**(1): 44–5.

Osayimwese, I., 1991, 'Oil and the new Europe in the 1990s: on OPEC perspective', *OPEC Bulletin*, **22**(6): 7–13, 19.

Paladian, M., 1967, 'Construcţiile forestiere şi dezvoltarea turismului în România', *Revista Pădurilor*, **82**: 546–51.

Pasarica, I., 1935, *Monografia Uzinelor de Fier şi Domeniilor din Reşiţa*, Imprimerie Centrală, Bucharest.

Pavić, R., 1980, 'Socialist republic of Croatia – political geographical and economic geographical characteristics', *Geographica Iugoslavica*, **2**: 149–56.

Petch, T., 1991, 'Eastern Europe must think again', *Financial Times*, 9 September.

Peto, I., 1937, 'Utilitatea publică căilor ferate forestiere', *Viaţa Forestieră*, **5**: 206–9.

Petrović, R., 1992, 'The national composition of Yugoslavia's population', *Yugoslav Survey*, **33**(1): 3–24.

Pop, G.P., 1984, *Rômania: geografia circulaiei*, Editura Ştiinţifică şi Enciclopediă, Bucharest.

Popescu, I., 1987, *Căi ferate: transporturi clasice şi moderne*, Editura Ştiinţifică şi Enciclopediă, Bucharest.

Potrykowski, M. and Taylor, Z., 1986, 'Shipping policy and seaport development in Poland', *GeoJournal*, **12**(1): 281–8.

Pounds, N.J.G., 1985, *An historical geography of Europe 1800–1914*, Cambridge University Press, Cambridge.

Rausser, V., 1977, *Repartizarea teritorială a industriei*, Editura Scrisul Romanesc, Craiova.

Rey, R., 1979, *Viitor în Carpatii*, Editura Scrisul Romanesc, Craiova.

Reynolds, P. and Young, P., 1992, *Eastern promise*, Adam Smith Institute, London.

Rogić, V., 1982, *Regionalna geografija Jugoslavije, vol. I*, Skolska knjiga, Zagreb.

Rothengatter, W. and Kowalski, J., 1991, 'Development prospects for European transport between East and West: passenger transport', in ECMT, *Prospects for East–West European transport, international seminar, Paris*, ECMT, Paris, pp. 189–226.

Rzeczpospolita, 1991, Polska – Wspólnoty Europejskie: zagrożenia i korzyści, *Rzeczpospolita*, 19 December, supplement.

Rzeczpospolita, 1992, 'Polska – Wspólnoty Europejskie: stowarzyszenie', *Rzeczpospolita*, 21 January, supplement.

Sawiczewska, Z., 1986, *Konferencje zeglugowe*, Wydawnictwo Morskie, Gdańsk.

Sawiczewska, Z., 1992, 'Reconstructing Polish ports and shipping', *Maritime Policy and Management*, **19**(1): 69–76.

Sburlan, D.A., 1938, *Contribuţiuni la studiul pădurilor inaccesibile din România*, Institutul de Cercetări şi Experimentatie Forestieră, Bucharest.

Seidenfus, H.S., 1987, 'From the "Rhine–Main–Danube Canal" to the "Main–Danube connection"', in Tismer, J.F., *et al.* (eds), *Transport and economic development – Soviet Union and Eastern Europe*, Duncker and Humblot, Berlin, pp. 429–48.

Seidenfus, H.S., 1991, 'Development prospects for European transport between East and West: railway transport', in ECMT, *Prospects for East–West European transport, international seminar, Paris*, ECMT, Paris, pp. 263–309.

Sharman, T., 1983, 'Canal on the Danube delta', *Geographical Magazine*, **55**: 317–21.

Sić, M., 1980–1, 'Auto-cesta Zagreb-Karlovac', *Radovi PMF Zagreb*, **15–16**: 33–46.

Šimičić, V., 1981, 'Ekonomska potreba i opravdanost izgradnje dolinske željez-ničke pruge Zagreb-Rijeka', *Suvremeni Promet*, **3**: 267–72.

Simmons, M., 1991, 'Gdańsk floats plans for market success', *The Guardian*, 21 May.

Simmons, M., 1992, 'Privatisation dream "a sham"', *The Guardian*, 19 October.

Singleton, F.B. and Carter, B., 1982, *The economy of Yugoslavia*, Croom Helm, London.

Singleton, F.B., and Wilson, J., 1977, 'The Belgrade–Bar railway', *Geography*, **62**(2): 121–5.

Sirotković, M. and Stipetić, V. (eds), 1982, *Ekonomika Jugoslavije*, Informator, Zagreb.

Sjöberg, Ö., 1991a, *Rural change and development in Albania*, Westview Press, Boulder and Oxford.

Sjöberg, Ö., 1991b, 'Rural retention in Albania: administrative restrictions on urban-bound migration', *East European Quarterly*.

Sjöberg, Ö., 1991c, *Urbanisation under central planning: the case of Albania*, Uppsala University, Uppsala.

Solimano, A., 1991, 'Central and Eastern Europe: an historical and international perspective', in Corbo, V. *et al.* (eds), *Reforming Central and Eastern Europe economies: initial results and challenges*, The World Bank, Washington D.C., pp. 7–24.

Space Technology, London, weekly.

Spulber, N., 1954, 'The Danube–Black Sea Canal and Russian control of the Danube', *Economic Geography*, **30**: 241–4.

Stan, C. and Pasoi-Barco, A., 1964, 'Dezvoltarea căilor de comunicaţii şi transporturi în Vrancea', *Comunicăre de Geografie*, **3**: 203–10.

Stanković, M., 1975, 'Transport and communications', *Yugoslav Survey*, **16**(4): 91–106.

Stražičić, N., 1989, *Pomorska geografija Jugoslavije*, Školska knjiga, Zagreb.

Tarski, I., 1981, *System transportowy RWPG*, Państwowe Wydaynictwo Ekonomiczne, Warsaw.

Taylor, J.W.R., 1976, *Jane's all the world's aircraft, 1976–77*, Jane's, London.

Taylor, J.W.R., 1982, *Jane's all the world's aircraft, 1982-3*, Jane's London.

Taylor, Z., 1984a, 'Seaport development and the role of the state: the case of Poland', in Hoyle, B.S. and Hilling, D. (eds), *Seaport systems and spatial change*, Wiley, Chichester, pp. 217–38.

Taylor, Z., 1984b, 'The diffusion of railway network in Poland as a space-time process', *Geographia Polonica*, **50**: 75–87.

Taylor, Z., 1987, 'Investment policy in the Polish transport sector: an appraisal', *GeoJournal*, **15**(1): 107–12.

Taylor, Z., 1988, *Transport system and regional development*, Papers and Proceedings of the First Japan–Poland Economic Geography Seminar, Tokyo, pp. 225–36.

Taylor, Z., 1989, 'Contemporary trends in the Polish transport system', *Geographia Polonica*, **56**: 179–94.

Thomas, C., 1973, 'The Iron Gates project: its context and problems', *Revue Géographique de l'Est*, **13**(4): 481–9.

Thomas, C., 1978, 'Decay and development in Mediterranean Yugoslavia', *Geography*, **63**(3): 179–87.

Thomas, C., 1982, 'Migration and urban growth in Yugoslavia', *East European Quarterly*, **16**(2): 199–216.

Thomas, C., 1987, 'Ethnic minorities in Yugoslavia', *Irish Slavonic Studies*, **8**: 59–85.

Thomas, C., 1990, 'Yugoslavia: the enduring dilemmas', *Geography*, **75**(3): 265–8.

Thrash, L.A. (ed.), 1991, 'Worldwide refining', *Oil and Gas Journal*, **89**(51): 39–82.

Timar, A., 1991, 'Prospective trends in passenger transport in the East European countries', in ECMT, *Prospects for East–West European transport, international seminar, Paris*, ECMT, Paris, pp. 227–62.

Timiş, D., 1962, 'Deschiderea bazinului forestier Lăpuş-Căvnic', *Revista Pădurilor*, **77**: 483–5.

Tismer, J.F. *et al.* (eds), 1987, *Transport and economic development – Soviet Union and Eastern Europe*, Duncker and Humblot, Berlin.

Tomoioaga, G., 1968, 'Dezvolarea reţelei de drumuri forestiere în intreprinderea forestieră Bocşa', *Revista Pădurilor*, **83**: 500–3.

Turbut, G., 1981, *Sistemul unitar de transport al RSR*, Editura Tehnică, Bucharest.

Turnock, D., 1979, 'The Europe Canal and its Central European context', *Bulletin, Society of University Cartographers*, **13**: 32–6.

Turnock, D., 1986, 'The Danube–Black Sea Canal and its impact on Southern Romania', *Geojournal*, **12**: 65–79.

Turnock, D., 1987a, 'The Danube–Black Sea Canal and its impact on southern Romania', in Tismer, J.F. *et al.*, (eds), *Transport and economic development – Soviet Union and Eastern Europe*, Duncker and Humblot, Berlin, pp. 400–28.

Turnock, D., 1987b, *The development of the Romanian railway network since the First World War*, Leicester University Geography Department, Occasional Paper 16, Leicester.

Turnock, D., 1989a, *Eastern Europe: an economic and political geography*, Routledge, London.

Turnock, D., 1989b, *The human geography of Eastern Europe*, Routledge, London.

Turnock, D., 1990, 'Transport for Romania's Carpathian forests: improved accessibility through technological change', *GeoJournal*, **22**: 409–28.

Turnock, D., 1991a, 'The changing Romanian countryside: the Ceausescu Epoch and prospects for reform following the revolution', *Environment and Planning C*, **9**: 319–40.

Turnock, D., 1991b, 'Forest exploitation and its impact on transport and settlement in the Romanian Carpathians', *Journal of Transport History*, **12**: 37–60.

Turnock, D., 1991c, 'Forest railway of Romania', *Industrial Railway Record*, **125**: 270–80.

Turnock, D., 1992, *The Romanian countryside at the end of state socialism*, Leicester University Geography Department, Occasional Paper 22.

Urry, J., 1990, *The tourist gaze*, Sage, London.

Urry, J., 1992, 'The tourist gaze and the "environment"', *Theory, Culture and Society*, **9**(3): 1–26.

Vankov, S., 1991, 'Balkan Airlines, what's new' *Chasove*, 21 January.

Vasilijević, V., 1989, 'Motorisation and road traffic safety, 1978–1987', *Yugoslav Survey*, **30**(4): 85–106.

Vickers, J. and Yarrow, G., 1988, *Privatisation – an economic analysis*, MIT Press, Cambridge Mass.

Vickers, J. and Yarrow, G., 1991, 'Economic perspectives on privatisation', *Journal of Economic Perspectives*, **5**(2): 111–32.

Vinski, I., 1963, 'Regional growth of fixed assets in Yugoslavia 1946–60', *Papers, Regional Science Association*, **12**: 127–51.

Vozdushniy Transport, Moscow, irregular.

Vrišer, I., 1988, 'Centralna naselja v SR Sloveniji leta 1987', *Geografski Zbornik*, **28**: 129–51.

Vrišer, I., 1990, 'Industrijska naselja v Republiki Sloveniji', *Urejanje Prostora*, **2**: 16–19.

Warr, J., 1992, 'Where investors land on their feet', *The European*, 24 September, p. 45.

Warren, K., 1978, 'The establishment of the modern automobile industry in Poland', *Geography*, **63**: 362–3.

Weigand, G.G., 1956, 'The problem of hinterland and foreland as illustrated by the Port of Hamburg', *Economic Geography*, **32**: 1–16.

Wellisz, C., 1992, 'Poland's auto industry gets boost from joint ventures with GM, FIAT, and Volkswagen', *Radio Free Europe Post-Soviet/East European Report*, **9**(32): 2, 6.

White, H.P. and Senior, M.L., 1983, *Transport geography*, Longman, London.

Williams, A.M. and Shaw, G. (eds), 1988, *Tourism and economic development: Western European experiences*, Belhaven, London.

Wilson, O., 1971, 'The Belgrade–Bar railroad: an essay in economic and political geography', in Hoffman, G.W. (ed.), *Eastern Europe: essays in geographical problems*, Praeger, New York, pp. 365–84.

Winiecki, J., 1988, *The distorted world of Soviet-type economies*, Routledge, London.

WTO (World Tourism Organisation), annual, *Yearbook of tourism statistics*, WTO, Madrid.

Wulf, D., 1983, 'Der Schiffahrtsweg Rhein–Main–Donau', *Geowissenschaften in unserer Zeit*, **1**: 19–28.

Zahorsky-Suchodolski, A.M., 1962, *Triest, Schicksal einer Stadt*, Bergland Verlag, Vienna.

Zečević, P., 1991, 'The social and economic development of Yugoslavia, 1970–1990', *Yugoslav Survey*, **32**(1): 33–54.

Zloch-Christy, L., 1991, *East–West financial relations: current problems and future prospects*, Cambridge University Press, Cambridge.

Žuljić, S., 1978, 'Razvoj sistema magistralnih zeleznickih pruga na podrucju SR Hrvatske', *Geografski Glasnik*, **40**: 41–58.

Zurek, J., 1991, 'Shipping and seaborne foreign trade: some economic correlations and relationships, 1991', in University of Gdańsk Maritime Transport Economics Institute/University of Antwerp (RUCA) Department of Transport Economics (eds), *Shipping and port in the national economy*, RUCA, Antwerp, pp. 87–106.

Index